Western Frontiersmen Series
XI

GEORGE DROUILLARD

HUNTER AND INTERPRETER

for

LEWIS AND CLARK

and

Fur Trader, 1807-1810

by

M. O. SKARSTEN

INTRODUCTION TO THE SECOND EDITION BY
ROBERT C. CARRIKER

THE ARTHUR H. CLARK COMPANY
Spokane, Washington
2003

The reprint edition of *George Drouillard: Hunter and Interpreter
for Lewis and Clark and Fur Trader, 1807–1810*, omits two half-
title pages, pages 13–14 and 341–342; a blank page between the
illustrations on pages 277–278; and Clark's Map and Notes, a
folding map on pages 339–340. There is no text missing as a
result.

Contents

Illustrations

Maps

Introduction to the Second Printing

by ROBERT C. CARRIKER, GONZAGA UNIVERSITY

George Drouillard left historians only a slight factual record. He apparently wrote no journals and the documents which he signed are very few in number. Yet his economy of written words has not obscured Drouillard's importance to the Lewis and Clark Expedition, his role in opening the Missouri River fur trade, or his achievements as an independent explorer in the trans-Mississippi West. That record is clearly set forth in the journals left by five members of the Corps of Discovery, in the recollections of fur entrepreneur Thomas James, and in the precision with which William Clark's 1810 manuscript map of the American West details the Yellowstone River basin and the Big Horn country.

Assembling these varied bits and pieces of a life lived on a frontier, where deeds counted more than what one penned into a journal, is a tremendous task. It is one to which Malvin Olai Skarsten devoted himself for years before his research resulted in the publication of *George Drouillard: Hunter and Interpreter of the Lewis and Clark Expedition and Fur Trader, 1807–1810*. Born the son of Norwegian immigrants in 1892, Skarsten early on gravitated to education in his native state of Minnesota. He became an elementary teacher in rural schools before graduating from high school, a secondary school teacher after attending college, and ultimately, following the completion of a doctorate in 1944, he spent the remainder of his career in higher education. For eighteen years Skarsten served on the faculty at Black Hills State University, South Dakota. Then, in 1944 he relocated to Pacific University in Forest Grove, Oregon, where he held various administrative positions, including director of the graduate school. A second book by Skarsten, *Their Hearts Were Right*, also focused on the Lewis and Clark Expedition, this time paying tribute to the Indians who helped along the journey. A third, *Those Remarkable People: The*

Dakota/Lakota, is a view of Lakota history and culture, but his biography of Drouillard remains his best-known work. Skarsten retired from teaching in 1965 and died at the age of 101 in 1993.

Lewis and Clark scholar Ernest S. Osgood, after reading Skarsten's work, commented that "He has combed the pages of the various journals and has given the reader a fair and judicious account of the important role this man played. . . ."[1] Donald Jackson, the premier Lewis and Clark scholar of his time and editor of the University of Illinois Press, agreed that "Making something full and well integrated out of bits and pieces is not an easy task."[2] A book reviewer for the *Pacific Historical Review,* however, missed the point and believed that Drouillard was the subject of only "occasional references found in the Lewis and Clark journals."[3] For his research, Skarsten relied upon the seven printed volumes of the Lewis and Clark journals edited by Reuben Gold Thwaites in 1904 and 1905.[4] Making the index by hand, Thwaites identified 202 places in the journals where Drouillard played a role, a number considerably larger than usually associated with the term 'occasional.' Interestingly, between 1986 and 1997 the University of Nebraska Press published a new edition of the original journals of the Lewis and Clark Expedition, edited by Gary Moulton, using computers to make the index.[5] The Moulton edition of the journals contains 641 references to Drouillard, 355 of them involving his hunting exploits alone.

Skarsten's interpretation of Drouillard has stood the test of time. Meriwether Lewis called Drouillard "A man of much merit; he has been peculiarly useful from his knowledge of the common language of gesticulation, and his uncommon skill as a hunter and woodsman. . . ."[6] Indeed, except for the captains who led the expe-

[1] Ernest S. Osgood, Book Reviews, *Journal of American History* 52 (Spring 1965): 359.

[2] Donald Jackson, Book Reviews, *American Historical Review* 70 (January 1965): 573.

[3] Wilbur R. Jacons, Book Reviews, *Pacific Historical Review* 33 (Winter 1964): 470.

[4] Thwaites, Reuben Gold, ed. *Original Journals of the Lewis and Clark Expedition, 1804–1806.* 8 vols. New York: Dodd, Mead & Co., 1904–1905.

[5] Gary E. Moulton, ed., *The Journals of the Lewis and Clark Expedition.* Vols. 2–11. (Lincoln: University of Nebraska Press, 1986–1997).

[6] Meriwether Lewis to Henry Dearborn, January 15, 1807, in Donald Jackson, ed., *Letters of the Lewis and Clark Expedition.* 2nd ed. (Chicago: University of Illinois Press, 1978): 368.

dition, Drouillard received higher compensation than anyone else on the expedition: $833 in total salary, a sum more than twice as much as the only other civilian member of the expedition, plus 320 acres of public land. And he was worth it. Skarsten got it right when, on the first page of the first chapter, he began a list of Drouillard's contributions to the overall success of the expedition: interpreter, hunter, diplomat, Lewis's friend, tracker, pilot, horse trader, negotiator, messenger, stalwart during a gun fight. As the chapters unfold, so too do the additional accomplishments of George Drouillard.

"It was his fate," Lewis explained to Secretary of War Henry Dearborn in 1807, for Drouillard "to have encountered, on various occasions, with either Captain Clark or myself, all the most dangerous and trying scenes of the voyage, in which he uniformly acquitted himself with honor."[7] He accompanied Lewis, for example, when Euro-Americans viewed for the first time the Great Falls of the Missouri, he was there when Lewis made contact with the Shoshone Indians, and he stood firm when Lewis was confronted by Piegan warriors on the return journey. In Skarsten's narrative Drouillard seems to always be present at the critical junctures of the expedition. Moreover, his hunting parties brought in the most meat, but still avoided territorial confrontations with the Indians who lived beyond the stockades of Fort Mandan and Fort Clatsop. Drouillard never stepped aside for a grizzly bear, however. Lewis once confided to his journal that he worried about Drouillard when his right-hand man spent two days alone near Great Falls searching for stolen horses, because he knew that if Drouillard met with a bear in the plains "he would attack him. [A]nd that if any accedent should happen to separate him from his horse in that situation the chances in favour of his being killed would be as 9 to 10. I felt so perfectly satisfyed that he had returned in safety that I thought but little of the horses although they were seven of the best I had."[8]

The Lewis and Clark Bicentennial commemoration has

[7] Ibid.

[8] Moulton, ed., *The Journals of the Lewis and Clark Expedition.* Vol. 8: 109–110.

brought forth many new books on the Corps of Discovery, plus some 'historically-based' novels. One novel is centered on George Drouillard, advertising itself as a history of the Lewis and Clark Expedition from a Native American perspective inasmuch as the central character is half-Indian. Drouillard, in novels, appears as a man reluctant to join the expedition, harboring a grudge against William Clark's brother, George Rogers, an American Revolution hero who may or may not have attacked a Shawnee Indian village and harmed tribal relatives. He silently seethes with contempt for the way the expedition treats Native Americans and disdains the management team of the expedition—especially the leader who exhibits mercurial, possibly even demonic tendencies—as the men move clumsily across the western landscape. Drouillard in these novels bears no relationship to the historical evidence, meager though it may be.

The most accurate recounting of Drouillard's life remains Skarsten's biography. In addition to presenting a text based upon serious Lewis and Clark research, it follows Drouillard's brief fur trade career following the expedition with St. Louis businessman Manuel Lisa. More important than any pelts Drouillard may have found are the geographic insights he provided in 1808 to his former boss, William Clark, about the Yellowstone River region. Clark's 1809 map, along with five of his handwritten notes, are presented as facsimile documents. This edition of Skarsten's work is 'new and improved' only in the instances where obvious errors, such as transposed dates, have been corrected. Skarsten himself refined parts of the text in his chapter on Drouillard that appeared in 1966 in *The Mountain Men and the Fur Trade*.[9] As a result, the only part of the original manuscript requiring an update is the bibliography. Volumes issued after Skarsten completed his manuscript, and which would have been included by the author, had he the opportunity to oversee this new edition, are:

- Ambrose, Stephen E. *Undaunted Courage: Meriwether Lewis, Thomas*

---

[9] LeRoy R. Hafen, ed., *Mountain Men and the Fur Trade of the Far West*. Vol. 4. (Glendale: Arthur H. Clark Co., 1966): 69–82.

Jefferson and the Opening of the American West. New York: Simon & Schuster, 1996. Paperback edition 1997.

• Appleman, Roy. *Lewis and Clark: Historic Places Associated with Their Transcontinental Exploration.* Washington, D.C.: United States Department of the Interior, National Park Service, 1975. New printing at St. Louis, Jefferson National Expansion Historical Association, 1993.

• Clark, William. *The Field Notes of Captain William Clark, 1803–1805.* Edited by Ernest S. Osgood. New Haven: Yale University Press, 1964.

• Clarke, Charles G. *The Men of the Lewis and Clark Expedition: A Biographical roster of the Fifty-one Members and a Composite Diary of their Activities from All Known Sources.* Glendale: Arthur H. Clark Co., 1970. New Introduction by Dayton Duncan. Lincoln: University of Nebraska Press, 2002.

• Duncan, Dayton and Ken Burns. *Lewis & Clark: The Journey of the Corps of Discovery.* New York: Alfred A. Knopf, 1997. Paperback edition 1999.

• Gass, Patrick. *The Journals of Patrick Gass: Member of the Lewis and Clark Expedition.* Edited and annotated by Carol Lynn MacGregor. Missoula, Mont.: Mountain Press Pub. Co., 1997.

• Lavender, David. *The Way to the Western Sea: Lewis and Clark Across the Continent.* New York: Harper & Row, 1988. New edition, Lincoln, Neb.: Bison Books, 2001.

• Lewis, Meriwether and William Clark. *The Journals of the Lewis and Clark Expedition.* Lincoln: University of Nebraska Press, 1983–2001. Edited by Gary E. Moulton.

Vol. 1, *Atlas of the Lewis and Clark Expedition.* (1983);

Vol. 2, *The Journals of the Lewis and Clark Expedition. August 30, 1803–August 24, 1804.* (1986) Paperback edition, 2002;

Vol. 3, *The Journals of the Lewis and Clark Expedition. August 25, 1804–April 6, 1805.* (1987) Paperback edition, 2002;

Vol. 4, *The Journals of the Lewis and Clark Expedition. April 7–July 27, 1805.* (1987) Paperback edition, 2002;

Vol. 5, *The Journals of the Lewis and Clark Expedition. July 28–November 1, 1805.* (1988) Paperback edition, 2002;

Vol. 6, *The Journals of the Lewis and Clark Expedition. November 2, 1805–March 22, 1806.* (1990) Paperback edition, 2002;

Vol. 7, *The Journals of the Lewis and Clark Expedition. March 23–June 9, 1806.* (1991) Paperback edition, 2002;

Vol. 8, *The Journals of the Lewis and Clark Expedition. June 10–September 26, 1806.* (1993) Paperback edition, 2002;

Vol. 9, *The Journals of John Ordway, May 14, 1804–September 23, 1806, and Charles Floyd, May 14–August 18, 1804.* (1996);

Vol. 10, *The Journal of Patrick Gass, May 14, 1804–September 23, 1806.* (1996);

Vol. 11, *The Journal of Joseph Whitehouse, May 14, 1804–April 2, 1806*. (1997);

Vol. 12, *Herbarium of the Lewis and Clark Expedition*. (1999);

Vol. 13, *Comprehensive Index*. (2001).

• Oglesby, Richard Edward. *Manuel Lisa and the Opening of the Missouri Fur Trade*. Norman: University of Oklahoma Press, 1963.

• Ronda, James P. *Lewis and Clark among the Indians*. Lincoln: University of Nebraska Press, 1984. New introduction, 2002.

The final paragraph of Skarsten's biography expresses the author's hope "that some day a marker will be erected in commemoration of the services of this man. . . ." That hope was realized on June 22, 1974, at the mouth of the Palouse River in southeastern Washington, when the Washington State Lewis and Clark Trail Committee and the Franklin County Historical Society dedicated an interpretive sign, set atop a basalt stone base, to the memory of George Drouillard. The marker notes a bit of the history of the region. On October 13, 1805, the Corps of Discovery was on the Snake River, called by them 'Lewis's River,' racing toward the Columbia River. At the tributary known today as Palouse River, they conferred the phonetic spelling of George Drouillard's surname: 'drewyers River.' Dr. Skarsten could not have been more pleased, for this site is today a National Historic Landmark. Gravesites in the Palouse River canyon contain bodies dating back 10,000 years, making it one of the most important archaeological sites in the Pacific Northwest. In ancient times Indian canoes crossed the Snake River at this point, and from the 1850s to the 1960s a cable-ferry accomplished the same task for wagons, then cattle, and finally cars. When the railroad completed the Joso Bridge here in 1914 it was hailed as the longest, highest trestle bridge in the world. On the day of the marker's dedication in 1974 three collateral descendants of the legendary interpreter traveled from Iowa and Ohio to be present when the Washington State Parks and Recreation Commission accepted the sign on behalf of the citizens of Washington State. Establishing the 'Drewyer's River' monument, ten years after the publication of his book, accomplished the most sincere wish of M. O. Skarsten and brought respect and recognition to the name of George Drouillard.

Preface

If you have been fortunate enough to read the journals of Lewis and Clark, you may have become impressed, as I was, with the number and variety of responsibilities assigned to one, George Drouillard, employed by the leaders of the expedition to serve them as interpreter. But for the efforts and accomplishments of this man it is certain the Lewis and Clark expedition would not have attained the success acclaimed for it today. One may even hazard the assertion that, but for him, and particularly for the role he played in assisting Lewis in negotiating with the Shoshones for horses, the explorers would not have been able to cross the mountains between the headwaters of the Missouri and the Columbia and so would not have reached the Pacific. It is my hope that the study herewith presented may make some contribution toward bringing to this man the recognition and acclaim his services in behalf of the expedition merit.

I trust that what is presented may serve to give, not merely an account of the pursuits in which George Drouillard engaged, but an idea, also, as to the kind of man he was, as a member of the expedition under Lewis and Clark, and as a partner of Manuel Lisa in fur trading ventures afterward.

In the preparation of the manuscript, I have used as my primary reference the original journals of Lewis and Clark as edited by Reuben Gold Thwaites. This multi-volume work, besides containing the accounts kept by the leaders of the expedition, contains also maps, the journal kept by Joseph Whitehouse, and, in addition, a vast amount of pertinent material compiled by Mr. Thwaites. This and other references consulted are given in the bibliography.

I might add that I have traveled, by automobile, over nearly the entire route followed by the explorers between Yankton, South Dakota, and the mouth of the Columbia. My route has taken me over the Continental Divide via not only Lemhi Pass but Lost Trail Pass as well. In the course of these travels I have visited and stopped to examine most of the points of interest along the entire route. That is, I have personally traveled over and seen much of that great west which so thrilled George Drouillard when he also traveled over it and saw it as a member of the Lewis and Clark expedition over a century and a half ago.

I am indebted to the Missouri Historical Society for permission to reproduce, in whole or in part, certain documents, hereafter mentioned. I am indebted, also, to Miss Barbara Kell, Reference Librarian of the same society, for calling my attention to certain maps and documents pertinent to my subject, and for arranging to have photostat copies of these made available to me. To Ernest S. Osgood, of the Department of History, University of Minnesota, and editor of the recently-discovered notes of William Clark, I am indebted for the service he rendered in examining the Clark notes for possible new references to George Drouillard. To Lucille M. Kane, Curator of Manuscripts, University of Minnesota, I am indebted for the assistance she gave in the same respect. I am indebted, also, to Harry J. Dubester, Acting Chief, General Reference and Bibliography Division, Library of Congress, for valuable assistance offered me in my search for materials. For the courteous assistance extended to me in Oregon by the staffs of the Portland Public Library, the Oregon Historical Society, and the Pacific University Library, I wish to express my appreciation.

Throughout the present volume may be found quotations for which no references are cited. Unless otherwise indicated, these quotations, with or without dates of entry, are from the Thwaites edition of the Lewis and Clark journals.

1
A Promising Recruit

When Lewis and Clark engaged George Drouillard as interpreter for the expedition which they proposed to lead to the Pacific, they transacted a piece of business that yielded them returns beyond their most sanguine expectations; and this for the reason that George Drouillard was to demonstrate to them an ability and a willingness to serve them, not merely in the capacity of interpreter, but in several other capacities as well.

For example, George Drouillard proved himself invaluable as a hunter. He demonstrated more than ordinary success in diplomatic ventures to the Indians. He became a boon companion of Lewis. To him fell the task of pursuing the trail of horses which had strayed from camp at night, or which had been spirited away by Indians. To him fell the task, also, of finding and bringing to justice a deserter. Drouillard was one of those who took a hand at steering pirogues on the Missouri. He became a horse trader on the Columbia. He bartered for canoes at Fort Clatsop. He gelded horses on the Kooskooske. He pleaded for guides to direct the explorers homeward over the Bitterroot Mountains. He played a leading role in a knife and gun struggle with a band of Piegan Blackfeet. To him, finally, fell the task of serving as Lewis' right-hand man at a time when the latter was desperately attempting to persuade the Shoshones to lend him the assistance which the explorers so sorely needed.

A cursory examination of the accomplishments of George Drouillard in behalf of the Lewis and Clark expedition will disclose that here lived a man of strong yet nimble physique, equally at home in the woods, on the plains, and in the mountains; a man of quick decision and vigorous action; enthusiastic, ardent, courageous, resourceful, likeable. It was the all-out competence of the man, his willingness – nay, even eagerness – to serve on any occasion, his unfailing reliability, his courage, tact, good judgment, and resourcefulness – it was qualities such as these that served, singly and in combination, to make him well-nigh indispensable in the furtherance of the project to which he had committed himself. Of him can it truthfully be said: He ranked high among those energetic, gallant men whose claim to recognition lay in the fact that they served with honor and distinction the expedition commanded by Lewis and Clark; and, in so doing, the country to which they owed allegiance.

George Drouillard was the son of a French Canadian father and a Shawnee mother. His father, Pierre Drouillard, a British subject, resided in Detroit, where he served the British as interpreter. In 1776 Pierre married Angelique Descamps. From this marriage issued several children.[1]

George appears to have found acceptance in the home of his stepmother, Angelique Descamps. For his

---

[1] Walter B. Douglas, in Appendix to Thomas James, *Three Years Among the Indians and Mexicans,* 285-86. (Hereafter referred to as Douglas).

"brothers and sisters" there, he formed an attachment sufficiently strong to have caused him to state, in a letter to one of them years later, that he wished to be remembered to them. The letter suggests that he held his "family" in high esteem, and that he sought to merit their good will. The letter follows, in part:

St. Louis,   May 23, 1809

MY DEAR MARIE LOUISE: . . . I would have had the pleasure of seeing you all last winter if it had not been for the lack of money to cover the expenses of such a voyage. . .

I do not think I can return from the Upper Missouri before three years and just as soon as I return I shall be delighted to see you all. If some of my family will be kind enough to write to me they will address their letters to Monsieur Pascal Cerré at St. Louis. He and his wife although not known to my family in Detroit join with me and beg you to accept their civilities . . . My respects to our Mother who I embrace well, also all my brothers and sisters who I would like very much to see.

Your very affectionate brother,

(Signed) GEORGE DROUILLARD

P.S. Remember please to Madam Maisonville and her family Madam Jacque Parrent, Detroit, Sandwich.[2]

Young George appears to have had the benefit of some schooling. This again suggests that he had found acceptance in the home of his father Pierre and his stepmother Angelique. In school he was taught reading and writing, and possibly cyphering. If he wrote, instead of dictated, the letter to which reference has been made, then he wrote very well. But whether he did or not, the solicitude revealed by the letter suggests that its author was, if not a man of refinement, then at least

---

[2] Quoted from his letter to "Marie Louise," dated at St. Louis, May 23, 1809, as quoted in Olin D. Wheeler, *The Trail of Lewis and Clark*, I, pp. 110-11. (Hereafter referred to as Wheeler).

one blessed with some knowledge of the social amenities. If, along with writing, he could also read, then his schooling must have been more extensive than that of many of his day.

If Drouillard's birth occurred before his father's marriage to Angelique Descamps in 1776, he would have been about twenty-seven years of age, or older, when he joined the Lewis and Clark expedition in 1803. If, however, this "marriage" to George's Shawnee mother occurred *after* the father's marriage to Angelique Descamps, then Drouillard would have been younger than this, at the time he joined the expedition. Whatever his age, the energy and enthusiasm he displayed, and the hardships he endured, as a member of the expedition, suggest that, if he were not a young man, he was, at least, a man blessed with a generous amount of vitality.[3]

Early in his youth, Drouillard migrated with his mother's people to Missouri.[4] According to one authority, he described himself "as of the District of Cape Girardeau," [5] a thriving Spanish community on the west side of the Mississippi (that is, in Missouri), somewhat over a hundred miles south of St. Louis.

There is reason to believe that Drouillard made his place of residence, also, at Fort Massac, a military post on the Ohio, fifty or more miles above the junction of the Ohio with the Mississippi. It is entirely possible

---

[3] Most of the members of the expedition were between twenty and thirty years of age. Clark was thirty-three, Gass thirty-two, and Lewis twenty-nine. Shannon, the youngest, was seventeen. See James Kendall Hosmer, *Gass' Journal of the Lewis and Clark Expedition*. (Hereafter referred to as Hosmer).

[4] Douglas, 285-86.   [5] *Ibid.*

that he betook himself to this place after having resided at Cape Girardeau. At any rate, it was at Fort Massac that Lewis and Clark found him in 1803. At Fort Massac, also, resided a "Mr Drewyer."[6] If a relative of George, the presence of this man there would furnish additional ground for believing that George was also a resident of this place. Furthermore, it was at Fort Massac that Drouillard, on February 11, 1804, contracted a debt to one William Graeter, amounting to $301.63 1/3 – a fact which suggests that he had resided at Fort Massac long enough to form an acquaintanceship with Graeter sufficiently matured to have caused the latter to be willing to lend him an amount equal to the face value of the debt.[7]

It may have been at Fort Massac – if not at Cape Girardeau – that Drouillard began in earnest his life as a hunter. Here he came in contact with the hardworking, liberty-loving, danger-flaunting Americans who were at this time seeking to establish themselves along the Ohio. Eventually he joined these Americans in an enterprise that was to take him to the Pacific.

One day, at Sandusky, Ohio, George Drouillard's father, Pierre, came upon a band of Indians who had in their possession an American prisoner. The prisoner was none other than Simon Kenton, a contemporary of Daniel Boone.[8] The Indians were jubilant over their capture of this prisoner, a Long Knife of some im-

[6] Milo M. Quaife (ed.), *The Journals of Captain Meriwether Lewis and Sergeant John Ordway*, 59. (Hereafter referred to as Quaife).

[7] "Early Litigation Papers," Missouri Historical Society. Used by permission of the Society. See also Appendix F herein.

[8] Reuben Gold Thwaites (ed.) *Original Journals of the Lewis and Clark Expedition*, I, p. 227. (Hereafter referred to as Thwaites).

portance. They were about to burn him at the stake when Pierre Drouillard intervened.[9]

It is not to be presumed the Indians were enthusiastic about giving up the prisoner who had fallen into their hands. But give him up they did, and Kenton found his way to liberty. The incident suggests the presence, in the make-up of Pierre Drouillard, of a trait of humanity; a trait which, may it be added, can be detected also in the make-up of his son George.

Pierre Drouillard fell into disfavor with the British after the cession of Detroit in 1796. Kenton, however, offered to help him establish himself among the Americans.[10] This offer Pierre accepted, at least in part. That is, with or without his family, he moved to Ohio, and there became an interpreter for the Americans.[11]

If George Drouillard was a relative of the "Mr Drewyer" to whom reference has been made, then he was a relative also, of Louis Lorimer, commander of the Spanish garrison at Cape Girardeau; for Lorimer was an uncle of the "Mr Drewyer" residing at Fort Massac.[12] If the two were, actually, related, as seems likely, then Drouillard's blood connections on his father's side were by no means despicable. By which it must not be inferred that his blood connections on his mother's side were inferior. The truth is, George Drouillard was the energetic, capable, courageous man he demonstrated himself to be because of a happy combination of qualities which he had inherited from both sides of the family tree, and nurtured by an environment which brought to bear upon him influences

[9] Eva Emery Dye, *The Conquest*, 46.
[10] *Ibid.*, 117.   [11] Douglas, 285.   [12] Quaife, p. 59.

from red men and white men alike. From the standpoint of heredity, therefore, and from the standpoint of culture and training, Drouillard compared favorably with most, if not all, of the men who placed their services at the disposal of Captain Meriwether Lewis and Captain William Clark.[13]

It was stated above that on February 11, 1804, Drouillard negotiated at Fort Massac a promissory note in the amount of $301.63 1/3, to one Graeter. On that same February 11, 1804, Drouillard was supposed to be either at the mouth of Wood River, nearly opposite St. Louis, where the explorers had established themselves for the winter, or in St. Louis itself, where Lewis spent some of his time. The fact that he executed a note on that date at Fort Massac would indicate that he actually was at Fort Massac at that time.

As a matter of fact, Drouillard had been permitted to go to Fort Massac to "settle his affairs."[14] Included among those affairs was, undoubtedly, his debt to Graeter. At any rate, the business must have seemed important enough to the commanding officers of the expedition to cause them to be willing to allow their new recruit to go there for the purpose of settling it — a round trip distance of over three hundred miles. At

[13] William Clark was actually a lieutenant. In soliciting his services in behalf of the expedition, Lewis wrote him that the President had "authorized" him to say that "in the event of your accepting this proposition he will grant you a Captain's commission which of course will entitle you to pay and emoluments attached to that office." The commission was not ratified, however, and Clark remained actually a lieutenant, though addressed and referred to as a captain by Lewis and the other members of the expedition. — Thwaites, VII, p. 230.

[14] The quotes are from Donald Jackson, *Letters of the Lewis and Clark Expedition*, 144. (Hereafter referred to as Jackson).

the same time they may already have come to regard
him as of such value to the expedition as to make them
feel that they had better grant him his request lest he
decide not to go with them. The fact that they were
willing to let him go probably indicated that they were
confident he would return.

GEORGE DROUILLARD'S PROMISSORY NOTE TO FREDERICK GRAETER, SHOWING HIS PRESENCE IN FORT MASSAC, FEBRUARY 11, 1804. From the Lisa Papers, courtesy of the Missouri Historical Society, St. Louis.

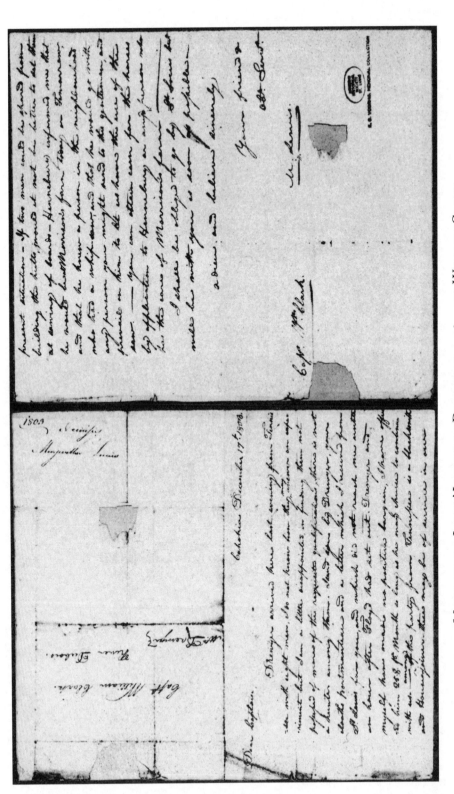

MERIWETHER LEWIS' LETTER OF DECEMBER 17, 1803, TO WILLIAM CLARK
GEORGE DROUILLARD ACTED AS MESSAGE BEARER IN DELIVERING THE LETTER.

2

No Positive Bargain

In the journal which Lewis kept on his journey down
the Ohio in 1803 occurs this entry:

11th NOVEMBER   Arrived at Massac engaged George Drewyer
in the public service as an Indian Interpretter, contracted to pay
him 25 Dollars pr month for his services. – Mr Swan Assistant
Millitary agent at that place advanced him *thirty* dollars on
account of his pay.

One could deduce from this statement that Drouillard accompanied the expedition from Fort Massac to
the mouth of the Ohio and then up the Mississippi as
far as Wood River, where the explorers established
themselves for the winter.

A letter from Lewis to Clark from Cahokia, dated
December 17, contains information which would indicate that this was not the case. The captain said:
"Drewyer arrived here last evening from Tennissee
with eight men.   . ."[1]

There is reason to believe that Lewis expected to
recruit men from Tennessee at Fort Massac.[2] The fact
that these prospective recruits were not there when he
arrived may have induced him to send George Drouillard into Tennessee for them, or for others to take their
place. His choice of a comparative stranger for so
important a task must have meant, either that Drouil-

---

[1] Thwaites, VII, p. 288.
[2] Jackson, 144.

lard had come to him highly recommended, or that
Lewis had become so favorably impressed with him
upon short acquaintance as to make him willing to
entrust him with the responsibility he had in mind. At
any rate, while the expedition continued its course
down the Ohio and up the Mississippi, Drouillard
went south, into Tennessee, found his men, and presented these to Lewis at Cahokia on December 16, after
having brought them a distance of upwards of two
hundred miles. This was probably Drouillard's first
task in behalf of the expedition. How well had he
performed it?

In his letter to Clark the next morning, Lewis said,
with reference to the men recruited by Drouillard: "I
do not know how they may answer on experiment but
I am a little disappointed, in finding them not possessed
of more of the requisite qualifications; there is not a
hunter among them." That is, Drouillard's recruitment
of men in Tennessee had been no outstanding success.

But Drouillard was not the only one who failed at
the business of recruitment of personnel for the Lewis
and Clark expedition. Lewis himself had, on occasion,
failed in this respect, due to the high standards he had
set. Months before, while he was yet in Pittsburg super-
vising the construction of the keelboat, he had given
Clark to understand that he did not consider "young
gentlemen" desirable, but, rather, "stout, healthy, un-
married men, accustomed to the woods, and capable of
bearing bodily fatigue in a pretty considerable degree.   ." [3]

Drouillard on his part may not at this time have had
any very clear idea as to the exacting qualifications

---

[3] Thwaites I, pp. 227, 266.

Lewis had in mind. If he had, he might not have disappointed the captain in the type of men he did bring.

Lewis had other things to say in his letter to Clark of December 17:

> I send you, by Drewyer, your cloaths portmanteau and a letter which I received from St. Louis for you and which did not reach me untill an hour after Floyd had set out. Drewyer and myself have made no positive bargain, I have offered him 25$ pr. month so long as he may chuise to continue with us.

The letter referred to, though it may have been his first, was not the last letter to be delivered by Drouillard in behalf of the Lewis and Clark expedition. This responsibility he continued to discharge throughout the rest of the winter, delivering letters, or carrying messages and articles, between Clark on the one hand, at Wood River, across from St. Louis, and Lewis, on the other hand, busy in various ways in St. Louis.

As a bearer of messages, Drouillard succeeded Charles Floyd, a competent man, who, had he lived, would, without doubt, have become one of the most valuable of the men in the entire expedition. The fact that he had been employed as a bearer of messages indicates that he enjoyed the confidence of both captains. His replacement by Drouillard indicates that the captains had confidence in Drouillard also.

It may be noted from the letter that Lewis had offered Drouillard twenty-five dollars per month but that Drouillard and himself had "made no positive bargain." Is this to be construed as meaning that Drouillard had not yet committed himself definitely to the enterprise for which he had been employed? Was he hesitant about surrendering his independence as a

hunter for the routine and the discipline to which he
would be subjected as a member of an army expedi-
tionary force? Did he prefer his present station in life
to that offered him by Lewis? Had he attachments in
Fort Massac, Cape Girardeau, or elsewhere, acting as
a deterrent to ambitions he may have had for joining
the expedition? Did he feel doubtful of his ability to
get along with the hard-driving, exacting American
captain? On the other hand, was Lewis the one responsible for the delay in arriving at a definite understanding between them?

In this connection it should be noted that Drouillard
was not the first candidate who had been considered for
the important position of interpreter. One, John Conner, had, and with Jefferson's approval, been considered
before him. In reporting for duty, Conner was to bring,
not only himself, but two Indians, if he could find any
who would qualify.

On August 3 Lewis wrote Clark from Pittsburg,
informing the latter that Conner resided among the
Delawares, and suggested he "spare no pains" in attempting to obtain his services as interpreter. Should
Conner fail to present himself, then Clark was to dis-
patch a man to the Delawares to inquire concerning
him and offer him an annual wage of three hundred
dollars, in addition to board and clothing.

Acting upon this recommendation, Clark, on August
20, dispatched a letter to Conner by Charles Floyd,
offering Conner a salary of three hundred dollars, and
urging him to report for duty. Conner, however, was
never employed. An explanation of this fact is contained in a letter which Lewis wrote Clark on September 28, on his way down the Ohio with the keelboat.

In this letter Lewis declared that he did not regret their failure to obtain the services of this man, "for several reasons," adding: "he has deceived me very much." [4] When the captains met at Louisville, therefore, where Clark resided, neither had obtained the services of an interpreter. It may have been at this time that the name of George Drouillard came in for consideration.

It could have been Lewis, therefore, instead of Drouillard, who was holding off in the matter of consummating a "bargain" between them. Was Lewis counting on chances of obtaining someone better qualified than Drouillard; someone who had consorted among the Indians of the Missouri, who knew their ways, who could converse with them by word of mouth as well as by signs, in whom the Indians had confidence, or for whom they entertained respect? Having been a British subject, which was true for Drouillard as well as for Conner, was there any likelihood that Drouillard, in the discharge of his duties, would be influenced by sympathies for the British, a people for whom Lewis entertained none too high an admiration? Would it be better to give Drouillard a probationary period, so to speak, and then, during the winter, perhaps, or in the spring, decide whether he was the man to be entrusted with the important position the captain had in mind?

Whatever the reason for the failure of the captain and Drouillard to come to a definite agreement, the matter did not long remain an issue; for among several names added to the Lewis and Clark roster on January 1, 1804, was the name of a hunter from Fort Massac — one, "George Drullier." [5]

---

[4] Thwaites I, p. 273. See also pp. 213, 218, 267, 268.
[5] Thwaites VII, pp. 360-61.

The interview at Fort Massac on November 11, 1803, between Lewis and Drouillard must have been, to each of them, one of some importance.

There was, on the one hand, the captain, in need of a man who could qualify for the important position of interpreter, and who, in addition to these qualities, must be young (preferably), accustomed to the out-of-doors, strong of body, intelligent, inured to hardships, unafraid, able, cooperative, loyal, resourceful. Was the man recommended to him the man for whom he had been looking?

There was, on the other hand, George Drouillard, for whose bold, adventurous, ardent spirit the proposed expedition must have seemed more than ordinarily attractive; finding himself, now, in the presence of the man who had stopped at Fort Massac in the interests of recruitment of personnel; in the presence of a man, that is, in a uniform of the United States Army – tall, slender, intent upon what he was doing, alert, self-assured, dignified – the man appointed by the President of the United States to command this expedition to the Pacific.

The prospect of becoming a member of an expedition as unprecedented as this one must have struck the sensitive, alert, imaginative, adventure-seeking Drouillard with compelling force. Whether he betrayed eagerness, enthusiasm, or reserve, in response to the proposition put to him by Lewis, in the course of the interview, is not known. The result of the interview was that the captain "engaged" him, "in the public service," as indicated.

When Drouillard enrolled with the Lewis and Clark expedition, the discovery of the Northwest Passage to the Pacific was still, as it had been for more than a century, pretty much an unrealized dream. Any account pertaining to such passage must, for George Drouillard, have had more than an ordinary connotation. It is not unlikely that, as a boy, he had listened to tales concerning this passage of swarthy Algonquins piloting their canoes down the St. Lawrence, and bringing accounts of a forked river to the west, in a land devoid of trees, that led toward unlimited hunting grounds. It is not unlikely that he had heard rumors of yet another river, (one beyond the mountains, this time), that flowed toward the Lake of Ill-Tasted Water. So alluring must have been these tales, and other tales on the same subject, and so fraught with promise of fame and adventure, that it probably did not seem at all strange to young Drouillard they should have prompted the untiring efforts of explorers, adventurers, fur traders, and even statesmen, among the French, the British, the Spaniards, and even among the Americans, in heroic attempts to be the first to discover and traverse this sought-after route to the Pacific. It can be taken for granted that Drouillard knew enough about the attempts to discover the Northwest Passage to make him realize that the enterprise upon which he had now agreed to embark was one which was at least as important as any that had gone before. He knew enough, also, to make him realize that in attempting to discharge the various responsibilities placed upon it, this enterprise was, more than the others, designed to perform a service of no mean importance to the America which had now become the country of his adoption. A realization such as this, coupled with whatever knowledge he had relative to the Northwest Passage, and coupled with his own insatiable love of adventure, must have kindled in him an enthusiasm for the enterprise which can perhaps better be imagined than described.

3

Anchor's Aweigh

The camp at Wood River saw greater activity than usual on May 14, in the year 1804; for this was the day on which the long-prepared-for expedition to the Pacific was to start.

Everything to be taken along – firearms, powder, ball, fishing tackle, ink powder, medicines, astronomical instruments, blankets, jackets, flannel shirts, socks, shoes, cornmeal, flour, biscuit, salt pork, coffee, beans, Indian presents – had been packed and stored in one or the other of the three boats which were to make the ascent of the Missouri as far as the Mandans.

The largest of the three, namely, the keelboat which Lewis had laboriously brought down the Ohio from Pittsburg, was designed to be manned by twenty-two oars. It was fifty-five feet in length, equipped with a square sail, a ten-foot deck in the bow, a forecastle and cabin in the stern, and with a set of lockers which could be raised, if occasion demanded, to form a breastwork for defense. The two smaller boats were pirogues, one of seven oars, the other of six, both having been procured by Lewis during the early stages of his trip down the Ohio.

Rainy and windy though the day, the moment of departure must have been a memorable one for those who participated in it: the army privates and their sergeants, equipped with muskets, pistols, shot pouches,

powder horns, hunting knives, and knapsacks; intrepid
Kentuckians, rigged out in buckskins; "gay, grimacing,
singing, good-humored" voyageurs (to paraphrase
Washington Irving)[1]; Corporal Richard Warfington
and his contingent of men, pressed into service to go as
far as the Mandans; William Clark, tall, dignified,
red-headed, clad in a United States Army uniform. The
moment must have been impressive, also, for the various
habitants who had been attracted to the spot to see the
flotilla get under way. Only two were absent, among
those slated to take the trip: Captain Meriwether
Lewis; and George Drouillard.

As it happened, these two were, at the time, in St.
Louis: Lewis, for the purpose of conferring with some
Osage chiefs who had come down the Missouri to do
business with their Spanish father; and Drouillard,
who had been dispatched to St. Louis the day before
with a letter from Clark informing Lewis that the
expedition would be getting under way on the fourteenth but would go no further than St. Charles, about
twenty-two or more miles up the river by boat, where it
would await Lewis' approval.

Drouillard's trip across the Missouri to St. Louis
from the camp at Wood River on May 13 may have
been like many another which he had made in the
course of that winter and spring, except that on this
day he was making the trip for the last time. For that
reason he may have paid more than ordinary attention
to the quaint but colorful village that presented itself
to view from, and above, the tree-fringed shore opposite. He may have been more than ordinarily inter-

---

[1] Washington Irving, *Astoria,* I, p. 142.

ested in the whitewashed log huts and pretentious stone
mansions that occupied the first of two limestone ter-
races; and equally interested in the clusters of buildings
below that constituted the trading houses, the shops,
the inns, the taverns, and the billiard parlors. He had
mental pictures of the polyglot population in this fron-
tier-situated, up-and-coming little metropolis: enterprising Spanish merchants; thrifty shopkeepers; gay-
hearted Canadian voyageurs; dark-skinned, burden-
bearing Creoles; painted, sober-faced, blanket-en-
shrouded Indians.[2]

Only a few weeks before (on March 9 and 10), the
village and, in fact, all of Louisiana, had been trans-
ferred from the Spaniards to the French, then from the
French to the Americans. Under the command of
Major Amos Stoddard, American soldiers from Cahokia had come over, as had Clark and his men from
Wood River. They had marched up the narrow,
crooked lane that led to the government house on the
hill. There, in the presence of a large assemblage of
people, Don Carlos De Hault De Lassus, the Spanish
governor (a Frenchman by nationality), had met them
and, with suppressed feelings, delivered himself of an
address, after which he had handed to Major Stoddard
the keys to the village.

Drouillard had retained vivid memories of the scenes
of those two days: the tense, emotion-suppressed silence
that gripped the crowd as the Spanish flag was lowered
to the ground; the weeping of De Lassus as he gathered

---

[2] Florence L. Dorsey, in her book, *Masters of the Mississippi,* gives a vivid
description of St. Louis and its inhabitants at a time which follows the departure of the Lewis and Clark expedition by only a few years. Descriptions
of the village are also found in Eva Emery Dye's, *The Conquest,* and in
Washington Irving's, *Astoria.*

the folds of the precious emblem in his hands; the
cheering of the French and the Creoles as the Lilies of
France were hoisted to the top of the mast; the rule of
the French flag during the day and throughout the
night. He may have experienced something akin to
sadness on the following morning as he listened to the
dirge-like roll of drums, and as he witnessed the weeping of the Creoles, during that breath-choking moment
while the once proud emblem of France was making
its humiliating descent to the ground. The feeling of
sadness must have been quickly dispelled, however, as
his senses became attuned to the whistling of fifes and
the rattling of drums during the interval which saw
the Stars and Stripes briskly hoisted to the top of the
mast, from where they seemed to proclaim that from
henceforth the village, and all of the vast country
around and beyond it, belonged, not to the Spaniards,
not to the French, but to the Americans, whose country
he would now have an opportunity of serving in a
magnificent way as a member of the expedition that
was to take him to the Pacific.

Having arrived at the opposite bank, Drouillard
secured his craft and made his way up one of the narrow lanes that led to the second terrace and the mansion
of Peter Chouteau.

Lewis was occupied with the matter of arranging for
the sending of a delegation of Osage chiefs to the nation's capital and could not get away at once to join
Clark at St. Charles. He instructed Drouillard to hold
himself in readiness to take a message to Clark.[3]

---

[3] On May 21, Clark wrote his brother-in-law, Maj. William Croghan, from
St. Charles, that he had waited for five days while Lewis in St. Louis was
attempting to "fix off the Osage chiefs." – Thwaites VII, p. 301.

Four days later (May 17) found Drouillard in St. Charles, with a message to Clark from Lewis. He returned to St. Louis the next day with a letter from Clark. Lewis promptly sent him back the following day with another letter, and with ninety-nine dollars. What the money was for is not disclosed. Clark states that, for some reason not given, Drouillard was not able to locate the letter until the next day (May 20).

In the afternoon of that day (May 20), accompanied by "Officers & Several Gentlemen of St Louis," Lewis arrived in "a heavy Showr of Rain." He and Clark, and presumably those who had accompanied the former, dined in the evening with a "Monsr." Charles Tayong, a Spanish Ensign & late commandant of St. Charles."

The next day, at half-past-three in the afternoon, in a downpour of rain driven by a hard wind, and to the accompaniment of *bon voyage* and other expressions of goodwill from the "gentlemen" on shore, and possibly to the accompaniment of lusty chants from the one-eyed Missouri waterman Peter Cruzette and his intrepid voyageurs, all of the explorers but two pushed off, upstream, heading, at last, for the unknown regions which had beckoned them for so long. The two who did not embark were Alexander Willard and George Drouillard. These had been left behind, temporarily, to receive any official who might come out from St. Louis. That is, Drouillard was to do the receiving; Willard was to accompany him on the journey to rejoin the expedition, or stand ready to take any message to the captains. As it happened, no official showed up, and Drouillard and Willard joined their companions, up river, three days later.

4

Westward Bound

Drouillard did not have long to wait, after rejoining the explorers, before he was to taste the experience of serving as a hunter for the more than forty men who made up the party at this time. The very next morning, at seven o'clock, in a heavy rain, he started out on horseback, ahead of the main party, accompanied by John Shields, mounted on the other of the expedition's two horses.

They were gone a week. During this week they rafted or swam several creeks. They sat down beside their fire at night to partake of roasted venison or bear steak or such other food as they had been able to procure. They experienced the discomfort of sleeping in the rain. At the end of the week they rejoined their companions, somewhat "worsted," as Clark put it, but with a "flattering" account of the country.

The plan of hunting was then modified so as to permit Drouillard and whoever went with him to return to the main party at night instead of camping by themselves for several days at a time.

Drouillard continued to serve as the chief hunter. He was accompanied, generally, by one of the men. They would fell their game, skin it, remove the entrails, and bring it to camp or to the river, on horseback. Here enough of the meat would be cooked to serve the party for the evening meal, and enough for the journey the next day, thereby eliminating the necessity, during this part of the journey, of doing any cooking on the march. It may be added that, since his official position was that of interpreter, Drouillard did not participate in any of the menial work in or about camp.

Two instances from Clark's journal mentioning Drouillard's hunting activity are: (1) "Several hunters sent out to day on both sides of the river, *Seven* Deer killed today, Drewyer killed six of them." (dated July 11, 1804); and (2) "George Drewyer our hunter and one man came in with 2 Deer & a Bear, also a young Horse, they had found in the Prarie." (dated June 17, 1804).

On his excursions up the river or across the plains Drouillard served, also, as scout, reporting to his superiors on the characteristics of the country, on his experiences, and, in general, on whatever he believed might be of interest or value to the expedition. Clark's journal for July 2, 1804, bears the entry: "George Drewyer informs that the Lands he passed through, yesterday and to day on the S.S. was verry fine, few Springs." And Sergeant Ordway, who accompanied Drouillard on June 21, was moved to write in his journal: "I went on Shore with Drewyer all day & I never Saw as fine Timbered land in my life nor Such Rich bottom land, Drewyer killed one Deer & him & me brought it to the River, one Turkey likewise."

Drouillard had not been with the expedition long before he discovered that other travelers, mostly in fur-laden canoes or rafts from the Platte, the Kansas, and other western tributaries of the Missouri, were also using the river, and bound for St. Louis. These craft were encountered, for the most part, during the early progress of the expedition – as many as eight of them, for example, in as many days.

Drouillard enjoyed those days of early summer, as he rode his horse leisurely along the river or out across the prairies in quest of game, and as he rejoined his rollicking companions at night and satisfied his healthy appetite on roasted venison or bear steak. He must have thrilled, of an early morning, as he beheld the vast, treeless plains unfolding before him, and as he filled his lungs with the pure, invigorating air and leaned into the robust, playful, prairie wind. His eyes must have sparkled as they beheld the herds of buffalo, elk, deer, and, further north, antelope, that populated the vast plains, accompanied, invariably, by packs of wolves, and occasionally by turkeys.

There were incidents without number, on this journey up the Missouri.[1] For instance, the snapping of the mast as the keelboat passed under an overhanging tree; the attempts of the men to coax a half-starved dog to follow them; the visit of a large wolf, which, from a nearby river bank, studiously observed the personnel and activities of the camp; the attempt of a snake to reach some venison which had been hung over the river; the taming of a beaver which someone – most likely Drouillard – had brought to camp; the discovery and capture, by Drouillard, of a fat young horse; the jerking of the meat of two bear killed by Drouillard; the swimming of the river by the Negro York, for the purpose of procuring wild cresses for "Dinner"; the efforts of the men to save their boats from being dashed against the shore by waves raised by a high wind which

---

[1] The incidents referred to may be found in Thwaites, I, pp. 40-119; the prairie dogs, in Quaife, 127.

had come upon them suddenly; the unsuccessful attempt of Drouillard to catch a glimpse of some aquatic creature that made a sound resembling the gobbling of a turkey; the invasion, by the men, of a village of prairie dogs, and the capture, by Drouillard, of one of the animals, after the expenditure, by himself and his companions, of several barrels of water.

There were other incidents: the memorable visit to Spirit Mound; the Fourth of July celebration; the day Drouillard brought in a "Missourie" Indian; the day Drouillard and Colter were sent in search of the horses which had strayed from camp; the time when Drouillard and Cruzatte were dispatched with a twist of tobacco to the Ottoes; the day Collins was court martialed for getting drunk while serving as sentinel and for having permitted Hall to draw whiskey, followed two weeks later by the court martial of Willard for having fallen asleep while standing guard; the night they camped in a "deserted trading house," near which they found a "fat" horse; the day a man suffered a sunstroke but found relief when bled by Lewis; the day Lewis and twelve men caught upwards of eight hundred fish in a pond; the day they passed the trading post where Cruzatte had spent two years as a trader among the Omahas. There were still other incidents, for the most part trivial, yet interesting; until finally occurred one which had in it not only important implications for the success of the expedition, but showed Drouillard in a role in which he had not heretofore participated.

5

Desertion

The incidents referred to followed in the wake of a succession of episodes, the first of which was Drouillard's discovery, on July 28, of the "Missourie" Indian, already mentioned. The captains persuaded this man to go with one of their own, La Liberté, the next day, to the Ottoes with an invitation to the latter to come to the fires of the white men for a smoke.[1]

Four days later saw the arrival of a fairly large group of Ottoes. They were accompanied by their interpreter, Fairfang, but La Liberté was not with them. When pressed for a reason as to the absence of the white man, the Ottoes evinced surprise, declaring they had supposed the white man had already arrived, since he had started a sleep's journey ahead of them.

No suspicion of desertion appears to have entered the minds of the captains at this time. Clark stated in his journal the next day they feared either that La Liberté's horse had tired or that the horseman had lost his way.

A council with the Ottoes was duly held on August 3 on a high point of land overlooking the Missouri,

---

[1] Ordway records in his journal for this date (July 28) that Drouillard came upon *three* Indians. They were "dressing an Elk. they were friendly and gave him a part of it and one of them came with him." In his entry for the next day, Ordway says: "Jo Barter a Frenchman who could Speak the Zotau language went with the Indian in order to Git as many of them together as possible & bring them to the River treat them &.C." – Quaife, 102.

which the explorers called Council Bluffs, near the present Council Bluffs, Iowa. The day following the council the Indians took their departure, presumably heading west or south. The explorers on their part, broke camp and headed north; but they had not gone far before one of their hands, Moses B. Reed, turned back, explaining to a companion that he intended to look for his knife, which, he declared, he had inadvertently left behind at the Council Bluffs camp ground. He did not rejoin his companions that day, or the next, or the next.

At one o'clock on the seventh, the captains dispatched Drouillard to find this man, with orders to shoot to kill, if necessary. Having taken Reed into custody, or otherwise disposed of him, he was to journey on to the Ottoes, find and apprehend La Liberté, then invite and escort the Ottoes to the camp of the explorers for a second conference, this one for the purpose of negotiating a peace between them, on the one hand, and the Omahas and the Sioux on the other.

It should have occasioned Drouillard no surprise to learn that, of all the men in the expedition, he was the one to be chosen for a task as important and as difficult as this one. He was well aware that the captains had at their disposal other men, and good ones, who could have been selected: the three sergeants, Charles Floyd, Nathaniel Pryor, and John Ordway; John Colter, courageous, resourceful, loyal, although lacking in experience in parleys with Indians; Cruzatte, a man who had consorted among the Omahas for two years, and who was acquainted to some extent with their language and customs. There were, also, the Fields brothers, and Patrick Gass, William Labiche, and others. Instead of any of these, the captains had chosen him, Drouillard, and at a time when his services might be needed as interpreter to the Indians whom the captains were now expecting to meet at any time. Whatever may have been his reactions to the assignment, and to the choice of himself as the one to carry it out, it must have afforded him some satisfaction to realize that his superior officers had been willing to entrust to him a responsibility in the successful discharge of which depended, in part, the morale, if not the fate, of the expedition.

Clark's journal for August 7, 1804, states: "at 1 oClock dispatched George Drewyer, R. Fields, Wm. Bratten & Wm. Labieche back after the Diserter reed with order if he did not give up Peaceibly to put him to Death &c. to go to the Ottoes Village & enquire for LaLiberty and bring him to the Mahar Village also with a Speech on the occasion to the Ottoes & Missouries, and derecting a few of their Chiefs to come to the Mahars, & we would make a peace between them & the Mahars and Soue."

Drouillard and his three companions made as good time down the river as they could. Very likely they were mounted, for the explorers had found, and probably appropriated, at least three horses en route.[2] Once Reed was apprehended, the journey was to continue until La Liberté had also been found and taken into custody, and the consent of the Ottoes obtained to visit the white men.

Several factors contributed toward making this task not only dangerous but difficult.

[2] On June 17, Drouillard and some of the men came in with a fat young horse, found on the prairie: On July 3, one or more of the men found another horse; on July 11, a third. Possibly Drouillard was instrumental in finding all three. The references to these horses are made by Clark.

For one thing, Reed had the advantage of a three-and-a-half-day start. During these days he may have traveled fifty or sixty miles to the south while the explorers traveled as many to the north.[3] When Drouillard started in pursuit of him, therefore, the two may have been one hundred twenty miles apart. If Reed traveled at the rate of fifteen miles per day, and Drouillard pushed himself so as to average fifty or more miles per day, then it would have taken Drouillard three days, or until the evening of August 9, in which to overtake Reed. By this time he would be close to two hundred miles distant from the main party, since this traveled north, during these days, a distance of forty miles; and seventy-six and three-fourths miles farther still during the succeeding four days before reaching the spot on which they chose to await Drouillard's arrival.[4]

For another thing, Reed could be counted on to put as much distance as possible between himself and his former comrades. Knowing, as he must, the intolerance of the captains of infractions of discipline, and anticipating, as he also must, what might happen to him were he caught and proved guilty of desertion, it is safe to assume he would take reasonable precautions against being detected and brought to trial.

---

[3] By their own estimates, the explorers traveled 15, 20½, 20½, and 17 mi. respectively, on Aug. 4, 5, 6, and 7, a total distance of 73 mi. They traveled 56 mi. on the first three of these four days. By noon on the fourth day they may have come 10 of the 17 mi. traveled that day, or possibly 66 mi. when they reached the point from which Drouillard was dispatched on his mission.

[4] Distances traveled (again by the explorers' own estimates): Aug. 10, 22¼ mi.; Aug. 11, 17 mi.; Aug. 12, 20¼ mi.; Aug. 13, 17¼ mi., or a total of 76¾ mi.

Wheeler, I, p. 377, states that the explorers were inclined to overstate distances traveled by themselves.

Upon contact with Reed would follow the dangerous and disagreeable task of capturing him without injury either to him or to those attempting to apprehend him. There would follow the still more disagreeable task of "shooting to kill," should Reed prove intractable; or, if captured, the inconvenience of keeping Reed under guard; and, finally, the task of persuading the Ottoes to cooperate with Drouillard and his companions in finding another prisoner when they already had one in tow.

Furthermore, nine days had elapsed since La Liberté had been sent to the Ottoes. If he had headed for the Missouri, upon leaving the Ottoes, and followed this south, there would be no point in attempting to overtake him.

As regards the Ottoes, they might be out on a buffalo hunt, as they had on a previous occasion when Drouillard had gone forth to find them, and might not, therefore, be easy to locate. Finally, when located, would follow the task of persuading them again to visit the camp of the white men.

Drouillard and his party were gone on this mission eleven days. They found, and captured, Reed. They brought Reed to the Ottoes. They inquired about La Liberté. With the help of the Ottoes, they ascertained La Liberté's whereabouts. They took La Liberté into custody. Drouillard obtained a hearing before the chiefs of the Ottoes, smoked the pipe, delivered himself of his "speech," and invited them to accompany him to the Omahas to smoke the pipe with the Omahas and the Sioux. After conferring among themselves, the chiefs agreed to accompany Drouillard to the white men.

The party, some two hundred miles to the south of where the main party was camping, started out. Included in the party were: three chiefs; a number of lesser Indians; Drouillard, Reuben Fields, Bratten, Labiche; and the two prisoners, Moses Reed and La Liberté. The Indians rode their horses. Since the two hundred miles were covered in fewer than six full days, the white men must also have been mounted. Possibly Drouillard had negotiated with the Indians for the use of some horses.

At six o'clock in the evening of August 17, ten days after the departure of Drouillard and his party, a messenger arrived at the Lewis and Clark camp on the Missouri (below the site of the present Sioux City, Iowa), to report that Drouillard and his party were behind, with Reed and three of the principal chiefs of the Ottoes, but that La Liberté had "deceived them" and got away.

In what the deception consisted, does not appear. It may be stated that, but for this deception, Drouillard and the men who accompanied him would have been completely successful in their mission.

The trial of Reed occurred on the day he was turned over to the captains by Drouillard. He confessed that he had "Deserted & stold a public Rifle Shot-pouch Powder & Ball." He requested his prosecutors to be "as favourable with him" as they could consistent with their "oathes."

The leniency for which he begged was granted, inasmuch as he was not required to suffer any greater punishment than that of running the gauntlet and of forfeiting his right to be considered henceforth a member of the expedition. The running of the gauntlet,

however, he had to do four times. Every time he ran
it, each man stood ready to lash him with nine switches.
The three Otto chiefs were among those, if others there
were, who petitioned that the prisoner be pardoned.

Whether Lewis, or Clark, personally thanked
Drouillard for what he had accomplished, is not recorded in the Lewis and Clark journals. It can be
assumed that they were pleased at the success of the
mission, and relieved to learn that Drouillard and his
subordinates had returned in safety. Drouillard had,
thus far, served the expedition well.

6

Enter, the Red Men

There was one question of never failing interest to Drouillard and to every member of the expedition – What would happen were they to encounter Indians? It had come to their attention that the natives of the Missouri did not believe the country had fallen into the hands of the Americans. How would these natives feel when the Americans themselves came and told them so?

It had become clearly obvious to Drouillard that any rumor to the effect that they were to meet Indians had a most salutary effect upon all of the members of the expedition, including the captains. On such occasions, firearms would be examined, supplies of powder and ball checked and replenished, and camp sites selected with a view to defense. The men would be assigned to strategic positions, and instructed on what to do in case of emergency. If a conference was expected, a suitable spot would be selected for the purpose, an awning or some other shelter would be erected, and presents of various sorts, including medals and tobacco, meticulously laid out. A flag of the United States would be flown from a mast.

Drouillard had no doubt formed a pretty accurate estimate of the fighting potential of the men in the expedition. Neither they nor their leaders could in any sense of the term be said to be lacking in courage or in determination. The men, moreover, as Drouillard well knew, had been carefully selected. They were young, bold, vigorous, hardy, in excellent condition physically, inured to hardships, well-trained, well-armed, well-disciplined, eager for whatever might befall, especially those who had been chosen to accompany the expedition all the way to the Pacific.

An incident which had in it the earmarks of an encounter with Indians occurred on the evening of July 9. Some of the men were camped on shore, as had been the practice up to this time, while the rest, including Drouillard and the captains, slept on board the keelboat. It was customary on such occasions for Clark, before retiring for the night, to communicate with the men on shore. When Clark flashed his signal on this particular night, there was no response. Could it be that those on shore were the much-vaunted Sioux? If so, where were their own men?

Without hesitation, Clark ordered all hands to prepare for action, and, at the same time, directed that a shot be fired from the swivel gun in the bow of the keelboat.

Drouillard was not likely the last to reach for his gun. Here was, finally, a chance for action. Were they Indians, those on shore? The Sioux? He strained his eyes in the darkness in a vain attempt to make out those who were camping or lurking there.

He might have spared himself. Those on shore, as it developed the next morning, were none other than their own men. They had failed to respond adequately to Clark's signal.

Drouillard knew that one of the important objects of the expedition was that of establishing friendly rela-

tionships with Indians along the route of travel. He
had observed that during the early stages of the expedition the captains had made no overt attempt to get in
touch with Indians for this purpose, first, because they
had met few Indians, and, second, because the Indians
with whom the captains did wish to confer were the
Ottoes, the Pawnees, the Omahas, and the Sioux —
tribes residing or roaming more than six hundred miles
up the river, at and above the mouth of the Platte.
After their arrival, on the twenty-first of July, however, at the mouth of the Platte, and from then on, for
the rest of their journey up the Missouri as far as the
Mandan villages, Indians were to figure in an important way in the daily routine of every man.

The first conference, as noted, had been with the
Ottoes, on August 3, at Council Bluffs; the second, also
with the Ottoes, on August 19, after Drouillard had
returned with the prisoner Reed. The Ottoes had been
amenable to the measures proposed to them. What
might be the attitude of the Pawnees, the Omahas, the
Sioux — and especially the Sioux — that was another
matter.

These latter Indians were reputed to be a fierce,
warlike, treacherous people, comprising several bands,
roaming up and down the Missouri, and to the far
reaches of both sides of it, in larger numbers than
could be mustered by any of the other Missouri tribes.
They possessed an abundance of firearms, kettles, axes,
knives, and a variety of other tools and equipment, procured from British trading posts at the headwaters of
the St. Peter (now the Minnesota) River, in exchange
for lodges and buffalo robes obtained by them through
hunting, theft, or war upon their neighbors. A realiza-

tion on their part that they possessed arms and equipment in excess of what other tribes possessed served but to heighten the feeling of boldness and arrogance with which they deported themselves anyhow. Moreover, they well realized their strength in numbers.

Drouillard was one of those who recalled the day on which the explorers met one, "M. Louisell," coming down the Missouri, fresh from these very people. This meeting had occurred on the fourth day of the departure of the expedition from St. Charles. Lewis had eagerly questioned Louisell in regard to the Sioux. What was their number, their strength? Where did they reside? What was their relationship to the British? What was their probable attitude toward Americans?

Drouillard recalled the day (June 12) on which they had met Pierre Dorion, the man who, according to his own statement, had resided among the Sioux for twenty years; who claimed to be a friend of the Sioux; who had married a Sioux woman; in whose children ran Sioux blood. What did he have to tell about the Sioux? The captains considered the probable services of this man to themselves so highly that they engaged him then and there to accompany them into the domains of the people who had aroused so much speculation among the members of the expedition.

This matter of holding themselves in readiness, day and night, and every hour of the day, for a possible meeting with the Sioux, may have begun to tell upon all of them. Would the Sioux ever show themselves? And if and when they did, what would be the result?

Cruzatte and others had reported to Drouillard that while he was gone in search of Reed and La Liberté, Lewis had dispatched Pryor, Dorion, and others to the vicinity of an immense smoke which they had beheld, on the chance that the smoke might have been started by the Sioux. The captain had also tried to get in touch with the Omahas. All of these attempts had failed. Nor was the captain to succeed any better after Drouillard's return and the expedition again began to move north. Yet Drouillard knew – the captains knew, everybody knew – that they were now in Sioux territory and might expect to encounter the miscreants of the plains at any hour.

To make matters worse, a number of misfortunes overtook them at this time. First, Floyd took suddenly ill of "Biliose Chorlick," as Clark put it, and died. He was buried that same day, within the present city limits of Sioux City, Iowa.[1] Second, two days later, several of the men, including Lewis, came down with upset stomachs, induced, so they believed, by the water of the Missouri which they drank, and which was here, to use Clark's words, coated with the "fumes & tast of the *Cobalt,*" and "had the appearance of Soft Isonglass Copperas & alum" – a mixture which the captain labeled "verry pisen." Then, shortly after this, their horses took it into their heads to stray from camp during the night.

It fell to Drouillard and Shannon to be sent out in search of the horses. One of them took to the plains.

---

[1] Thwaites I, pp. 37, 114. A relative of Floyd's, possibly his brother, began, in 1820, a crusade for the establishment of an American government in Oregon. "On December 20," of that year, "he exploded his first bombshell by asking Congress that a committee be appointed 'to inquire into the situation of the settlements upon the Pacific Ocean, and the expediency of occupying the Columbia River.' The House approved, and Floyd became chairman of the new committee which one month later (January 25, 1821) reported a bill authorizing occupation by the United States of the Columbia River Valley." – Oscar Osborn Winther, *The Great Northwest,* 141.

The other followed the river bottom. When, the next
day, Drouillard returned to camp, without having
found the horses, he became the recipient, not only of
the disquieting news that Shannon had not returned,
but that Joseph Fields and John Shields had been sent
back to look for both of them.

It was on that same day, at two in the afternoon, at
the mouth of the James River, that they came, unexpectedly, upon an Indian!

No sooner had this Indian discovered the boats than
he plunged into the water and swam out to one of the
pirogues. He was taken aboard, and the boats ordered
to pull for shore. Here two other Indians made their
appearance. These Indians informed the explorers that
a large band of their people were camped but a short
distance above the mouth of the river.

The captains lost no time in sending Sergeant Pryor
and a Frenchman, along with Dorion, to invite the
principal chiefs of this nation to a council at the foot
of a certain bluff which may have been discernable a
short distance up the river. Two of the Indians accompanied these emissaries. The third, who said he was an
Omaha, remained on board one of the boats.

The boats then continued upstream for a mile and a
half, when the captains ordered that camp be struck. It
did not escape Drouillard's observation that the site
selected was, this time, a sand bar, instead of the river
bank. The sand bar, did, however, lie toward the north
side of the river, which was the side into which the
James River flowed.

It was a cool, pleasant evening. A refreshing breeze
was blowing from the south. Even nature, it seemed,
was doing her part to lend life and zest to the events
that now seemed imminent.

The breeze was still blowing sharply from the south the next morning when the boats got under way.

After four miles, the explorers arrived at a high bluff which sloped gradually away from the river to their right. Here the Omaha Indian left them. He intended, he said, to go to the camp of the Sioux.

Drouillard soon learned they were not to be free from the series of misfortunes which had first visited them on the nineteenth of August, the day that brought on the fatal illness of Floyd. For one thing, the captains felt much "indisposed" during the day, due to some cause which they were unable to determine. For another, one of the pirogues ran a "Snag thro her" and, in the stiff breeze, was on the point of sinking before the damage could be temporarily repaired. For a third, Shields and Fields returned in the evening to report that Shannon and the two horses had passed them at some point and were now so far ahead that they could not be overtaken.

Drouillard knew that this last bit of news worried the captains not a little, for they realized that Shannon was not a first-rate hunter. They realized, also, there were dangers, other than the danger of starvation, to which Shannon might now be exposed. It did not surprise him, therefore, to learn that the captains had "deturmined" to send a man to his aid with provisions.

The man chosen was Colter. Without protest, the latter donned his knapsack, grasped his gun, and started out the next morning, on foot, leaving Drouillard free to act as interpreter, should his services as such be needed.

The site chosen for the conference with the notorious Sioux was located some eight miles above the sand bar

on which they had camped the night before. It occupied a "Butifull Plain," on the west, or larboard,
side of the river, nearly opposite the present site of
Yankton, South Dakota, and near the foot of "Calumet
Bluff," sloping gradually back from the river. Oaks,
elms, and other trees grew in abundance throughout
the entire lovely valley.

Drouillard realized as much as any one the importance which the captains attached to this forthcoming meeting with the Sioux, for upon the success of
this meeting, and upon the success of further meetings
with other bands of this notorious nation, might depend
the fate of the expedition. He observed the care with
which the captains set their camp in order. The men
were instructed in respect to their duties. A spot under
an oak was selected on which to meet the Indians.
Presents, consisting of medals, coats, hats, tobacco,
wampum, and other articles, were selected, to be meticulously laid out the next day, prior to the council
proper. The American flag was already flying on a
staff. An additional spot, at some distance from the oak,
was reserved as a camp site for the Indians.

Drouillard, the captains, and the entire personnel of
the camp, save Shannon and Colter and the men who
had been sent to the Indian village, waited at the foot
of Calumet Bluff the rest of that day, and until four
o'clock the next afternoon, before the Indians made
their appearance on the river bluffs across the river.

There were seventy or more of them, all men except
for a few boys. They came on horseback and on foot,
leisurely, the chiefs and Pryor and his party in front,
the rest following. Conspicuous among them were five
chiefs, easily detected because of their elaborate feather
headdresses. Bows and arrows, and a few guns, were in

evidence. Hunks of meat had been loaded onto some of the horses.

What sense of the dramatic, or the symbolic, Drouillard may have experienced, as he stood and gazed at the red men across the river, is not known. He may not have caught either the spirit or the historic significance of that first important meeting of white men and red men, each confronting the other across the broad expanse of the Missouri, the one group at the foot of the now historic Calumet Bluff, the other from atop the bluffs across the river. It would be a matter for comment, though, if, in common with the captains and the other men, he did not experience something akin to a thrill, or at least a feeling of expectancy, as he first beheld those dignified red men who had come forth in their finest regalia, upon invitation of the white men, to smoke.

Lewis was not slow in sending over a pirogue. The pirogue brought back, not the Indians, but Pryor, Dorion, and Dorion's son. They reported that the Indians were Yankton Sioux and that these Indians had accepted the invitation of the white men for a smoke.

The captains sent Pryor and young Dorion back to these people, with tobacco, corn, kettles, and with the information that the white man chiefs would smoke with them after the next sun.

The council was held at twelve o'clock noon the next day (August 30). Some of the Indians, however, had, long before then, swum the river and were privileged to sit down with the white men for breakfast. Ordway has this to say about what happened:

at the hour of 9 oClock the commanding officers had all things in readiness . . . they sent a pearogue across for them, they all [c]ame into our Camp in the most friendly manner &.C.

their was four of them which were always a Singing & playing their curious Instruments . . . the head man of the[m] was painted white, the rest of them were painted different colours. When they arrived at our Camp & took the commanding officers by the hand 2 Guns was fired from our bow peace. The colours displaying &.C. Each man of our party Gave the 4 men of [the] Band a peace of Tobacco, they Sang around our camp during the time of the counsel. . .[2]

The council itself, held under the spreading branches of the oak, at the foot of the bluff, was a dignified, colorful affair. Lewis carefully explained to the Indians why the white men had come. Upon the conclusion of the speech the chiefs were formally recognized and treated to gifts, after which they retired to a bower of bushes prepared by the young braves, to smoke, eat, and decide how to answer the speech of the white man.

The afternoon and evening were spent in amusements. Whitehouse, in his journal, states that

they [their] Boys Shot with their Bows and arrows for Beeds and appeared to be merry, and behaved wel among our parte[y]. Capt. Lewis Shot his air gun told them that their was medicien in hir & that She would doe Great execution, they were all amazed at the curiosity, & as Soon as he had Shot a fiew times they all ran hastily to See the Ball holes in the tree they Shouted aloud at the Site of the execution She would do &c.[3]

There followed, the next day, a continuation of the council, when the Indians gave their answer to the white man's words of the day before. The Indians stated they had opened their hearts and would do as the white man had suggested, even to the extent of going with their friend Dorion on a visit to their American Father.

Drouillard must have gained a vivid impression of

[2] Quaife, 119.   [3] Thwaites VII, pp. 54-55.

the Yankton chiefs, as they sat and listened to the white man, and as they spoke themselves. He noted their solemn demeanor, the poise with which they deported themselves, the dignity and yet at the same time the eloquence with which they spoke, as they emphasized their words with timely pauses and with appropriate gestures. He studied their appearance, as they sat upon their painted buffalo robes, undressed to the waist (except for their headdresses). He noted their painted, brown faces, the high cheek bones, the slightly aquiline noses, the thin lips. He was not unaware of the embroidered moccasins, the richly-adorned buckskin leggings. He saw the long, supple arms extended in passing the pipe, or raised in gesture. He observed the pipe itself, long stemmed, ornamented, made of pipe stone.

So these were the vaunted Sioux, the talk and terror of the plains, the untrammeled savages who ruled both man and beast on all the vast expanse of the western plains! Savages they may have been. But one could hardly have asked for a finer display of courtesy and decorum than was here demonstrated by these Yankton chiefs and their followers, or their real enjoyment of the festivities that accompanied the more formal aspects of the gathering.

Nor had they been less considerate of Pryor and his party, upon the arrival of the latter at the village four days before. Hardly had the sergeant and his men come within sight of the village than they had been met by a delegation of braves who, in spite of the sergeant's declaration that he and his men were not chiefs, had promptly carried them on painted buffalo robes to the village itself and there placed them upon robes before the chiefs, who, on their part, had treated them to fat dog, a delicacy served only on special occasions and to special guests. Not content with this, the Indian braves had, upon request of their chiefs, gone out of their way, on their journey to the white man camp, to shoot the two elk and the six deer which they had brought along as a gift to these same white men who had been willing to stop on their journey to see them.

Untrammeled savages? Blood-spilling wildmen? Hardly.

But what would be the reaction of the Tetons farther up the river, into whose domain the explorers would soon be moving? How would they be received – by the Tetons?

7

The Tetons

George Drouillard and, for that matter, every member of the expedition, were certainly more than ordinarily interested in an announcement brought to them by three Indian boys one Sunday afternoon in late September. The boys had swum out to the boats and there, aboard the already overloaded keelboat, had informed every one on board that, on the creek above, were camped eighty lodges of Teton Sioux and, a short distance above these, sixty lodges more – upwards of fourteen hundred souls! [1]

The captains were not slow in offering the boys tobacco, and in sending word to their chiefs to come, at the next sun, for a smoke.

Trouble was in store for the explorers the next day.

In the first place, when the keelboat, accompanied by the red and the white pirogues, picked up Colter, who had been sent ahead to hunt, the latter reported that some Indians had stolen his horse. In the second place, the captains had angered a small group of Indians by refusing to pull up at the sand bar upon which the latter were standing.

That night the keelboat anchored off the mouth of the Teton (now Bad) River, deploying into the Mis-

---

[1] Quaife, 141. Ordway states that Gass told him he had been to one of these villages and had counted eighty lodges, "which contain ten persons each."

souri from the southwest (in the vicinity of the present city of Pierre, South Dakota).

In the course of the evening, Clark stepped ashore to smoke with some "chiefs" who had approached, but who did nothing to indicate they were anything but friendly. Five Indians ate with those of the Lewis and Clark men who camped on shore. According to Ordway, these men "Slept with us friendly." Nevertheless, and contrary to custom, two-thirds of the entire party of nearly forty-five persons received orders that night to sleep on board the keelboat. The captains were taking no chances.

It did not help the interests of the explorers to discover, the next day, at a critical moment, that they were without the services of a competent interpreter. Why did they not use Drouillard?

The answer was, mainly, for the reason that the captains preferred communication by word of mouth to the cumbersome method of communication by signs. This was the method they adopted among the Ottoes, where Fairfang had been on hand to act as interpreter. It was the method employed among the Yanktons, where Pierre Dorion had officiated. It was the method they had expected to use now, among the Tetons, in the absence of Dorion (who had been dispatched with some Yankton chiefs to the seat of government at Washington). It was the method which they employed later, among the Mandans and the Minnetarees. But the question may be asked: When they discovered the inadequacy of the man engaged by them to serve them as interpreter – a Frenchman whom they had picked up – why did they not rely upon Drouillard?

The answer is, they did, to some extent, later, although not as a substitute for the Frenchman, but, rather, as a complement to him. That is, Drouillard supplemented by signs such communication as the captains, through the Frenchman, found it necessary to have with the Indians; using, for this purpose, either the system of signs which he had learned, or adapting this system to that used by the Indians. It is probable that the Indians responded in kind, with the result that communication between the whites and the Indians was accomplished through the use of two media rather than one, and with satisfactory results, if one may judge from the ease with which one side understood the other in the conversations and speeches that followed.[2]

The morning of September 25 was "fair." It was the morning on which the explorers expected the arrival of the chiefs. Clark delivered himself of appropriate instructions to his men, especially as regarded the manner in which they were to escort the chiefs, military fashion, to the place of council. He was explicit in his instructions, taking nothing for granted.

Along with other members of the expedition, Drouillard experienced the tenseness, the sense of expectancy, that pervaded the morning air. Along with others, he stood at attention while the Stars and Stripes were being hoisted to the top of a staff erected on a sand bar. He observed the men on this same sand bar as they rigged the awning that was to serve as a council lodge. He may have assisted in laying out the presents intended for the chiefs.

All this while, out on the river at the safe distance of seventy yards, lay the keelboat, jealously guarded by

[2] See Appendix A.

the boat crew. The red and the white pirogues floated
lazily near the sand bar.

At "about 10 o'c. A. M.," wrote Ordway, the Indians
"Came flocking in from boath Sides of the River. When
30 odd was selected under the American coullours Capt
Clark went out to speak and treat with them." The
captains "gave them pork in return" for the "Buffaloe
meat" offered by the Indians, and carried on the backs
of "squars." [3] There followed the ceremony of smoking, Lewis' "talk," the recognition of the chiefs, the
distribution of presents, and a visit to the keelboat.

On board the keelboat the captains made the mistake
of treating the Indians to whisky. In a short while, the
Second Chief began to pretend he was drunk. He stag-
gered and reeled, now against one of the men, now
against Clark, uttering insolent remarks, laughing
harshly, smacking his lips, sucking the bottle (to which
he still clung), and, in general, acting in an insulting
manner. It was only through the exercise of tact and
firmness on the part of the captains, with the help of
Drouillard and other men, that the captains were able
to persuade the Indians it was time to depart. To Clark,
accompanied by five men, including the "two interpreters," fell the task of escorting them to the opposite
shore in one of the pirogues.

When the pirogue grated on the gravel, Drouillard,
Clark, and the others, including the Indians, got out.

Scarcely had this been accomplished than three of
the Indians on shore ran forward and seized the cable.
A fourth rushed into the water and flung his arms
around the mast. The others, with gleaming eyes, and

---

[3] Clark states that the Indians came at eleven o'clock and that they were
accompanied by three "squars," who carried "vast quantities" of buffalo meat.

armed with bows and arrows, swarmed in from all sides, upon the heels of their chiefs, as the latter edged up close to Clark and Drouillard and the French interpreter and the three men who had accompanied them.

The Second Chief made himself especially obnoxious. Feigning drunkenness, and staggering up against Clark, he declared insolently, in words and gestures, that Clark should not be permitted to continue his journey, inasmuch as the white men had not given him enough presents.

An animated exchange of words and gestures followed, in the course of which Clark told the Second Chief that he (Clark) "would not be prevented from going on"; that he and his men "were not squaws, but warriors";[4] and that they had on board the big canoe warriors and medicine that could, in one day, destroy twenty nations such as that of the Tetons.[5] The "justures" of the Second Chief, wrote Clark in his journal afterward, "were of Such a personal nature I felt My self Compeled to Draw my Sword *(and Made a Signal to the boat to prepare for action).* . ."[6]

It was a tense moment. There were, on the one hand, the hostile Indians, crowding in close, their eyes gleaming with hatred and determination, their hands itching to let loose a volley of arrows into the hides of the provocative white men; on the other hand, the white men themselves – a handful of them – standing close, one of them with sword in mid-air, the others with hands on guns or pistols, all of them as determined as any white men could be to take it out on the red men should the

[4] Paul Allen, *History of the Expedition under the Command of Captains Lewis and Clark,* 98. (Hereafter referred to as Allen).
[5] Hosmer, 37.   [6] Thwaites I, p. 165.

latter have the audacity to start even the semblance of a fight.

"I felt My Self warm," declared Clark, "& Spoke in verry positive terms . . . those with me also Showed a Disposition to Defend themselves and me. . ." Had it not been for the intervention of the judicious-minded Black Buffalo, it is doubtful whether the situation would have been resolved without resort to combat. Black Buffalo, however, at the psychological moment, and aware of the ominous fact that the medicine gun in the big canoe was directed upon him, turned on his heel and, striding toward the pirogue, jerked the cable from out of the hands of those who held it and ordered them gruffly away.

Upon receiving this command from their head chief, the Indians did, grudgingly, yield the rope and withdrew to a short distance, followed by the man who had hugged the mast.

Perceiving that those surrounding him were determined to prevent his escape, Clark barked a sharp command to "all" of his men, except the "2" interpreters, to take the pirogue to the keelboat for reinforcements. The reinforcements came, posthaste, in the form of twelve determined, well-armed men. Said Clark:

> this movement caused a no: of the Indians to withdraw at a distance, *(leaving their chiefs & soldiers alone with me)* . . . they all left my Perogue, and Councild. with themselves the result I could not lern and nearly all went off. . .
>
> After remaining in this situation Some time, I offered my hand to the 1. & 2. Chiefs who refused to receive it. . .

Disdaining further attempts at saving the day, Clark then ordered his men to the pirogue.

Hardly had they gone ten paces before Black Buffalo, accompanied by the "3rd." chief "& 2 Brave Men Waded in," regalia and all, after them, grabbed the gunwales, and made signs to indicate they wished to be taken aboard. Clark grudgingly consented.

Once on the keelboat, the entire party, accompanied by the pirogues, proceeded about a mile. Anchor was cast for the night off an island of willows, which Clark dubbed Bad Humored Island. The pirogues were fastened to the keelboat. A guard was stationed on shore; another on the boat.

In the morning, Black Buffalo and the others on board the keelboat professed friendliness. They importuned the captains to permit their women and children to see the big canoe. They desired the white men to visit the village. To all of which the captains finally consented, agreeing between themselves that Lewis be the one to go for the purpose. Accompanied by a handful of men, including Drouillard and the French interpreter, he started off, in one of the pirogues.

The shore was lined with men, women, and children who had come forth, in all their finery of grease, paint, and "calumet feathers." In the crowd was the Second Chief, who met the white men with an apologetic smile, and with the explanation that the white man's milk had made his heart bad the day before but that now it was good. Why the change of front?

For one thing, the tactics of the Indians the day before had failed. It was incumbent upon them to do something to save face.

For another, the council, started the day before, had not been completed. A council between white men and Indians, in those days, ordinarily consisted of three sessions: the first, in which the white men made a proposition to the Indians; the second, in which the Indians retired to their council lodge to deliberate among themselves; the third, in which the Indians gave their formal answer to the proposition. The first and third sessions were invariably accompanied by the ceremony of smoking, by eating, and by the exchange of gifts. As a matter of fact, the Teton Sioux had not yet formally delivered their answer to the white man's speech of the day before. They had failed to extend to him the courtesies that a situation such as this demanded. They would do so today.

Finally, and just as important, if not more so, in view of their ultimate design to exact tribute, was the matter of expediency. Should they fail to change their tactics, the white men – these obstinate new white men who could not be cowed either by threat of force or by a display of overwhelming numbers – might decide to leave without bothering further about any exchange of gifts whatever! In such event, they (the Tetons) would be defeated in their designs anyhow. Better try a different approach. They might win by diplomacy what they had failed to accomplish by threat.

As a result, the explorers were treated, that day, first to a tour of the village, then, later, to a grand council, followed by feasting and dancing.

The village was a large one, consisting of trim-looking, artistically-decorated tepees, placed in concentric circles around a larger tepee which occupied an open court in the center.

Even though many of the inhabitants had gone to view the big canoe, still the village was by no means deserted. Women of all ages, including girls, attired in deerskin dresses, were – or might have been – occupied in tanning buffalo skins for clothing and shelter. Men lounged about. Dogs scampered everywhere. Horses were grazing in the distance, except for such as may have been kept tied to tepee poles.

Through this village, later in the day, six stalwart warriors carried, on a painted buffalo robe, first Clark, then Lewis. Neither was permitted to touch the ground until he had been taken to the grand council lodge in the center of the village and placed on a white, dressed robe, next to Black Buffalo, who also sat on a robe.

The lodge itself was a large tepee, forming three-fourths of a circle, the remaining fourth being open. About seventy of the more important of the Teton men had gathered and were now seated within the circle. To the front of the captains and the chiefs, Drouillard, from his position near that of the captains, may have noted an open, circular space, about six feet across. In this space had been placed the pipe of peace, raised on forked sticks so as to hold it about six or eight inches from the ground. The ground under the pipe had been strewn with swan's down. On one side of the circle was another pipe, and directly across from it a third. The flag of Spain and the Stars and Stripes held sway from a staff. Near the sacred circle was a large fire, over which "provisions" were cooking. Near the fire, neatly piled on a robe, lay about four hundred pounds of excellent buffalo meat – a present to the white men.

In a few minutes an old man rose. By word and gesture he informed the white men that he approved of their conduct. He ended by asking them to have pity on the red men.

Black Buffalo rose with great state and spoke to the same purpose. With great solemnity he took the pipe and, observed in silence by everybody, pointed it, first to the Heavens, then to the Four Winds, then to the Earth, their Mother. He presented the stem to Lewis, who took a puff, then to Clark, who likewise took a puff. Upon the conclusion of the ceremony he made a short speech. Then, turning to his guests, he offered them dog, pemmican, and ground potato. The meal was followed by an hour of smoking. There was no hurrying, no noise, nothing frivolous. The entire affair was carried out with the solemnity of a sacred ceremonial, witnessed patiently by painted men, women, and children.

Were they sincere? If Drouillard had been asked the question, he would have answered in the affirmative. But, they had been the day before, too, when they had laid hands on the pirogues. But sincerity would not necessarily deter them from attempting to carry out their original intention, if such it had been, of preventing the strangers from continuing their journey up the river.

By the time the smoking had been concluded it was dark. Everything was then cleared away. A large fire was built in the center of the court. Ten musicians appeared, played on tambourines and rattles, and sang. Women, in their finery of paint, feathers, and porcupine quills, came forward and, while the musicians played, danced Indian style, displaying, during this performance, scalps and other trophies of war won by their braves in battle. The Teton women were joined in the dancing by five or six of the braves, who had been selected to perform in pantomime praise-worthy deeds enacted by themselves or other braves in combat.

The festivities lasted until midnight. When Drouil-

lard and his companions finally stood up to leave, Black
Buffalo and three other chiefs rose to accompany them,
as far as the keelboat, on board of which these chiefs
spent the night.

Clark states in his journal for the next day (September 27) that "P. C. our Bowman who cd. Speek Mahar
informed us in the night that the Maha Prisoners informed him we were to be Stoped. we Shew as little
Sighns of a Knowledge of their intentions as possible
all prepared on board for any thing which might hapen,
we kept a Strong guard all night in the boat, no Sleep."

Drouillard had noticed these prisoners, the day before: twenty-five women and thirteen boys; sitting on
the ground, huddled together, hair disheveled, grief-
stricken – the victims of despair. And why not? Had
not the Sioux only thirteen days before destroyed forty
lodges, killed seventy-five men and a number of boys,
and carried, in triumph, these women and boys to the
Sioux lodges? Their homes destroyed, their husbands,
brothers, and sons killed, they themselves carried off by
these ruffiians, who regarded them with contempt and
had it in their power to taunt them, ridicule them,
torture them, take their lives, or inflict upon them such
other indignities as their cunning might devise – why
should they not feel dejected? The scalps flaunted in
triumph during the festivities that very night had undoubtedly been the scalps of the nearest of kin to these
prisoners.

September 27 was pretty much a repetition of the day
before, except for an incident which occurred as the
party was returning to the keelboat late in the night.
The man steering the pirogue, not skilled in the act,
instead of easing the pirogue against the sides of the

boat, brought it broadside against the cable by which
the boat was anchored. The cable snapped. Clark
ordered all hands to the oars. The Second Chief, who
had accompanied the party in the place of Black Buffalo, "hollowaed" the camp at the top of his lungs,
shouting to the effect that the Omahas were about to
attack. Two hundred warriors rushed to the river bank,
armed for battle, headed by Black Buffalo.

Clark was dubious. Omahas, my liver! The chief's
outcry was made because the latter feared the explorers
were attempting to slip away in the darkness. Clark
might have added: "They'll probably try murder next."
Nothing further happened, however, except that sixty
of the warriors remained on the river bank throughout
the night.

The loss of the anchor compelled the explorers to
draw the keelboat up against an overhanging bank,
where it lay exposed to whatever hostile intentions the
Indians may have had. A strong guard was stationed
on board the boat, and probably on shore, for the rest
of the night. Nobody slept. The men were prepared for
anything.

Several unsuccessful attempts were made the next
morning (September 28) to retrieve the anchor. This
had become so immersed in the sand that it could not
be found.

Drouillard was aboard the keelboat. He kept an
observant eye upon Black Buffalo, who had replaced
the Second Chief, and upon the other Indians aboard,
as these studied with some show of interest the efforts
of the Lewis and Clark men feverishly searching in
the water for the anchor. At every obvious failure, or
new mode of attack, on the part of the workers, these

dignitaries grunted, or curved their lips in smug satisfaction.

Drouillard felt more concerned, however, about the crowd on shore than about the chiefs on board the keelboat. Some two hundred warriors, armed with "fire arms . . . Spears . . . Cutlashes . . . and Bows and steel or Iron pointed arrows," [7] had gathered on the gravel, near the edge of the water, but far enough away from the workers not to be too much in the way. These warriors surveyed with interest the efforts of the men who were attempting to retrieve the anchor. Now and then, like their chiefs on board the keelboat, they grunted or smiled. They may even have laughed outright, or given expression to taunting remarks. A goodly number of them were near the keelboat. Some of them were sitting on the cable.

Some idea of what was going on, and what happened, may be gained from Ordway, who wrote:

> . . . Capt Clark was Speaking to the chiefs in the cabin. Capt Lewis asked the chiefs if they were going out of the boat. they did not incline to. then Capt Lewis came out [and] ordered every man to his place ordered the Sail hoisted, then one man went out [and] untied the chord, which the warrier had in his hand, then 2 or 3 more of their warries caught hold of the chord and tyed it faster than before. Capt Lewis then appeared to be angarry, and told [them] to go out of the Boat and the chief then went out and Sayd we are sorry to have you go, But if you will Give us one carret of tobacco we will be willing for you to go on & will not try to stop you. Capt Lewis Gave it to them. the head chief Sayd then that we must Give him one more carrit of tobacco more for his warries who held the chord and then we might go, boath of our Captains told him that we did not mean to be trifled with. nor would not humer them any more, but would Give him 1 carrit more for the warriers, if he would be a

---

[7] Quaife, 142.

man of his word and Stand to his word like a man. the chief
Sayd he was mad too, to See us Stand So much for 1 carrit of
tobacco. if we would Give it we might go on. Capt Lewis gave
it to him.[8]

It was at this critical moment that Black Buffalo
flung the tobacco to his warriors, jerked the cable out
of their hands, and handed it to the bowsman. The deck
hands applied the oars, and, under a gentle breeze, the
boat, accompanied by the pirogues, got under way, the
object of angry taunts and jibes hurled at it from shore.

The departure of the boats on September 28 did not
mark the end of the contacts which the explorers had
with the Sioux. The latter, in large or small numbers,
continued to crowd the river front, or to follow the
boats, for the rest of that day, and the two days after
that. The explorers, however, had no more dealing with
them than their sense of expediency dictated.[9] They
arrived safely among the Arikaras, spent an enjoyable
week there, then journeyed on to the Mandans, among
whom they established themselves for the winter.[10]

---

[8] *Ibid.*

[9] The Teton Sioux continued for some time their practice of annoying
various boat parties which ascended the Missouri on their way to the Indians
to the north. So persistent were they in this practice that they came to be
known as the "pirates of the Missouri." Yet, strangely enough, the Tetons
discontinued their hostile attitude sooner than did their neighbors and kins-
men, the Yanktons. Of all the Sioux tribes, the latter came to be the most
dreaded by the Missouri traders. The "loss of life and property at their hands
during the period of the fur trade was such as to cause never-ending solicitude on the part of those who did business with them." – Hiram Martin
Chittenden, *The American Fur Trade in the Far West,* II, p. 865. (Hereafter referred to as Chittenden).

[10] The Arikaras gave the explorers a most cordial reception. Bernard De
Voto ascribes this hospitality as due to the fact that the latter had, through
the "Indian underground," gained information with respect to the firmness
and success with which Lewis and Clark had met the rapacious demands of
the Teton Sioux only two weeks before. – De Voto, *Journals of Lewis and
Clark,* 34. (Hereafter referred to as De Voto). Judging by the speeches
which the Arikara chiefs delivered to the white men when the latter arrived

among them, this could very well have been the case. The grand chief
Kakawissasa, for example, said: "My Fathers! My heart is gladder than it
ever was before to see my fathers. . . If you want the road open no one
can prevent it. It will always be open for you. Can you think any one Dare
put their hands on your rope of your boat, No! Not one dar[e]." – Thwaites,
VII, p. 303.

It may be recalled that it was by laying hands on the "rope" that the Teton
Sioux had attempted to stop the explorers.

8

Danger Ahead

April 7, 1805, was a memorable day in the lives of the members of the Lewis and Clark expedition, for it was on that day, at four o'clock in the afternoon, after an enjoyable winter among the friendly Mandans, that the explorers again resumed their journey toward that faraway western land beyond the Shining Mountains that had beckoned them so long.

In the presence of whatever Indians may have been on hand to see them off, and to the accompaniment of shouts and cheers among themselves, they launched forth, in their two pirogues and six dugout canoes, leaving the keelboat, under Corporal Richard Warfington, to make its way back to St. Louis, loaded with biological and zoological specimens, and with messages for the country from which the men had now been separated a long time.

The last-minute preparations for the journey northward were accomplished without any lack of enthusiasm on the part of the men as these hurried forward with packages and bundles for the boats, and as each sought to further the venture which held in it so much of promise for all of them.

"At this moment," wrote Lewis, "every individual of the party is in good health, and excellent spirits; zealously attached to the enterprise, and anxious to proceed; not a whisper of discontent or murmur is to be heard among them; but all in unison, act with the most perfect harmony. With such men I have every thing to hope, and but little to fear." [1]

The men themselves were not lacking in praise and appreciation of their leaders, if one may judge from the reports brought back by those who returned to St. Louis with Warfington, and if one may judge, further, from the contents of the letters sent back with this same party by some of those who went on to the Pacific. According to a newspaper account, the men who returned spoke in the "highest terms of the humanity, and uncommon pains and attention of both Captains, *Lewis* and *Clark,* toward the whole of them; and that they left them in good spirits, fully convinced that they would winter on the Pacific Ocean." [2]

Two there were, that day, who did not embark with the enthusiastic men as these took their places at the oars: one, Meriwether Lewis, co-captain of the expedition; the other, George Drouillard, hunter and interpreter. These two found themselves standing side by side at the edge of the water, silent but admiring observers of the two flotillas as these pulled away, one pushing north, the other south. This separation from their comrades, however, was merely to permit the captain a last word of farewell with his friend, Black Cat, head chief of the Mandans, whose lodge was situated a few miles up the river. In the furtherance of this purpose, he had asked Drouillard to go with him as interpreter. Accompanying the two of them, was, without doubt, the captain's esteemed dog, a Newfoundland, for which the captain had paid twenty

---

[1] Thwaites, VII, p. 321; I, p. 285.
[2] Thwaites, VII, p. 326.

dollars, and which had been with him ever since his trip down the Ohio – and was to accompany him on many a tour by foot in the future.[3]

Drouillard had spent a comparatively quiet winter at the establishment which the Lewis and Clark men had erected on the Missouri, about three miles to the south of the lower Mandan village.[4] He had not been called upon extensively to act as interpreter, because the captains had engaged for this purpose Rene Jessaume, to assist them in communicating with the Mandans, and Toussaint Charbonneau to do likewise when they communicated with the Minnetarees (Hidatsa), whose villages were located on Knife River, seven or eight miles above the villages of the Mandans.

But he had hunted. This latter responsibility made it necessary for him, along with those who accompanied him, to venture far out onto the wind-swept, snow-covered prairie, at one time to a distance of twenty-four miles, and on another occasion to a distance of thirty miles. Frequently he was out over night. Once he was set upon by a band of a hundred Indians whom he and his companions judged to have been Sioux. The Indians unhitched the hunters' three horses from the sleighs, but, upon command of their leader, returned one. Clark noted in his journal that the hunters were "not disposed to be robed of all they had tamely."

Three new recruits had been added to the expedition when it departed from Fort Mandan on April 7. One of these was Toussaint Charbonneau. Another was Charbonneau's wife, Sacajawea, a young Shoshone who had been taken captive a few years before by the Minnetarees of Knife River on one of their war-raiding or

---

[3] Quaife, 48.   [4] Thwaites, I, p. 216.

horse-stealing expeditions. The third was Baptiste Lepage, who was engaged at Fort Mandan to replace John Newman.[5] These, added to the old recruits, made a total of thirty-one men and one woman. To this group should be added, also, Sacajawea's two-months old son, Baptiste, whom Clark came in time to speak of as Pomp.[6] A Mandan man was with them when they started but turned back two days later.

The expedition had not long been gone from Fort Mandan before Drouillard found himself back at his job of hunting. He was accompanied, now, sometimes by Lewis, sometimes by Clark, each of whom would

[5] John Newman was tried by court martial for "certain mutinous expressions" uttered in "an unguarded moment." Though his conduct was "highly meritorious" from then on, as it had before then been "generally correct," and though he showed an "ardent wish" to attone for his crime, and even "asked forgiveness for what had passed," still Lewis, even though the man stood acquitted in his own mind, deemed it "impolitic to relax from the sentence," and accordingly sent him back to St. Louis from Fort Mandan. In a letter to Secretary of War Dearborn, however, Lewis stated that he would feel "much gratified" if the Secretary could think it "proper to give Newman the remaining third" of the gratuity due Baptiste Le Page, who was employed in Newman's place. – Thwaites VII, pp. 356-57.

[6] Born Feb. 11, 1805. Clark called this infant "Pomp" in his letter to Charbonneau, "On Board the Perogue near the Ricara Village," on his return trip down the Missouri August 20, 1806. – Thwaites VII, p. 329.

". . . about five Oclock this evening [Feb. 11, 1805]," wrote Lewis, "one of the wives of Charbono was delivered of a fine boy. it is worthy of remark that this was the first child which this woman had boarn, and as is common in such cases her labour was tedious and the pain violent; Mr. Jessome informed me that he had frequently administered a small portion of the rattle of the rattle-snake, which he assured me had never failed to produce the desired effect, that of hastening the birth of the child; having the rattle of a snake by me I gave it to him and he administered two rings of it to the woman broken in small pieces with the fingers and added to a small quantity of water. Whether this medicine was truly the cause or not I shall not undertake to determine, but I was informed that she had not taken it more than ten minutes before she brought forth perhaps this remedy may be worthy of future experiments, but I must confess that I want faith as to its efficacy." – Thwaites I, p. 258.

take turns at walking on shore while the other took
charge of the boats.

This stage of the journey did not prove strenuous
insofar as Drouillard was concerned, due mainly to the
fact that, except in the vicinity of the villages of the
Mandans and the Minnetarees, game was plentiful and
easy to procure. Even though the healthy appetites of
the explorers required well nigh the equivalent of one
buffalo per day, still this was not a difficult assignment,
especially when, as was the case in the vicinity of the
Yellowstone, the animals hunted were so unafraid as
to make it possible to walk up to them and touch them
with sticks.

Drouillard knew that the Assiniboines roamed the
country to the north. Farther to the west were the Indians of "Fort de Prarie," [7] who traded at a post established by the British in Canada. The captains, Drouillard knew, did not wish to meet Indians now. They
were particularly desirous of avoiding a meeting with
the Assiniboines and the Indians of "Fort de Prarie,"
either of whom might prove troublesome. Aware of
this, and also because it was in the nature of his duties
and his training to do so, Drouillard kept himself ever
on the alert for signs of these or other Indians.

With unfeigned interest he examined abandoned
hunting camps and village campsites. He scrutinized
discarded, worn-out moccasins. Whenever possible, he,
or others in the expedition, retrieved articles that
floated down the river; as, for example, lodge poles;
and, once, a football. He studied any smoke that might
disclose itself in the distance.

[7] Lewis' designation (Thwaites II, p. 92). He may have had in mind the
Gros Ventres of the Prairies.

A man with a zest for the out-of-doors, such as that possessed by Drouillard, could be depended upon to keep himself on the alert, not only for signs of Indians, but for other signs as well.

He saw and heard, for example, the flocks of geese that winged their way northward. He observed these birds as they fed on the green grass on the prairies, and again when they were shedding their feathers and could no longer fly. He noted the nests of the bald eagle in the trees along the river, and may have asked himself why these nests were invariably accompanied by the nests of two or three magpies. He passed numerous carcasses of buffalo, scattered along the edge of the water, where they had been washed ashore after the animals had lost their lives in attempting to swim the river, or because of having broken through the ice while crossing the river in the spring.

He came upon the industrious beaver, contentedly feeding on the bark of young trees. Upon taking to the bluffs, he would behold at a glance, buffalo, elk, deer, antelope, grazing peacefully as in a common pasture.

The bleached hair of the buffalo, clinging to a thorny bush, did not escape his attention, nor the cast-off antlers of the elk, nor the wrapped-up body of a dead woman, placed on a scaffold, with the carcass of a dog underneath.

He beheld packs of wolves, from six to ten animals per pack, stalking the buffalo. He observed how the wolves would pounce upon any luckless buffalo calf indiscreet enough to separate itself from the herd, or lacking in strength to keep up with its elders. He discovered that the wolves caught the fleet-footed antelope, not on the ground, but while the animals were attempting to swim the river.[8]

Nor did facts about the country escape his attention. Day after day he would cast his eyes over the treeless, undulating prairies, now green with the fresh grass of spring. He inhaled the pure, crisp, invigorating morning air; noted the almost entire absence of dew on the grass; observed the thin ice along the edge of the river, or in the kettles, after a frosty night. He braced himself against the ever-present prairie wind; avoided the prickly pear; scraped ponderous clumps of clay off his moccasins on a rainy day. With Lewis, he thrilled at the colors and shapes of geologic formations known today as badlands. He noted the clarity with which he could discern objects at a distance, due to the rarity of the air.

In the vicinity of the Yellowstone, along with several of the other members of the expedition, he experienced a soreness of the eyes, due, the captains believed, to the fine sand picked up by the wind from sand bars in the river and carried for miles in the form of clouds. These clouds were at times so thick as to make it impossible to discern the bluffs or the tree line across the river. It was impossible to keep the sand from these clouds out of their food. In fact, as Lewis remarked, they were "compelled to eat, drink, and breath it very freely." The sand even penetrated to the inner workings of the captain's watch, in spite of the fact that the instrument had the protection of a double case. One dust storm, which struck them toward evening on the twenty-first

---

[8] Thwaites II, p. 351. In his journal for July 15, 1805, Lewis states that, after Drouillard had wounded a deer, the captain's dog pursued it into the river, "drowned it and brought it to shore at our camp."

of May, was so violent as not only to make it impossible for them to "cook, eat, nor sleep," but compelled them, at eight o'clock, to move to the foot of an adjacent hill.

Another annoyance was that caused by the blowing fly, about which Lewis wrote on May 20: "They infest our meat while roasting or boiling. . . we are obliged to brush them off our provision as we eat." Mosquitoes, gnats, ticks, and the prickly pear also came in for comment.

Some of the annoyances actually amounted to hardships, as witness the occasions when the men who navigated the boats came upon rapids, or when they attempted, from slippery river banks, to tow the boats against a current too swift for oars and too deep for poles. Drouillard must occasionally have come upon these men as they laboriously towed the boats upstream, while wading in water, or while toiling on river banks too slippery for walking; unable, at times, to wear moccasins because of the "tenacious" clay; compelled, at other times, to walk barefoot on "fragments of rock" that had "tumbled from the river bluffs" – performing labor which Lewis characterized as "incredibly painful and great." In all of this the men did not resort to even a "murmur" of complaint.

This journey up the Missouri had dangers as well as hardships. One night, to cite an example, Drouillard was aroused by a shout from the sentinel, who awoke the occupants of the tepee (Lewis, Clark, Charbonneau, Sacajawea, York and Drouillard) just in time to enable them to move the tepee to a place of safety before the top of a tall tree, which had caught fire, came crashing down upon the spot where the tepee had stood. On another night a buffalo bull, after having swum the river and made quite a racket as it clambered over the white pirogue, became frightened and started on a run through camp, rousing not only Lewis' dog but all hands, and causing each man to spring to his feet, gun in hand, to inquire of his neighbor what had happened.

There was the ever-present danger of being "swallowed up by . . . masses of earth" from perpendicular banks "eternally precipitating themselves into the river"; and the danger of having their boats swamped by sudden squalls.

One sample of this latter danger is furnished by an incident which occurred on April 13. Regarding this incident, Lewis wrote:

> . . . the wind was in our favour after 9 A.M. and continued favourable untill 3 P.M. we therefore hoisted both sails in the White Perogue, consisting of a small squar sail, and spritsail, which carried her at a pretty good gate, untill about 2 in the afternoon when a sudden squall of wind struck us and turned the perogue so much on the side as to allarm Sharbono who was steering at the time, in this state of alarm he threw the perogue with her side to the wind, when the spritsail gibing was as near oversetting the perogue as it was possible to have missed. the wind however abating for an instant I ordered Drewyer to the helm and the sails to be taken in, which was instant[ly] executed and the perogue being steered before the wind was agin plased in a state of security. this accedent was very near costing us dearly. beleiving this vessel to be the most steady and safe, we had embarked on board of it our instruments, Papers, medicine and the more valuable part of the merchandize which we had still in reserve as presents for the Indians. we had also embarked on board ourselves, with three men who could not swim and the squaw with the young child, all of whom, had the perogue overset, would most probably have perished, as the waves were high, and the perogue upwards of 200 yards from the nearest shore; however we fortunately escaped and pursued our journey under the squar sail, which shortly after the accident I directed to be again hoisted.

An incident of this sort on May 14 was even more dramatic, and again involved Drouillard, though to a lesser degree than this one. The two incidents, besides serving as samples of a danger to which the explorers were exposed, serve also to illustrate another skill attained by Drouillard, if navigating a pirogue under sail may be classified as such; a skill, howbeit, which stood the expedition in good stead on April 13, in view of what might have happened had the pirogue upset.[9]

The grizzly was another source of danger, and one to which Drouillard was subjected more than the others, partly because of his responsibilities as hunter, and partly because of a bent in his nature to test his prowess against that of a bear whenever circumstances should bring him and a bear together.[10]

Drouillard had not been gone many days out of Fort Mandan before he began to catch glimpses of this king of the plains and mountains; but not until the departure of the explorers from the Yellowstone was he to experience the gratification of having his first real encounter with him. This first experience with *ursus horribilis* was followed by many another, involving not only Drouillard but other members of the expedition as well, and compelling them, at times, to run for their lives, seek refuge in trees or behind clumps of willows, or jump over precipices into the river.

At the Great Falls of the Missouri the grizzlies became so bold, in spite of Lewis' dog, as to venture into camp at night. Here they would proceed to help themselves to meat, soup, or to whatever they found handy, forcing Lewis to the necessity of issuing orders, first,

[9] See Appendix B.   [10] See Appendix C.

that no man leave camp except when accompanied by at least one other person, and second, that the men sleep on their arms at night the same as if they expected an attack by Indians.

At the Great Falls of the Missouri, also, it may be added, the explorers, including the captains, organized themselves into an expedition de luxe to "beat up" on the bears. Only one bear was encountered, however, and that by the party led by Drouillard, who, in a thick brush, and "at the distance of about 20 feet," felled it by a well-placed bullet.

One additional danger may be mentioned – that of losing their footing while making their way on steep river bluffs.

This danger resulted in near tragedy on a trip of exploration which Lewis, Drouillard, Windsor, Cruzatte, Shields, Lepage, and Pryor took, on foot, up the Marias River on June 4-8. The trip started off happily enough. The presence of numerous birds, as the adventurers journeyed across the prairie, added "much to the gayety and cheerfulness of the scene." They encountered "meriads of small grasshoppers." When, after eight miles, Drouillard was dispatched to kill one of two deer for their breakfast, "this excellent hunter," wrote the enthusiastic captain, "so[o]n exceeded his orders by killing of them both. . . we soon kindled a fire cooked and made a hearty meal."

On the fourth day, as they were making the return trip, they were compelled to take to the river bluffs, due to the swollen waters of the river as a result of a rain which had fallen the day before and most of the night. While treading his way along these bluffs, one of them – Windsor – slipped and fell.

It was an exclamation from the prostrate man that called his plight to the attention of the captain, at the head of the line, and probably to Drouillard also, who may have been close behind. The exclamation was: "Good God, Captain! What shall I do"

As recorded in his journal, the captain said that Windsor had slipped and fallen and was

> lying prostrate on his belley, with his wright hand arm and leg over the precipice while he was holding on with the left arm and foot as well as he could which appeared to be with much difficulty. I discovered his danger and the trepedation which he was in gave me still further concern for I expected every instant to see him loose his strength and slip off; altho' much allarmed at his situation I disguised my feelings and spoke very calmly to him and assured him that he was in no kind of danger, to take the knife out of his belt behind him with his wright hand and dig a hole with it in the face of the bank to receive his wright foot which he did and then raised himself to his knees; I then directed him to take off his mockersons and to come forward on his hands and knees holding the knife in one hand and the gun in the other   this he happily effected and escaped.

If Drouillard was the man behind Windsor, he must have stood stock still while the captain spoke and while Windsor tried to carry out the captain's instructions. Upon a directive from Lewis, he turned back to warn the others in the party not to come this way, but to descend to the river and to follow this as best they could. The captain and Windsor would join them there shortly.

It was not long before Drouillard, along with his companions, found himself in water to his "breast." When the water became too deep for wading, he and the others, including Lewis and Windsor, cut "footsteps in the face of the steep bluffs" with their hunting knives and proceeded as best they could, through "rain, mud, and water untill late in the evening," when they camped in an old Indian stick lodge, which afforded, in contrast to the night before, a "dry and comfortable shelter."

Beside a cheery fire in that stick lodge they dried themselves. They relaxed their weary muscles. They treated themselves to roasted venison. They listened to the slashing rain, the blustery wind. They recounted the day's adventures, and may even have dreamed of adventures to come. In his journal the captain wrote: "I now laid myself down on some willow boughs to a comfortable nights rest, and felt indeed as if I was fully repaid for the toil and pain of the day, so much will a dry bed, and comfortable supper revive the sperits of the w[e]aryed, wet and hungry traveler."

The next morning the birds – among whom the captain named the brown thrush, the robin, the turtle dove, the linnet, the gold finch, the large and small blackbird, the wren, "and several other birds of lesser note" – these birds sang "most enchantingly" in the trees along the river when the "sun began to shine." Was the captain enjoying his trip of exploration to the sea? Was one, George Drouillard?

There were moments on this trip that neither of them would ever forget.

9

In Search of the Red Men

Seven days after the mishap to Windsor found Lewis at the Great Falls of the Missouri, accompanied by Drouillard, Joseph Fields, Gibson, and Goodrich.

During more than half of the sixteen days it took the explorers to portage their supplies and equipment over the eighteen-mile stretch around the falls,[1] Drouillard occupied himself in the hunting of elk. These animals were in demand for their skins, to be used in encasing an iron boat frame that Lewis had brought from Harper's Ferry. The boat, when completed, floated "like a perfect cork," but soon began to leak and had to be abandoned. Drouillard, however, knew of two cottonwoods which, he believed, might be shaped into dugout canoes to supplement the six that had been portaged around the falls. When, on July 13, these had been finished, the explorers loaded their craft and resumed their long interrupted journey to the Pacific.

Drouillard was now to find himself the member of an expedition in pursuit of two objectives: that of reaching the Pacific; and that of coming in contact

[1] Coues says the portage "measured 17¾ miles, inclusive of the short course below Portage creek." Elliott Coues (ed) *History of the Expedition under the Command of Lewis and Clark,* II, p. 386. (Hereafter referred to as Coues). One of the Lewis and Clark maps shows the distance as 17 miles. – Thwaites II, p. 178.

with Indians who could supply them with horses and a guide for crossing the mountains.

The plan of operation was to send a party of four or five men ahead of the main party, in an attempt to make contact with Indians before the discharge of the guns of the hunters, or the discovery by the Indians of a large party, should cause the former to flee to the mountains.

Three such parties were sent out in succession. Each party traveled scores of miles in advance of the canoes. Each party was gone from the main party for about five days. Clark was in charge of the first and second; Lewis, of the third. Those among the men who accompanied them were Drouillard, Joseph and Reuben Fields, Charbonneau, York, Potts, Frazier, and Gass.

These parties traversed a terrain that was not only rough and rugged but so infested with the prickly pear as to make it difficult to proceed without stepping on the thorny plant time and again. The men in the parties endured a burning sun and thirst and fatigue by day, and cold, sore limbs, aching joints, and bruised feet by night. They climbed peaks, searched valleys, penetrated canyons, examined river bottoms, went up one stream, down another – all in the hope of coming in contact with Indians. Yet, during fifteen days of the most arduous toil, not one Indian did they see, nor even a sign of an Indian, other than signs which did not help them.[2]

---

[2] Thwaites II, pp. 249, 261, 263, 266-67, 279, 282, 315. De Voto thinks the failure of the explorers to encounter Indians between the villages of the Mandans and the Continental Divide may have been due to the "Indian underground," which traveled faster than they did and which told how the formidable Teton Sioux had been rebuffed by these same white men, after the former had attempted to prevent them from continuing their journey. – De Voto, 34.

They were not to complete these toilsome treks without mishaps to themselves. Clark came down with a fever. Charbonneau sprained an ankle, on one occasion, and, on another, was swept away by a mountain stream. In descending a peak, Drouillard injured a leg and sprained a finger, and had to rest twenty minutes before being able to go on.

Those toiling upstream with the canoes were not having an easier time of it. If they attempted navigation by pushing the canoes with poles, the poles were as apt as not to slip on the smooth stones that lined the river bottom. If they towed the canoes by wading through the current, pebbles in the river bed would blister their feet. If they pulled the canoes by walking along the bank, brush or tall grass would be in their way. Rapids, beaver dams, and blind channels would impede their progress. Canoes would upset, or fill with water. Along with all of these difficulties were their "trio of pests," the mosquitoes, the gnats, and the ever-present prickly pear – "equal," Lewis declared, "to any three curses that ever poor Egypt laiboured under, except the *Mahometant* Yoke. . ."

On the last day of July, Lewis wrote that two of the boat crew were lame, from "tumers or bad boils on various parts of them." A third was suffering from a "stone bruise." A fourth had "dislocated" an arm. A fifth – their burly Irishman, Patrick Gass – had strained his back as the result of slipping and falling backwards over one of the canoes. Whitehouse had been pinned under a canoe that glided over him while being swept down stream by a turbulent current.

On July 27, Lewis wrote:

> we begin to feel considerable anxiety with rispect to the Snake Indians. if we do not find them or some other nation who have

horses I fear the successfull issue of our voyage will be very
doubtfull or at all events much more difficult in it's accomplishment. we are now several hundred miles within the bosom of
this wild and mountanous country, where game may rationally
be expected shortly to become scarce and subsistence precarious
without any information with rispect to the country not knowing
how far these mountains continue, *or* where to direct our course
to pass them to advantage or intersept a navigable branch of the
Columbia, or even were we on such an one the probability is
that we should not find any timber within these mountains large
enough for canoes if we judge from the portion of them through
which we have passed. however I still hope for the best, and
intend taking a tramp myself in a few days to find these yellow
gentlemen if possible. my two principal consolations are that
from our present position it is impossible that the s. w. fork can
head with the waters of any other river but the Columbia, and
that if any Indians can subsist in the form of a nation in these
mountains with the means they have of acquiring food we can
also subsist.

Five days later Lewis made good his resolve. He
started out, as leader of the third advance party which
has been mentioned, in search of the "yellow gentlemen," accompanied by Drouillard, Charbonneau, and
the man who had sprained his back, Patrick Gass. After
five days of fruitless endeavor they rejoined the main
party, but remained with this party only three days.
Then Lewis started again, accompanied by John
Shields, Hugh McNeal, and George Drouillard; determined, this time, to find the elusive red men, though
the attempt cost him a month.

On this last, desperate venture into the unknown
regions ahead, Drouillard was to be given the opportunity of participating with his friend and superior
officer, Meriwether Lewis, in heroic attempts; first, to
find and gain audience with the red men, and second,

to enlist these red men in the services of the expedition.

On his third day out (August 11), Drouillard made a discovery which, on the face of it, gave early promise that their hopes would be realized, at least in part.

He was trudging along through the dry grass, on a mountain-enclosed tableland which the captain called the Cove, when, upon looking ahead, his eyes chanced to fall upon a lone horseman riding slowly toward him and his companions at a distance of two miles.

It would require no undue strain on the imagination to conjecture that Drouillard experienced a quickening of the heartbeat the moment his eyes lighted upon that lone horseman, the first human being, aside from his companions, he had seen since his departure from the Mandans and the Minnetarees in the spring. It would require little imagination to assume that, consequent upon that discovery, he neither increased nor decreased his rate of advance, nor gave the slightest outward indication that a chance meeting with an Indian was anything but an ordinary occurrence. He did take an occasional glance, though, in the direction of the captain and McNeal, advancing beyond calling distance to his left, and at Shields, as far away again from the captain and McNeal to the left. He noted that all three of them were continuing to advance as before. He noted also that the Indian, for so he supposed the horseman to be, continued to ride forward slowly, until he had permitted the four of them to come within a mile of him, when he stopped and assumed a position astride his pony as if to await their arrival.

A glance in Lewis' direction at the moment when the Indian stopped revealed to Drouillard that the captain and McNeal had also stopped. Drouillard noted, while continuing to move forward himself, that the captain was unstrapping the blanket from his pack. Having done this, the captain took hold of two corners of the blanket and, lifting it high over his head, allowed it to fall to the ground as if in the act of spreading it. Drouillard knew that this was a custom among plains Indians and intended as an invitation to come for a conference or visit. He knew that the captain had used this signal in an endeavor to inform the Indian of his friendly intentions. He knew the Indian should have heeded this gesture of friendship. But the Indian did not heed it. At least, he made no attempt to come forward; not even after the captain had performed the act three times. Instead, he continued to sit astride his pony as immovable as a statue, except when he cast his gaze, now in Drouillard's direction, now in a direction toward Shields, as if wondering what might be *their* intentions.

Soon the captain was striding forward again, some distance ahead of McNeal, and minus his gun and pouch, although equipped, as Drouillard learned afterward, with a mirror, beads, and a few trinkets. Proceeding forward thus alone, and flanked by Drouillard and Shields as before, he was able to get within two hundred paces of the Indian before the latter turned his horse and began to ride slowly away, looking back, however, over his shoulder from time to time, in the direction of Drouillard and Shields.

At this precarious moment Drouillard made the discovery that the captain was signaling him to stop advancing. *Sacré Dieu!* That was what Drouillard should have done long ere this, at the time the captain stopped. That was what Shields should have done. The captain had been too far away to call to them; and he had not wanted to signal them for fear of arousing the suspicions of the Indian!

Drouillard came to a stop. So did the Indian. In fact, the Indian turned his horse as if to wait for them, casting his eyes from Drouillard to the captain and then to Shields, who, however, on his part, was continuing to advance as before.

The captain, too, kept striding forward. He held high the trinkets for the Indian to see. He stripped his shirt sleeve to show the color of his skin. He called, at the top of his lungs (as Drouillard found out later), the ringing words, *"Tabba-bone! Tabba-bone!* White man! White man!"* Proceeding in this manner he was able to get, finally, to within one hundred paces of the Indian, when the latter gave whip to his horse, and disappeared behind some willows on the other side of the creek.

The captain was not slow in upbraiding Drouillard and Shields for their lack of "segacity" in not coming to a halt when he did, attributing his inability to gain an audience with the Indian "principally" to the failure of Shields to heed his signal. Well, the evil was done. Drouillard no doubt regretted his stupidity in the matter as much as did the captain. So did Shields, who claimed he had not seen the captain's signal. There was nothing more any of them could do about it now, except to try to follow the trail of the departed horseman. This they did, after Drouillard and Shields had been sent back for the "spye glass" which the captain had dropped with the blanket, and after McNeal had been made to carry on a pole a small flag of the United States.

It soon occurred to one of them – perhaps it was Drouillard, perhaps Lewis – that Indians might be

observing them from the hills, three miles away, toward
which the trail of the lone horseman led. Why in such
a hurry to find the trail? Why not advance slowly?
Why advance at all, except to yonder "elivated situation" near the creek, where they could build a fire, and
sit down to eat?

The thought had no sooner been suggested than it
was acted upon. While McNeal was kindling the fire
and preparing the meal, the captain got out an "assortment of trinkets" – moccasin awls, strings of beads,
paint, a looking glass. These he fastened to a pole
which he – or Drouillard – planted near the fire.

During these preparations a shower of rain came up,
accompanied by hail. The rain soaked the travelers to
the skin. This, however, did not matter. What did
matter, though, was the disappointing fact that the rain
had raised the grass trodden down by the pony of the
vanished Indian, making it difficult for them to track
the Indian.

Even so, Drouillard was able to follow the trail for
four miles. In doing so he led his companions past
"several places where Indians appeared to have been
diging roots. . ." He found the "fresh tracks" of
eight or ten horses. These, unfortunately, "had wan-
dered about in such a confused manner" as to cause
him to lose the trail of the horse he had been following. As for the tracks of the other horses, these criss-
crossed to such an extent that neither he nor his companions "could make nothing of them." They veered
to the left, therefore, and proceeded along the foothills
until they arrived at a small creek, where they camped,
after having traveled, during the day, twenty miles,
"in different directions," but only ten from their camp

of the night before. The day, which had begun with promise, had ended in failure.

As soon as it was light the next morning Drouillard set out in an attempt to discover the route taken by the Indians whose horses had but recently grazed in the Cove. He chanced to discover the trail of the lone horseman instead! In hopeful anticipation, he followed this trail until it entered the foothills. Realizing that it would be useless, or at best difficult, to attempt to follow the trail into the hills, he turned back and rejoined his companions. He had been gone about an hour and a half.

It was now agreed they should continue to skirt the foothills as they had done the day before, in the hope of discovering an Indian trail that might lead into and across the mountains to the west. Drouillard again took the flank to the right – that is, up against the foothills, this time. Shields was farther away, to the left. Lewis and McNeal, as before, held to the center.

They had gone, in a southwesterly direction, perhaps four miles, along the boundary of the Cove, when Lewis signaled that he had fallen in with an Indian trail from the northwest. This they now followed eagerly for about five miles to a point where it crossed a creek flowing in the direction of the West Fork. On this creek they sat down to breakfast on the last of their venison, keeping in reserve a small piece of salt pork.

After breakfast they again took to the trail, which was so plain, and appeared to have been so much traveled, that Drouillard, for one, now had no doubt but that it would lead them over the mountains to the waters of the Columbia.

He was in high spirits. So was Shields. So was McNeal. But, more to the point, so was the captain.

After some time they came to a creek that could in all probability be none other than the West Fork, the name by which they now knew the river they had been following for more than a year, here reduced to a rivulet so narrow as to prompt the imaginative McNeal to straddle it and, while so doing, to thank God that he had lived to see the day when he could bestride the mighty and heretofore seemingly endless Missouri. (The Missouri was here called the Beaverhead.)

Up this rivulet ran the Indian trail, plainly discernible, leading westward toward a gap in the mountains only a short distance away. Up this rivulet, also, went the enthusiastic adventurers, never pausing in their ascent until they had come near the top of the gap, when they halted for a brief interval to quench their thirst and to rest.

The sight Drouillard was to behold, when once he had gained the top of the pass, was one which neither he nor his companions would soon forget. Stretching forth in endless succession, to the west, the north, and the south, as far as his eyes could penetrate, was a vast array of rugged mountains, partially covered with snow. Must he cross these mountains to get to the Columbia? Was it in these mountains they would encounter the Indians, those elusive people of whom Sacajawea, the Indian woman, had said, "You will find them either on this river [the Beaverhead] or on a river beyond the mountains that flows toward the Lake of Ill-Tasted Water"? The Lake of Ill-Tasted Water? Beyond these mountains? And what river would, or could, lead them through mountains as formidable as these? Some river there would be, of course; the water falling on these vast slopes would have to make its way to the Columbia somehow, or to some other river heading for the Pacific. But would they be able to travel on this river? If not, what about horses? They would have to have horses. That meant they must, somehow, find Indians – Indians with horses; and they must be able to persuade these Indians to spare them as many horses as they themselves would need. All of which meant, in turn, they had work to do!

It is not likely Drouillard thought of all this while he stood on the crest of the Continental Divide and contemplated the scene before him. He was at that moment too thrilled to think of any plan for the future other than that of finding a river that would lead to the Columbia – and Indians with horses to help them. As for the view, it was grand beyond comparison, exceeding any of which he had knowledge. One comforting thought, no doubt, was that the trail they had been following continued unmistakably downward; it must inevitably lead from the brush-covered ridge upon which they were standing to some valley below. There was nothing to do but follow this trail.[3]

---

[3] The author had the pleasure of crossing this Divide, by automobile from the east, via Lemhi Pass, on Aug. 14, 1940 (Lewis crossed it on Aug. 12, 1805). The ascent was easy. The descent was so steep as to bring my car, in low gear, to a speed of twenty-five miles per hour in a few seconds. The trail, going down, was narrow and winding. The willows and other brush, which scraped against my car, crowded the trail so closely as almost to "cover" it. From the top of the pass, looking westward, the scenery was grand. As regards Horse Shoe Creek, this was reached after a descent of one and one-tenth of a mile. (Lewis estimated the distance, as traveled by himself and his party, as three-fourths of a mile.) This creek hugged my trail to the left. Steep mountain slopes rose abruptly from the edge of the trail to my right. The trail, though narrow and winding and steep, and all but crowded off the earth by the creek on the one side and the mountain slopes on the other, was not especially rough, though in my own mind I had no difficulty in conceiving it to have been exceedingly rough at the time when Lewis and Clark used it a hundred and forty years before.

Follow it they did, for about three-fourths of a mile,
to a "handsome bold running creek of cold clear water,"
where they stopped long enough to afford them their
first taste of the refreshing mountain waters of a branch
of the Columbia. After this they continued on, downward, "over steep hills and deep hollows," to a spring
where they found some dry willows and made their
camp. For supper McNeal boiled the last of their salt
pork, leaving them with no supply of food other than
a little flour and some parched meal.

The next morning their trail took them to the valley
of a northward-flowing river – the Lemhi. They had
proceeded some distance down this river when they
were delighted to discover, on a knoll ahead, at a distance of about a mile, a man, two women, and some
dogs. The women seated themselves as if to await their
arrival. The man remained standing, gazing in the
direction of the strangers. The dogs kept him, and the
women, company.

Once again it was to become Drouillard's fate to
witness the efforts of the leader of the intrepid adventurers in further attempts at gaining an audience with
Indians. He saw the captain dispose of his gun and
pouch; saw him begin his determined march in the
direction of those observing him from the knoll; heard
him call at the top of his voice: *"Tabba-bone! Tabba-
bone!"*; saw those on the knoll leave, first the women,
then the man, finally the dogs. He beheld the captain
ascending the knoll; saw the dogs return; watched the
captain as he tried to coax them toward him so that he
might tie a handkerchief and trinkets around the neck
of one of them. The dogs would not allow themselves
to be touched. In a little while they, also, were gone.

But the situation was not without hope. Drouillard
and his companions were now in Indian country; the
presence of those on the knoll augured the presence of
others not far away. Furthermore, the trail over which
they had come was now not only dusty but recently
traveled, a further evidence that Indians were probably
not far away. There remained for them again but the
one alternative – advance. Who could tell but at their
next discovery of an Indian they would be able to talk
to him?

Advance they did, along the dusty trail, in the hot
sunshine.

They had not gone more than a mile before they
came upon an elderly woman, a young woman, and a
girl. These three had been walking or standing near
the trail, but because of the shrubs and ravines had not
discovered the strangers until these were all but upon
them.

Without hesitation the young woman took to her
heels. The elderly woman threw one terror-inspired
glance at the strangers, then began to cast about for
some means of escape.

It was to become Drouillard's lot again to follow,
with his eyes, the progress of the captain as, minus his
gun, he strode forward toward the strangers alone. He
noted how the woman and the girl sank to the ground,
in a sitting posture, and bowed their heads, as if in
expectation of the death which must now have seemed
imminent. He observed the excited captain as he took
the woman gently by the hand; as he raised her to her
feet; as he repeated again the familiar words, *"Tabba-
bone! Tabba-bone!"* He observed him, further, as he
stripped to his elbow, to display the whiteness of his

skin; and as he fumbled in his pack for "some beads a few mockerson awls some pewter looking glasses and a little paint," which he offered to the woman and the girl.

When, finally, he beckoned Drouillard to come forward, Drouillard needed no prompting. What the captain wanted was for Drouillard to ask the woman to call her companion. This Drouillard did, through the medium of the language of signs. He was gratified to discover, not only that the old creature understood him, but that she obeyed. He was equally gratified when he beheld the young woman as she showed herself in the clearing, as she approached them hesitantly, and as she stood before them trembling, out of breath.

The captain was not slow in bestowing upon this wild creature gifts similar to those he had bestowed upon her kinswoman. Drouillard noted, however, that the young woman, as well as the older one, continued to view with fear and suspicion the captain and himself, as well as Shields and McNeal, who had also come forward. It was not until the persuasive captain had finally painted their "tawny cheeks" with vermilion that their faces and posture began to take on a semblance of composure sufficient to enable him, through Drouillard, to request them to lead the way to their village.

The party had hardly gone two miles before they were met by a band of sixty warriors, mounted on excellent horses, armed with shields, bows, arrows, battle-axes, and lances, and bearing down upon them at "nearly" full speed.

Again the captain was equal to the emergency. He handed his gun to one of his men. Displaying the flag of his country, he strode forward, followed, fifty paces back, by the group behind him.

It was a tense moment, packed with dramatic possibilities and prophetic of tragic consequences. Would the warriors cut them down, like so many coyotes, without an opportunity for explanation? Drouillard gripped his gun. He clamped tight his jaws. He allowed full play to the marshalling of forces within him. A glance at Shields and McNeal revealed that they evidently felt as he did, and were as prepared for whatever might happen.

The warriors were advancing at a reckless pace, disregarding the rough terrain over which they were riding, leaving behind them a cloud of dust. When they had all but descended upon the lone white man who had the temerity to stand up to them they drew to an abrupt halt. The chief, his two companions, and the men behind them, their faces smeared with paint, glared at the white man, and at the group behind him, with eyes which all too clearly bespoke a disposition on the part of their owners to fall upon the strangers and to hack them to pieces if someone did not come forward readily with an explanation.

It was the leader of the group, a man with blazing eyes and lanky jaw, who precipitated the action that followed. Holding his prancing steed in check, and darting his fiery eyes from one to the other of those who confronted him, he finally demanded of the elderly woman who the strangers were.

Stepping forward, the elderly woman declared that the strangers were white men – friends; and she excitedly held up the trinkets which the white man had given her.

Scarcely had the words escaped her lips than the swarthy, fierce-eyed chieftain, his black hair cropped close around his head, slid from his horse and, stepping forward, embraced the captain by slinging his left arm over the captain's right shoulder, and clasping the captain's back, while at the same time pressing his left, paint-besmeared cheek against the left cheek of the captain, and exclaiming rapturously: *"Ah-hi-e! A-hi-e!* (I am much pleased! I am much rejoiced!)" The warriors followed the example of their chief and treated not only the captain but Drouillard, Shields, and McNeal to the same affectionate welcome, causing the captain later to declare, in his journal, that he was "heartily tired of the national hug."

Drouillard needed no extensive knowledge of the language of signs to inform the chieftain that the strangers desired him and his companions to join them in a friendly smoke. While they were seating themselves, Lewis got out the pipe and gave them smoke.

Then a singular thing happened. Hardly had the captain started to extend the pipe toward the chieftain than he and his warriors, to a man, began to draw off their moccasins; an act intended to signify that were they to prove unfaithful to whatever they might agree upon in the forthcoming conference, they would walk barefoot, for ever afterward, summer and winter, for the rest of their lives.

It took more than one pipe, and more minutes than pipes, to make the rounds. Drouillard, who had not tasted of food since the evening before, and not of water for several hours, felt more in need of satiating his appetite and quenching his thirst than he felt in need of smoking. He was grateful, therefore, when, upon the conclusion of the ceremony, and after the inevitable distribution of presents, the captain instructed him to inform the chief that their visit was friendly; that they would explain who they were and where they were going as soon as they reached the Indian village; that now they wished to be moving on, since the sun was warm and they had no water.

As Drouillard translated this, in the language of signs, he could see that at least some of the warriors, as well as their chief, understood him; for no sooner had he stopped motioning than these, as well as the rest of the warriors, began to put on their moccasins, and would have risen to their feet had not their chief motioned them to remain seated.

The chief then took a few moments in which to address them (It was more of a harangue than a speech). When he had finished, he turned to the captain as if to indicate that now he was ready to start.

The captain had, meanwhile, taken the American flag from McNeal. Presenting this to the chief, he informed the latter that among white men this was an emblem of peace and that now that he had it the chief was to regard it as a bond of union between himself and the white men.

The chief received the flag with solemnity. His uncouth followers crowded unceremoniously around him, the better to obtain a look at this object of curiosity, and to touch it with their bony fingers.

Finally Lewis "desired" the chief, through Drouillard, to take him to his village. The chief ordered his party to start. On the way the chief held a second harangue with his followers, which had the effect of sending six or eight of his warriors on ahead.

The village was located about four miles from where
Drouillard and his companions first met the Shoshones.
It was situated on the beautiful mountain stream down
which the trail had led them. The stream flowed north,
between two ridges of mountains. The village itself was
one consisting of dome-shaped, grass-thatched huts and
one buffalo skin tepee.

Before this tepee the chief stopped. He motioned to
Drouillard and to the captain to enter.

Drouillard took a look at the tepee. It was in good
enough condition. The grass around it had not been
much trampled. That told him the tepee had just been
set up. It had probably been set up by the half-dozen
warriors who had galloped off; or, more likely, by
some women to whom these warriors had given orders.
Green willow boughs and dressed antelope skins had
been spread inside. A half-grown boy was pulling up
the grass in the center to form a circular space about
two feet across.

While Drouillard and those with him were seating
themselves, a young brave came forward with some
dried sticks and dead grass. Twirling one of the sticks
rapidly between the palms of his hands, he kindled a
fire. The chief then rose and delivered himself of a
speech.

While he spoke Drouillard found time, now and
then, to glance at the dirty, dust-begrimed, painted
warriors. He had a view of almost the entire village,
for the bottom edge of the tepee had been raised on
stakes driven into the ground, so that he could look
outside, upon the warriors seated there, and women
and children beyond these – maybe four hundred people in all.

The tall, lanky chief spoke solemnly for several minutes. The speech was followed by the ceremony of smoking, after which Lewis gave his address to the nation. This was followed by the distribution of presents to the women and children, and this, in turn, by a feast on sun-baked service berry and chokecherry cakes. It was not until then that Drouillard and his companions were finally able to betake themselves to the river to quench their thirst.

The sun was now on the point of dipping over the ridge of mountains across the river to the west. The air had begun to feel comfortable. And after the hefty meal – hefty enough – and the refreshing drink, Drouillard was well content to sit for awhile, on the low-lying river bank, for a chat with the gangly but seemingly well-meaning chief.

But not even then could Lewis forget the mission upon which he had come. He wanted to know about the river. Could one travel down this river to the Columbia?

The chief began to heap up hills of sand, to represent mountains. He drew crooked lines on the ground, with a stick, to represent rivers. As he answered the captain's questions, he traced his finger along the crooked lines and pointed out that the Lemhi flowed into the River-of-No-Return (the Salmon) ; that the River-of-No-Return was twice as large as the Lemhi; that the trees along the River-of-No-Return were not any larger than the trees along the Lemhi – not large enough for canoes; that one could not travel by canoe, or by horses, or on foot down the River-of-No-Return; that one could not even cross the mountains through which the

River-of-No-Return flowed. How, then, could one get to the Lake of Ill-Tasted Water? That was what the captain wanted to know.

It does not appear that the chief divulged his secret then. If he had, he might have pointed out that it would be necessary to go down the Lemhi, then down the River-of-No-Return, then north across the mountains and along a big river, then west, across the mountains again, then along a river to the west, then along another river to the west, and finally down a big river to the Lake of Ill-Tasted Water.

That could have been a bit confusing – if the chief had said it. As far as that went, what he did say *was* discouraging. The captain hoped it might have been exaggerated. Maybe Drouillard hoped so too. And yet – did Drouillard place greater confidence in the words of the chief than did Lewis?

While he sat beside the waters of the Lemhi and assisted Lewis and the Shoshone chief in the art of communication, Drouillard was not unaware of his surroundings. He saw the unkempt, half-starved warriors and other men crowding in rather close, and the women and children beyond these. He saw the grass-thatched huts, made from willows, and the trim-looking buffalo skin tepee. He counted hundreds of horses, some tied in close, but many others grazing in the lovely valley. He saw the mountains edging along both sides of the valley. He swept his eyes down the river itself, which was here about forty yards wide and three feet deep; a stream of clear, cool water flowing swiftly between steep, low-lying banks. When he first sat down beside this river he may even have asked, would it take them to the Pacific? Would they need horses, after all?

And yet – they *would* need horses, at least for the trans-
porting of their baggage to the Shoshone village. And
now that he had talked with the chieftain, he knew that
they would need horses, also, for crossing the mountains.

That night the Indians entertained their guests with
music and dance. Intermittently they talked, laughed,
shouted, and sang as if they did not have a care in the
world. Despite their wild appearance, they seemed no
more capable of evil intentions than if they had been
so many lambs in the fold.

Along with Shields and McNeal, Drouillard sat
with the captain and the chief during the fore part of
the evening, as the ever inquisitive captain again plied
the chief with questions. It may have been at this time
– if not earlier – that Drouillard learned that the chief's
name was Cameahwait, which was supposed to mean
He-Who-Never-Walks.[4] It may have been at this time,
also, that he learned that the Shoshones had been attacked that spring by the very people near whose
villages the explorers had spent the winter, the Minnetarees of Knife River, whom they called the Pahkees.
In this attack they had burned the Shoshones' tepees,
stolen their horses, and killed some of their number. It
was because of having lost their relatives at the hands
of these marauders that the Shoshones had shorn their
hair. Cameahwait, having lost more than the others,
had cropped his close around the head.

---

[4] On Aug. 24, Lewis wrote: "Cameahwait literally translated is *one who
never walks.* he told me that his nation had also given him another name by
which he was signalized as a warrior which was Too-et'-te-can'-e or *black
gun.* these people have many names in the course of their lives, particularly
if they become distinguished characters." Thwaites III, p. 29. Clark states
that "Ka-me-ah-wah," was the equivalent of come & Smoke." – *Ibid.*, II, p.
367.

At midnight the captain excused himself, leaving Drouillard, Shields, and McNeal to "amuse themselves" among the natives, who continued to entertain their guests "with dancing nearly all night."

Anon, Drouillard also sought repose in the tepee. It had been an adventure-packed day: the discovery of the Indians and the dogs on the knoll; the contact with the elderly woman, the young woman, and the girl; the dramatic meeting with Cameahwait and his warriors; the smoking that followed; the arrival at the village, and the welcoming ceremony; the plying of the chief with questions about a route to the Pacific; finally, the merrymaking of the villagers throughout most of the night. How would Cameahwait and his Shoshones react on the morrow when it would become Drouillard's responsibility to inform them about the brother chief and his warriors on the other side of the mountains? Would they lend them enough horses to take the baggage of this brother chief across the mountains to their village? Would they sell to the white men the horses these would need to take them to the Columbia?[5] Would they furnish a guide?

The morrow would tell. As for now, it behooved him to get an hour of sleep. Time enough on the morrow to speculate on the problems thereof.

---

[5] Thwaites II, p. 347. On Aug. 19, Lewis stated that the Shoshones had 700 horses, including 40 colts and 20 mules. *Ibid.* II, p. 372.

10

A Shoshone Chieftain

The captain was up and writing in his journal when
Drouillard rolled out of his blanket the next morning.
By the time the former had finished his writing, Shields
and McNeal were also up, and, in fact, the entire
village.

What did they have to eat?

Drouillard may have asked the question. He knew.
They had only flour, and not much of that. He would
probably be sent out to hunt.

He was. Shields went with him, and several of the
Shoshone braves. They came back with exactly nothing
except ravenous appetites.[1]

McNeal then mixed some of his flour with water and
with berries procured from the Indians. On this he

---

[1] On his first morning at the Shoshone village, Lewis witnessed a group of
Shoshone hunters drive a herd of antelope, back and forth, at full speed on
fresh horses, from one side of a valley to the other, *without getting a single
antelope.*

Gass, in his journal for July 28, 1806, describes how he had observed
wolves in the act of hunting these animals. "The wolves having fixed upon
their intended prey and taken their stations, a part of the pack commence
the chase, and running it in a circle, are at certain intervals relieved by
others. In this manner they are able to run a goat down. At the falls [of the
Missouri] where the wolves are plenty, I had an opportunity of seeing one
of these hunts." – Hosmer, 266.

While in central Montana, Lewis recorded in his journal that "we have
frequently seen the wolves in pursuit of the Antelope in the plains; they
appear to decoy a single one from a flock, and then pursue it, alturnately
releiving each other untill they take it." – Thwaites, I, p. 351.

and his companions made out their breakfast as best
they could. It was upon the conclusion of this sump-
tuous meal that Lewis, through Drouillard as interpreter, informed Cameahwait about the presence of
the brother chief and his group of young men at the
Place-Where-the-Two-Rivers-Meet, beyond the mountains, toward the Rising Sun.

As Drouillard rendered the captain's words into
signs, an expression of surprise – Or was it suspicion?
Or anger? – crept into the fierce-glowing eyes of the
chieftain. But he nodded his shorn head, and rose and
went to his followers, with whom he held a harangue
for an hour and a half. When he returned, he informed
Lewis that his people would assist the white men after
one sleep.

When it was time to depart the next morning, however, Drouillard noted that the Indians hung back. He
glanced at Lewis.

The captain was in favor of starting at once, before
the Indians changed their minds. He called for the
chief. And when the chief stood before him he demanded to know why his people did not come.

Cameahwait obligingly went and spoke to them. His
words seemed not to arouse them at all. He spoke again
and again, by word and gesture, with all the vigor at
his command, doing his best, so it seemed, to meet their
loudly-spoken objections. When he once more stood
before the captain, it is not likely that Drouillard failed
to notice the anger, the determination, the disgust, in
the burning eyes.

Some people were there, he motioned angrily, who
maintained that the white man was a friend of the
Pahkees, and that he would be leading them to their

enemies. He added, however, that he, on his part, did not believe this.

As Drouillard translated, the captain told Cameahwait he was sorry the chief had so little confidence in him. He said he would forgive him, however, for perhaps Cameahwait did not know the ways of white men. Among white men, declared the captain – and Drouillard was kept busy translating – it was considered a disgrace to lie, or to entrap even an enemy by falsehood. He said that if Cameahwait's people continued to think meanly of him, then Cameahwait could rely on it, that no white man would ever come to him or his people, or bring them arms and ammunition. If most of Cameahwait's nation still entertained their false opinion, the captain hoped, he said, that there "were some among them that were not afraid to die," who "were men" and would go with him and convince themselves of the truth of what he had said. He added that white men waited even now at the forks of the Beaverhead or a little below, with merchandise. He said, as for him, he was determined to go there; that he was not afraid to die. And then he added: "I soon found that I had touched him on the right string; to doubt the bravery of a savage is at once to put him on his mettle." Without hesitation, Cameahwait mounted his horse and "harangued" his followers for the second time that morning – and then came back to declare that he would go himself, even though it cost him his life. He added that he hoped there were some among his people who were not afraid to die with him, but would mount their horses and come. And hardly had he finished before some six or eight of them mounted their horses and joined him.

Drouillard was privileged to sit down, then and there, to smoke with these volunteers. Upon the conclusion of the smoke the captain ordered himself and Shields and McNeal to put on their packs, since he was "determined to set out" with the Indians while he had them "in the humour."

The start was made at 12:30 p.m. Drouillard noticed that several of the old women were crying and, as the captain put it, "imploring the great sperit to protect their warriors as if they were going to inevitable destruction."

The adventurers had not gone far before they were joined by ten or twelve men from the village; and before long by many others, until it seemed as if all the men in the village, and several of the women, had ventured forth. "This," wrote the captain, "may serve in some measure to ilustrate the capricious disposition of those people, who never act but from the impulse of the moment." They were now "very cheerfull and gay," while only two hours before had they looked "as sirly as so many imps of satturn."

Drouillard and his party had by this time left the Lemhi and were climbing the ridge forming the divide. When they reached the spring on which Drouillard and his three companions had camped on the twelfth, three days before, only a short distance to the west of the divide, Cameahwait drew to a halt. He insisted that the horses needed to graze.

Though this was not much to his liking, the captain agreed. He even got out the pipe. And for the second time that day, Drouillard had the satisfaction, if satisfaction it was, of sitting down for a smoke with the Indians. He would rather, at the moment, have had a steak of venison.

An hour later, when their journey was resumed, Drouillard was sent ahead to hunt. Hungry though he was, and tired, he hunted without success until dark. How they were to feed their guests, was no secret. All they had for the purpose was one pound of flour, which the captain divided among himself, his three companions, Cameahwait, and one other. The entire pound might have sufficed for one person.

The next morning Drouillard was out again, accompanied by Shields.

Before they left, Lewis, through Drouillard, requested Cameahwait to ask his followers not to go along, inasmuch as their incessant jabbering frightened away the game. When Cameahwait had made this request of his followers, Drouillard could tell, from the remonstrations they made, that it did not meet with their approval. It did not surprise him, therefore, to discover, later, that two small parties had gone forth, one to keep to the right of himself and Shields, the other to the left, as he and Shields made their way along the creek. The parties had not been sent out to hunt. They had been sent – rather, they had been permitted – by Cameahwait, to go out for the purpose of keeping an eye on the hunters, lest the latter lead them into an ambush!

Drouillard and Shields had not been gone much more than an hour before Drouillard killed a deer. Before long he had killed two more. The last he and Shields brought to camp.

Here he learned that all of the Indians, with the exception of twenty-eight men and three women, had returned to their village. He also learned that Lewis had given to the Indians three quarters of the first deer Drouillard had killed and that these had devoured it almost without cooking. Upon the entrails, which Drouillard had thrown out, they had pounced like so many starved wolves, each snatching or tearing away what he could, and greedily devouring what came into his possession. The second deer, after it had been cooked by McNeal, they had likewise devoured – to the soft part of the hoofs.

The Indians now seemed in no hurry about going on. Nor did Cameahwait attempt to influence them. He explained that their horses needed to graze.

The party finally did get under way, however. It was now that Lewis informed Cameahwait of the possibility that, due to the difficulty of navigation, his brother chief might not yet have arrived at the forks of which he had spoken.

No sooner had Cameahwait received this information than he swept his fiery eyes in the direction of the forks. He signaled a halt, got off his horse, and strode up to one of his men. Removing the tippet from this man's neck, he placed it, in solemn dignity, upon Lewis. Taking the hint, some of his followers favored Drouillard and Shields and McNeal in the same manner.[2]

Lewis, on his part, removed from his head his hat and placed it upon the head of Cameahwait. Drouillard placed his hat upon the head of one of the Indians. Shields and McNeal did the same. Then, after Lewis had again reminded Cameahwait of the possibility that Clark might not yet have arrived at the forks, the party

---

[2] Lewis describes a tippet as a collar made from a four to five-inch strip of otter skin with the fur left on. The eyes and nose were at one end of the strip, the tail at the other. To this strip would be attached from 100 to 250 ermine skins in such manner as to cause these, while the tippet was being worn, to hang down over the shoulders and body nearly to the waist. The "center" of the collar would be ornamented with shells. The article was held in high esteem by the Indians. – Thwaites II, p. 378.

journeyed on at a brisk trot, during which one of the Indians carried the American flag.

Drouillard directed his eyes from time to time in the direction of the forks, wondering, with some uneasiness, whether Clark was there. He realized that if Clark had not arrived, there was every possibility the Indians would desert them. With their departure would vanish whatever hope the captain may have had of obtaining horses.

Drouillard had participated in the heroic attempts of the captain to win and maintain the confidence of these Indians. He and the captain had not even neglected to mention that, traveling with the brother chief, was a woman of their own nation, taken captive by the Pahkees, who would help them understand that the white men had spoken with a straight tongue. They had told them of York, that monstrous man, whose skin was black, whose hair was short and curly, whose strength was prodigious. The Indians had evinced an interest in this man greater even than their interest in the goods which the white men had promised them. Yet so harassed were they by fear and suspicion lest they be betrayed into the hands of their enemies that it was useless to place any high degree of confidence either in their promises or in their conduct. Those moments before the travelers arrived at the forks of the Beaverhead were anxious moments, not only for the captain and his companions, but for Cameahwait and his Indians as well.

As it happened, Clark was *not* at the forks! This became evident to Drouillard when they had come within two miles of the place.

The Indians began to slacken their pace. They cast furtive glances in the direction of the place ahead.

Lewis called a halt. He handed Cameahwait his gun
and ordered the astonished chief, if his enemies were
in the bushes, to shoot him dead. Taking the hint,
Drouillard, Shields, and McNeal gave up their guns
too.

Restored to some measure of confidence, the chief
sent his "spies" on ahead. With set jaws and fuming
eyes, he followed himself, at the head of his cohorts.

Drouillard was, presumably, riding next to the captain. He had not ridden far before the captain turned
to him and instructed him to ride on to the forks and
there retrieve the notes which the captain had written
six days before and placed upon a pole, suggesting to
Clark not to attempt to bring the canoes any farther
than this particular spot.

Drouillard was not unaware of the close attention
with which he and the Indian were being regarded by
the warriors, and by Cameahwait, as they galloped off
in pursuit of their quest. Fortunately, the notes were
found where Lewis had left them. Making certain the
Indian was observing him, Drouillard removed them
from the pole, then rode back to the main party, and,
with all eyes upon him, handed the notes to the captain.

The captain took the notes with a show of interest,
read them – or pretended to – then informed Cameahwait – as Drouillard translated – that he and his brother
chief had agreed that if his brother chief found the
river to be slow he was to send a man up to the first
forks above with a message that would say that he was
just below and would be coming up slowly, and for
Lewis to wait for him there. The captain then added
that if the chief did not now believe him he would send
one of his men – his sign talker – down the river below

the forks to meet the brother chief, and that Cameah-wait might, if he wished, send one of *his* men along, too. As for the captain, he would wait at the forks until the brother chief arrived.

It was a "stratagem." And it worked, although several of the chief's followers volubly complained that their chief was exposing them to needless danger and that, furthermore, the white man chief was now, as before, telling them "different stories." All of the chief's followers, however, rode on, slowly, to the forks, where Lewis, "confident that there was not a moment to spare," sat down, in the evening, to write to Clark, "by the light from a willow bush," and to urge upon Drouillard to start with this message in the morning.

During the night, only the chief and five or six of his men had the courage to sleep beside the fire of their mysterious friends. The rest disbanded and concealed themselves in the willows. In his journal the captain wrote:

I . . . entertained various conjectures myself with rispect to the cause of Capt. Clarks detention and was even fearfull that he had found the river so difficult that he had halted below the Rattlesnake bluffs. I knew that if these people left me that they would immediately disperse and secret themselves in the mountains where it would be impossible to find them or at least in vain to pursue them and that they would spread the allarm to all other bands within our reach & of course we should be disappointed in obtaining horses, which would vastly retard and increase the labour of our voyage and I feared might so discourage the men as to defeat the expedition altogether, my mind was in reality quite as gloomy all this evening as the most affrighted indian but I affected cheerfulness to keep the Indians so who were about me. we finally laid down and the Chief placed himself by the side of my musquitoe bier. I slept but little as might be well expected, my mind dwelling on the state of the expedition which I have ever held in equal estimation with my

own existence, and the fait of which appeared at this moment to
depend in a great measure upon the caprice of a few savages who
are ever as fickle as the wind.   .   .

The events of the last two days had put to a test
Drouillard's skill in the use of the Indian language of
signs. He had been called upon to use this medium of
communication, not merely in an exchange of information, but in argument; and argument in the face of fear
and suspected treachery on the part of the Indians, and,
on the part of the whites, apprehension lest the enterprise to which they had given their lives fail. So ably
did Drouillard distinguish himself in the difficult role
he was being called upon to play as to cause Lewis then
and there to single him out for a citation, in which he
stated that Drouillard, "who understood perfectly the
common language of jesticulation or signs," was his
main dependence for such communication as he found
it necessary to have with the Indians. Had Drouillard
failed to make himself known to the Indians, during
those tense moments when Lewis was attempting to
enlist their services, the Lewis and Clark men would
in all probability have had a different story to tell
upon their return to St. Louis than the one they did
bring back – if, indeed, they would have been able to
come back at all. Thanks to Lewis for the courageous
and able manner in which he conducted his conferences with Cameahwait, and thanks to Drouillard for
the skill and efficiency with which he acted as intermediary in these conferences, the Shoshones were won
over sufficiently to make them willing to accompany
the white men as far as the Two Forks, where Cameahwait, for one, consented to lie down beside Lewis'
mosquito bier to sleep. What the morrow would bring
forth, was another matter.

11

Among the Shoshones

Drouillard was up and on his way, on horseback, to meet Clark early the next morning. He was accompanied, not only by the Indian who had promised to go with him, but by several others.

They had not been gone more than an hour before Drouillard discovered a woman and two men coming toward them on foot, up the river. It took but a glance to reveal to him that the woman was Sacajawea and that the men were Charbonneau and Clark.

It was not necessary for Drouillard to inform his companions who the strangers were. He may, however, have motioned to them that here, coming to meet them, was the very woman – one of their own people – about whom the white man chief had told them.

If he did, he could hardly have finished before the woman herself began to point them out to Clark behind her. Not only was she pointing, she began to dance out of sheer joy. Clark informed them later that she had also sucked her fingers, as an indication that the horsemen approaching her were her countrymen.

The discovery of the strangers had a most salutary effect upon Drouillard's companions. Their delight and excitement were plainly evident from the looks on their faces and the exclamations they made the moment they noticed that the woman, after pointing them out to the man behind, had begun to dance. Whereas before they had held their horses back, now they began, presumably, to urge them forward, so that Drouillard had to do likewise if he would keep abreast of them.

The meeting of these uncouth warriors with their long-lost country woman must have been a sight not easily forgotten by those who witnessed it, as Sacajawea ran forward, eagerly, to meet them, and then as eagerly pointed them out to Clark, after he also had arrived. As for the Indians themselves, these sang "aloud with the greatest appearance of delight," as they accompanied Drouillard and the newcomers to the forks, where Lewis and Cameahwait were awaiting them.

As they neared this spot, one of the young women there began to come forward, on foot, alone, hesitantly.

Sacajawea, among others, noticed this woman, for she stepped ahead as if to meet her. Hardly had she done so than, with a shout, the other woman began to run forward. Sacajawea did the same. When the two met, they fell upon each other and "embraced with the most tender affection," uttering cries of endearment, shedding tears, and, in general, carrying on in a "peculiarly touching" manner. Biddle says:

> The meeting of these two young women had in it something peculiarly touching, not only in the ardent manner in which their feelings were expressed, but from the real interest of their relation to each other. They had been companions in childhood; in the war with the Minnetarees they had both been taken prisoners in the same battle; and they had shared together and softened by mutual affection the rigours of captivity, till one of them had escaped from their enemies with scarce a hope of ever seeing her friend rescued from their hands.[1]

When they entered Lewis' camp, however, it was not

---

[1] Allen I, p. 318.

Sacajawea and this woman to whom either the captain or Cameahwait gave their attention, but to Clark. Drouillard witnessed again the ceremony of the national hug; heard again the words, *"Ah-hi-e, Ah-hi-e."* Later he observed Cameahwait as the latter fumbled in his medicine bag for six sea shells, and as he awkwardly fastened these to Clark's luxurious growth of red hair.

A council was held. At this council Sacajawea was summoned to act as interpreter.

> [She] came into the tent, sat down, and was beginning to enterpret, when in the person of Cameahwait she recognized her brother. She instantly jumped up, and ran and embraced him, throwing over him her blanket, and weeping profusely; the chief was himself moved, though not in the same degree. After some conversation between them she resumed her seat, and attempted to interpret . . . but her new situation seemed to overpower her, and she was frequently interrupted by her tears. After the council was finished, the unfortunate woman learned that all her family were dead except two brothers, one of whom was absent, and a son of her eldest sister, a small boy, who was immediately adopted by her.[2]

Drouillard may not have been present at this council. He had been sent out to hunt, but he no doubt learned, upon his return, what had happened. He also learned that Cameahwait had agreed to go, after one sleep, to his village to assist in procuring such horses as might be needed.

Why the chief did not ask those of his followers who were then with him to walk, or ride double with their companions, so that the baggage might be transported at once, was no surprise to Drouillard. For one thing, there were not enough horses at hand to afford each of

---

[2] *Ibid.* I, p. 319.

the Lewis and Clark men a mount, even though he did
ride double with an Indian. Besides, were this arrangement made, there would be no room for the baggage.
Furthermore, if a Shoshone had a horse, he could not
be expected to walk. That would be as unthinkable as
to expect an eagle not to fly.

Drouillard already knew the esteem with which a
Shoshone regarded his horse. To a Shoshone, a horse
was not merely a means of transportation, it was an
invaluable aid on the hunt, and in time of war. Upon
his horse a Shoshone would bestow ornaments similar
to those he bestowed upon himself, and, on the war path,
protect his horse by an arrow-proof shield, as he pro-
tected himself. If a Shoshone had two horses, and
found one of them unable to carry his woman along
with her pack, the woman would have to walk. To
tempt a Shoshone to part with his horse was like
tempting him to part with his nearest of kin. It was not
in the least a foregone conclusion, therefore, that either
Drouillard or Lewis or any other member of the gallant band of explorers would be able, at least not without the exercise of considerable effort, to persuade the
Shoshones to part with their horses.[3]

Upon his return from his hunting trip Drouillard
learned, also, of the plan which the captains had
formed for the immediate future. Clark, with eleven
workmen, was to accompany Cameahwait and the Indians to the Indian village. Clark and these men were
to descend the Lemhi, and then the Salmon, to determine whether the Salmon might be navigable, and, if
so, and provided they found trees large enough for the

3 Thwaites II, pp. 347, 371, 372; III, p. 43.

purpose, to start the construction of canoes. It was also agreed that Sacajawea and Charbonneau should accompany the party as far as the village, where Sacajawea was to use her influence in hastening the return of the Indians.

Cameahwait and his Indians, accompanied by Clark and his men, and by Sacajawea and Charbonneau and their infant, took off the next morning at ten o'clock. Lewis remained with the rest of the men in camp, and set about preparing packs for the horses, wrapping baggage into bundles suitable for transportation by horseback, caching such baggage as they could spare, disposing of the canoes, and preparing moccasins and clothing for the trek across the mountains.

Drouillard was more fully aware than most of the members of the expedition of the scarcity of game in the somewhat desolate country in which they now found themselves. Furthermore, he knew that Lewis was desirous, if possible, of laying in an extra supply of meat for their trek across the mountains. It occasioned him no surprise, therefore, when Lewis instructed him on the third day after the departure of Clark, to get himself in readiness to go to the Cove on the morrow for a one or even a two-day hunt.

He was on his way early the next day, on a horse which the captain, or he himself, had been able to procure from the Indians. It was a cool morning. The grass lay white with frost all around him. Ice had formed in the kettles.

At about noon, he came upon a party of six Indians: a young man, an old man, a boy, and three women. They were finishing their meal of roots when he discovered them. Their horses were grazing nearby.

Drouillard rode leisurely toward them. When he came up to them, he dismounted and turned his horse loose to graze. He noted that a willow basket, some bags, and the saddles of their horses lay scattered upon the ground. He began to speak to them in the language of signs.

One of them – mayhap the old man – answered him. He may have been small, thin, and, in common with many of the Shoshones, bow-legged. He did not volunteer more information than what was asked for, and hardly that. The other five, on their part, stood by, surly of face, suspicious, wary, but not otherwise unfriendly or hostile.

After awhile one of the women said something to the others, whereupon all of them, except the old man, went to bring in the horses.

When they had done so, and while they were putting on the saddles, Drouillard started for his own horse, without bothering to bring along his gun.

He had not gone fifty paces, before the young man sprang for the gun, snatched it up, and, before Drouillard could overtake him, was on his horse and away toward the mountains, followed by his companions.

Cursing himself for his negligence, Drouillard sprinted for his horse. In the matter of seconds he was on his way in pursuit.

His object was to regain possession of the gun. But how? All the young man had to do, should Drouillard overtake him, was to train the gun upon him and fire. And what hope could Drouillard have of overtaking him when the man rode a horse so swift he was able to ride circles around the horses of the women? Yet overtake him he must. He must at least try.

Mile after mile the chase continued, until the horses

of two of the women began to tire, enabling Drouillard to overtake them.

But this brought also the young man to the scene of action. Ever on the alert, Drouillard was upon him in an instant. Finding Drouillard too strong for him, and discovering that he must yield the gun, the man had enough presence of mind to open the pan and cast the priming before he allowed the gun to be wrested from him. Then, finding himself divested of the gun, he turned his horse about and galloped away, leaving the women to follow as best they could. Drouillard, on his part, retraced the ten miles he had come and helped himself to the supplies which the culprits had left in their haste to get away. These spoils consisted of skins, dried service berries, chokecherry cakes, dried roots, and an assortment of flint, including an "instrument of bone for manufacturing the flint into arrow points." With these in possession, and with his gun, he rejoined Lewis at the forks the next day.

Cameahwait had returned (August 22) from his village when Drouillard rode into camp. Accompanying Cameahwait were Sacajawea, Charbonneau, about fifty men, and a number of women and children. The captain had treated them to boiled corn and meal, since they had no meat of their own, and seemed half starved. He had also turned over to them nearly all of the five hundred fish, mostly "trout," which his men had caught by means of a "bush drag."

Lewis and his party would have been on their way the day following that which saw the return of Cameahwait had not Cameahwait persuaded him to await the arrival of a brother chief.

The brother chief, and about fifty of his people, including women and children, arrived at three o'clock in the afternoon on that same day (August 23), on their way to the buffalo country in quest of meat and robes for the winter. Cameahwait's Shoshones interpreted this as an opportunity for them to go also, inasmuch as they would, by so doing, have the protection of greater numbers against any enemy who might attack them while supplying themselves with food and clothing. To this Lewis said nothing, but he was resolved to start for the Shoshone village the next morning.

He was able to make good his resolve – by twelve o'clock, noon. He had the satisfaction, also, of knowing that he had been able to obtain nine horses and one mule. His prospects of obtaining additional horses at the Shoshone village seemed good.

But a piece of bad news was to strike him between the eyes the next day (August 25) : Charbonneau, with apparent unconcern, informed him that Cameahwait had sent one of his young men to the village to bid the people there to join him on the morrow, and he and they would all go to the buffalo country.

Would they, now? And leave him and his party in the lurch? Lewis lost no time in calling Cameahwait and two lesser chiefs together to ask them if they were men of their words.

It was a tense moment. The captain was hot under the collar. He spoke, not only with feeling, but at considerable length. Was Drouillard on hand to help him?

It is a strong probability. The length of the speech alone would suggest this, as would also the fact that Cameahwait and the two lesser chiefs appeared to understand perfectly well what was being said to them. The outcome of the incident was that Cameahwait agreed to send one of his young men to the village to bid the people there await his arrival.

In admitting his guilt – if guilt it was – Cameahwait submitted that he had done so because his people were hungry. Had not the white man himself seen how the chief's women felt under compunction to go out, every time the party came to a halt, to dig roots in the hard, crusty ground to keep their children from starving?

It was something the captain could understand. But had not he, on his part, shared his own food with these women? He was, in fact, to demonstrate this spirit of compassion again that very evening, when his hunters came in with one deer. He gave the meat to the women and children, and went supperless himself, as perhaps did also Drouillard and many others.

The captain performed one additional act of thoughtfulness that day, howbeit he was probably actuated by motives of self interest in doing it – he called together the Indian men and women who had helped him and gave each a "billet," along with a promise that he would exchange goods for this billet as soon as they arrived at the place on the Lemhi where he would establish his camp. Was Drouillard the man who helped him this time? The answer would seem to be that if Drouillard had been present to help Lewis in the conference, it is more than likely that Drouillard was present to help Lewis now.

The travelers were on the march the next morning at sunrise. At six in the evening they pulled in at the Shoshone village,[4] where Colter met them with a note from Clark to the effect that the route down the Salmon was impracticable. Lewis was not slow in making up his mind to buy horses. He asked for no fewer than twenty. To this request the chief did not display much

---

[4] The village was now located three miles farther up the river.

enthusiasm. The Pahkees, he said, had stolen many horses that spring. Yet he hoped his people could spare as many horses as might be needed.

Not entirely convinced of this possibility, Lewis decided to keep the natives in as good a humor as possible, by directing that the fiddle be played, and that his men dance.

> though I must confess that the state of my own mind at this moment did not well accord with the prevailing mirth as I somewhat feared that the caprice of the indians might suddenly induce them to withhold their horses from us without which my hopes of prosicuting my voyage to advantage was lost; however I deturmined to keep the indians in a good humour if possible, and to lose no time in obtaining the necessary number of horses.

To his hunters that evening he gave instructions to turn out "early" the next morning. He contented himself with a little parched corn for supper.

Clark arrived at one p.m. three days later (August 29). He and his men were half-starved. They found Lewis (probably with Drouillard's help) busy "counciling" and trying to buy horses.

Once Clark had arrived, the question arose, what route should they take – the one recommended by the old man, Toby, who was to guide them? As it happened, this route was "contradicted" by all the Shoshones. The captains ascribed the contradiction as being due to the desire of the Indians to have the white men spend the winter with them.[5]

If this was their desire, they were due for a disappointment, for their guests pulled up and left them the next morning (August 30), the proud possessors of twenty-nine horses – and old Toby to guide them.

---

[5] Thwaites III, p. 47; Allen I, p. 135.

12

Across the Bitterroots
to the Nez Perces

Old Toby led the explorers down the Lemhi, nineteen miles, to its junction with the Salmon; then down the Salmon, twenty-two miles, to the north fork of the Salmon; then up the north fork and over the Continental Divide via an unnamed pass,[1] about thirty miles, to the Bitterroot River; and finally down this, sixty or more miles, to the mouth of Lolo Creek, for a total distance of between one hundred fifty and one hundred sixty miles, all the time in a northerly direction. From Lolo Creek he led them another one hundred fifty miles, in a westerly direction, over the Bitterroot Mountains.

Except for acting as interpreter at a conference which the captains held with a band of Flatheads, Drouillard's main duty, on this three hundred-mile trek, during which the explorers crossed the Continental Divide and the mighty Bitterroots, was to serve as hunter. And quite some job that proved to be.

For one thing, game was scarce, especially on the one hundred fifty-mile trek across the Bitterroots. Whereas formerly he had been accustomed to shooting a deer or an elk or a buffalo, now he had to be content,

---

[1] This may be the pass which De Voto calls the "Lost Trail Pass." – De Voto, 219, 233.

for the most part, with a pheasant, a squirrel, or with nothing at all. One day, for example, all that he and his hunters could boast of when they returned to camp in the evening, after having tramped the mountains all day, was one pheasant.

So hard pressed were the explorers for food on their journey across the Bitterroots that they killed and ate three of their horses, in addition to a stray horse encountered by Clark. These, supplemented by pheasants, and by a meagre supply of "portable soupe . . . a little bears oil and about twenty lbs. of candles," enabled them to pull through, though when they arrived among the Nez Percés beyond the mountains, on the twentieth and twenty-second of September (about three weeks after their departure from Cameahwait's village), they were "lean and debilitated," and all but exhausted from fatigue and starvation.

The trail they followed has come to be known as the Lolo Trail. It ran, for the most part, along a ridge of the Bitterroots, between the Chopunnish or North Fork of the Clearwater on the north and the Lochsa, or Middle Fork, on the south. Richard L. Neuberger, in an article in the *Saturday Evening Post* for April 10, 1954, entitled, "They're Taming the Lolo Trail," quotes General William Tecumseh Sherman as designating the Lolo Trail as "one of the worst trails for man or beast on the North American continent." In the same article, he quotes Colonel Charles Erskine Scott Wood, General Howard's aide-de-camp in the Chief Joseph War, as having said about one portion of the Lolo Trail: "The descent into the gulf carved by Lolo Creek was like falling over a wall."

While they were crossing the mountains snow fell to

a depth of several inches. Clark said he felt as cold in "every part" as he had ever felt in his life, and was even fearful his feet would freeze in the "thin Mockersons" he wore. Whitehouse, in his journal, stated that some of the men wrapped rags around their feet. The heavy timber, too, impeded their progress, making it necessary for them at times to chop their way through.

The journey seemed to be just as hard on the horses as on the men. These became footsore, weak, and "jaded." They sometimes lost their footing and fell. One of them, with Clark's desk and trunk tied to its back, rolled down a one hundred twenty-foot slope, coming to a stop only when it collided with a tree. The incident resulted in the destruction of the desk, but in only minor injuries to the horse. Four days later another of the horses slid, or rolled, down a three hundred-foot slope, and landed in a creek, but escaped without injury.

Unable to find enough grass on which to satisfy their hunger, the horses would stray from camp at night. This would result in delays the following day, while the men searched for them. Two of the horses gave out entirely and had to be left behind.

Early in their three hundred-mile journey across the mountains to the northward and westward, Drouillard had the help, in his task of hunting, of three of the best hunters in the expedition. During the latter part of the journey, this number was increased to six. Clark was, generally, one of these six.

On the eighteenth of September this group of men – Clark, Drouillard, Colter, Shields, Reuben Fields, Joseph Fields (probably), and one other – advanced so far to the westward as to make it unlikely the main party would overtake them. (They traveled thirty-two miles, by Clark's estimate, as against eighteen covered by Lewis.) From a high point on the first day out, Drouillard, and those with him, beheld, for the first time, to their inexpressible delight, the welcome sight of the prairie country beyond, lying far to the south-west.

The sight of that prairie country (Kamas Prairie Plateau)[2] made Drouillard forget for a moment the fact that neither he nor his companions had had anything to eat during the long trek that day. There was some hope, now, they would reach the prairie country in another day, or two at the most. Surely there would they encounter game of some sort, or meet Indians from whom they could obtain food. At any rate, they crawled into their blankets that night, tired and hungry. Especially hungry. The creek on which they camped was appropriately named Hungry Creek.

The discovery of the prairie country was as welcome to Lewis and his men as it had been to Drouillard, Clark, and his hunters. In his journal for the day (September 19), Gass, who was with Lewis, states that they had some hope of

> getting soon out of this horrible mountainous desert, as we have discovered the appearance of a valley or level part of the country about 40 miles ahead. When this discovery was made there was as much joy and rejoicing among the corps, as happens among passengers at sea, who have experienced a dangerous and protracted voyage, when they first discover land.[3]

The discovery of the prairie country caused Clark to decide to press forward with all haste. Press forward he and his companions did, as rapidly as they could.

---

[2] Wheeler II, p. 102.   [3] Hosmer, 145.

In the course of the day they encountered a stray horse. This they killed. They ate some of the flesh and left the balance for Lewis, with a note from Clark in which he informed Lewis that he intended to proceed to the prairie country beyond, where he planned to remain and hunt until Lewis arrived. They arrived at the first Nez Percé village the next day.

A man came forward, cautiously, to meet them. He led them to a large, rectangular-shaped house of pine bushes thatched with mats and straw. He informed Drouillard that this was the residence of the chief, but that the chief and his warriors had departed for the war path three sleeps before.

Drouillard had noted the absence of men in the village. The women and children hung back, as if afraid.

When requested to do so, the women brought food. This consisted of a small piece of buffalo meat, dried salmon, camas cakes, and roots and berries. This food they placed, respectfully, at the feet of the strangers and then rejoined their companions, to study the newcomers with the same absorbed interest and apprehension as they had shown before.

Drouillard and his companions, delighted at the generosity shown them, sat down, with the old man, to feast upon the food. While thus engaged, Drouillard found time for a closer look at the women.

They wore deerskin dresses reaching to the knees, and fastened about the waist by a belt. Their hair hung in two queues down the front of their shoulders. (The Shoshones had worn theirs loose.) They were standing back at a respectful distance, attended by a group of children and a few men. They stared at Clark and his party as if they were creatures from another world.

Drouillard may have speculated on the buffalo meat. Had the Nez Percés obtained it in the buffalo country, beyond the formidable Bitterroots? And the salmon – did the salmon of the Pacific penetrate as far as the waters of these mountains?

No doubt Drouillard gave some attention to the camas cakes too. He had noticed piles of these tubers as he approached the large house toward which the old man had been leading him.

Early the next morning, after spending the night in a village two miles distant, Drouillard rode out in quest of venison. Two other hunters also went out, each in a different direction. When the three returned empty handed, Clark, with the help of Drouillard, bargained with the Indians for a horseload of tubers and three salmon, and sent this with Reuben Fields and an Indian to Lewis.

At four that afternoon, accompanied by a young Indian, they started for the river – the Kooskooske – and for the camp of the Twisted Hair, a Nez Percé chief believed to be hunting down this river. Upon arriving at their destination at eleven o'clock in the night, they learned that the man they sought had made his camp on an island. When they called to him, however, he came over.

The Twisted Hair may have seen forty or more summers. He was cheerful, talkative, sincere, and most willing to accommodate the strangers in any way he could. He smoked with his guests until one o'clock in the morning, when he left them. No sooner had he rejoined them later in the morning, however, than Clark started, with the chief and the chief's son, and with one or more of his own men, for one or the other of the villages from which Clark had departed two days before.

Whether Drouillard was one of those who accompanied him is not indicated. Clark's statement (in his journal), that he and Lewis "attempted to have some talk with those people but could not for the want of an Interpreter," suggests that Drouillard was not there.[4] His account of the activities for the next day, however, when he and Lewis assembled the principal men, "as well as the Chiefs," and "by Signs informed them where we came from where bound our wish to inculcate peace and good understanding between all the red people &c. . ."—this suggests that Drouillard was present.

Be that as it may, upon invitation of the Twisted Hair, they continued their journey the next day (August 24), arriving at the Twisted Hair's island at sunset. Two days later found them at the confluence of the north branch of the Clearwater (the Chopunnish) with the south or main branch (the Kooskooske). Here, in the bottom opposite the forks, they camped until the seventh of October, spending the interval in the construction of five dugout canoes, in which they proposed to travel down the Clearwater to the Snake, then down the Snake to the Columbia, and finally down the Columbia to the ocean.

[4] Wheeler recounts a Nez Percé legend to the effect that when Lewis and Clark first came among them, the Nez Percés intended to kill them but were dissuaded by a woman who, while held as a captive in Manitoba, Canada, had been befriended by some white people who helped her to escape. According to the legend, this woman urged her people to treat the strangers with kindness and hospitality. – Wheeler II, pp. 113-14.

It has been noted that after Clark and his men had descended, half-starved, from the mountains, they feasted upon the food which the Nez Percé women set before them.

Not many hours later they began to feel pain in their bowels. A similar disorder overtook Lewis and his men, also, who, although warned by Clark, had, like Clark and his men, eaten too freely of this same food served them by the Nez Percé women. The illness of these men – those under Lewis as well as those under Clark – became so severe as to compel several of them to lie down by the side of the road. Others had to be helped onto their ponies. Lewis could scarcely ride a gentle horse.

Clark ascribed the illness as being due, not merely to the fact that they had eaten too freely while in their famished condition, but to something in the "roots" themselves, a species of food which "Swelled us in Such a manner that we were Scercely able to breath for Several hours." Although Clark administered "rushes Pills," still the men continued ill for several days, unable to do but little work.

The illness affecting the Lewis and Clark men did not extend to Drouillard and Colter, or, if it did, affected these only so slightly as not to incapacitate them – at least, not for any considerable length of time. Colter, for one, was able to set out for the mountains in search of some horses which had strayed from Lewis' camp. Upon his return, three days later, he was sent out to hunt. As for Drouillard, he continued with his customary job of hunting as if nothing had happened to him.

It may be pertinent to remark on Drouillard's health in general during the time (two years, nine months, and ten days) which saw him in service in behalf of the expedition.

On August 20, 1804, two days after he had returned to the Lewis and Clark camp from a five hundred-mile trek, in quest of Reed, La Liberté, and the Otto Indians, Ordway had this to say in his journal: "George Drewyer Sick." On January 31, 1805, among the Mandans, Clark wrote: "George Drewyer taken with Pleurisy last evening. Bled. & gave him Some Sage tea, this morning he is much better." And on March 18, the day after Drouillard had returned late the evening before with a canoe which he had purchased in behalf of the expedition, Lewis wrote: "Drewyer was taken last night with a violent pain in his side. Capt. Clark blead him. several of the men are complaining of being unwell."

There may have been other illnesses. These three stand out. They were minor. By and large, Drouillard enjoyed excellent health.

In view of the numerous dangerous situations in which he found himself, Drouillard was singularly free from accidents. Two are reported in the Lewis and Clark journals: one, for November 21, 1804, the while the explorers were among the Mandans, when Clark states that "G D hurd his hand verry bad"; the other, for August 5, 1805, while Drouillard was descending a mountain with Lewis, with whom he had gone out in search of Indians. On this latter occasion Lewis wrote that "Drewyer missed his step and had a very dangerous fall," as a result of which he "sprained one of his fingers and hirt his leg very much." The captain states that it was "fifteen or 20 minutes" – it took that long – before "he was able to proceed and we continued our rout to the river. . ."

13

Down the Columbia

On October 5 the explorers collected and branded their thirty-eight horses. (They had purchased eleven additional horses from some Flatheads whom they had met before crossing the Bitterroots, on their westward trek.) They also cut off the "fore top" of the horses' manes, then delivered the horses to the Nez Percés for safekeeping until their expected return in the spring. Having cached such of their supplies as in their opinion could be left, they loaded their canoes and, on October 7, started out for the last lap of their journey to the sea. They were accompanied by We-ah-koo-nut, Te-toh-ar-sky, the Twisted Hair, and two young men, who were to act as guides and/or intermediaries to such Indians as might be encountered.[1] Old Toby and his son went along, too, for four days.

Their route took them, at first, for forty or more

---

[1] Three of the five Nez Percés who accompanied them left the explorers at the forks of the Columbia and the Snake, as witness the following statement: ". . . we took in our Two Chiefs, and set out on the great Columbia river, haveing left our guide and the two young men two of them enclined not to proceed on any further, and the 3d. could be of no service to us as he did not know the river below."—Thwaites III, p. 130. On May 8, 1806, Lewis states that the Twisted Hair had separated from them at the Falls of the Columbia. (Ibid., v, p. 6.) On May 4, 1806, Lewis says: ". . . here we met with Te-toh-ar-sky, the youngest of the two chiefs who accompanied us last fall [to] the great falls of the Columbia. we also met with our pilot who decended the river with us as far as the Columbia." (Ibid., III, p. 355.) That is, the "two chiefs" who accompanied the explorers all the way to the falls of the Columbia were the Twisted Hair and Te-toh-ar-sky.

miles, down the Clearwater; then, for one hundred fifty miles, down the Snake; and, finally, down the Columbia to the ocean. We-ah-koo-nut and the two young men accompanied them to the mouth of the Snake; the Twisted Hair and Te-toh-ar-sky, to a point just below the Dalles of the Columbia.

At a point a little better than half the one hundred fifty miles down the Snake, they came to the largest tributary of the Snake below the Clearwater, a river which they named in honor of Drouillard, but which is today known as the Palouse. The river rises in the Bitterroots in western Idaho, near the town of Potlatch, and, flowing westward for a hundred miles, turns south and, after another fifty or more miles, joins the Snake. Thus Drouillard, in common with other members of the expedition, was privileged to have a river named in his honor.

Travel down these rivers was so rapid as to make it impracticable to send out hunters, except occasionally. Furthermore, game was scarce. The result was that a new item was added to their bill of fare – dog, a delicacy which was relished, at first, only by "some Frenchmen" among them, who, according to Gass, preferred this to pounded fish. It was not long, however, until all the members of the expedition, except Clark, began to take to this kind of food. At the junction of the Snake with the Columbia, a large supply of dog was laid by, and, the next day (October 18), the day on which they began their descent of this river to the sea, forty dogs more.

Drouillard saw Indians daily, especially in the evening, when sometimes whole villages of them would come out to satisfy the curiosity previously aroused by those experts at advance publicity, the Nez Percé chiefs.

On the nineteenth of October Drouillard had the opportunity of observing what could happen among natives not reached by this advance publicity.

He and the Fields brothers had just succeeded in bringing their canoe and that of Clark down a series of rapids, and were waiting at the foot of the rapids, not only for the other canoes, in charge of Lewis, but, also, for Clark, Sacajawea, Charbonneau, and the two chiefs, who had walked past the rapids on foot.

Across from him, on the bluffs opposite, Drouillard made out the outlines of five Indian houses and a motley crowd of Indians gazing in his direction. A number of Indians at the foot of the bluffs were approaching Lewis and his men as these were attempting to make their way down the rapids.

In due time, Clark arrived. Scarcely had this occurred than a crane flew overhead. Clark raised his gun and fired. The bird fell with a splash into the river. The incident sent the Indians on the bluffs opposite scampering like frightened rabbits toward their huts.

Clark decided that the situation demanded he do what he could to pacify these Indians. Selecting Drouillard and the Fields brothers, therefore, to accompany him, he crossed the river in their small canoe, and after climbing the bluffs and finding no one in sight, entered one of the five houses.

The scene inside was one not easily forgotten. Some thirty or more men, women, and children, not to mention dogs, were "Setting permiscuisly" about, but burst forth in loud lamentation the moment the strangers entered; especially the women, who wept, wailed, and

wrung their hands; while others, including the men,
sat with bowed heads, as if unable or unwilling to
face the doom which they expected was about to descend
upon them.

Clark did not hesitate. After one glance around, he
stepped forward, pipe in hand, making the sign of
friendship, taking each of the inhabitants by the hand,
offering his pipe to the men, and fumbling in his
pockets for a few trinkets for the women and children.

These acts of friendship appeared to have "passified
those distressed people verry much"; so much so, in
fact, as to cause Clark to decide to repeat the experiment in the other houses. He recorded in his journal:

> I . . . sent one man into each lodge, and entered a Sec-
> ond myself the inhabitants of which I found more fritened than
> those of the first lodge I destributed Sundrey Small articles
> amongst them, and Smoked with the men, I then entered the
> third 4th. & fifth Lodge which I found Somewhat passified, the
> three men, Drewyer Jo. & R. Fields, haveing used everey means
> in their power to convince them of our friendly disposition to
> them, I then Set my self on a rock and made signs to the men to
> come and Smoke with me. . .

None of them came, however, until after the arrival
of the two Nez Percé chiefs, one of whom had some
knowledge of their language. It was then that some of
them began to come forward. As for the majority, these
remained unresponsive to any and all proffers of friendship on the part of the strangers – until their eyes fell
upon Lewis and the "Squar," coming up the bluff. Not
until then did they gain enough fortitude to come forward en masse, their assurance, now, being the "Squar";
since, according to their way of life, "no woman ever
accompanies a war party . . . in this quarter."
Before long, these same timorous men, and these same

strangers, were smoking together "in the greatest friendship."

In due time the Indians informed the explorers they had heard the shot which Clark had fired at the crane. They had seen the bird fall into the river. They had, at the same time, noted a few clouds in the sky. It had taken but little imagination to concoct a story to the effect that the strangers had arrived, not by canoe, but on the clouds; that they were, therefore, not men, but gods; for how could any but gods drop from the clouds and produce a noise like thunder or bring down fire from the sun? The fact that they had never seen a gun until then did not make it any easier for them to believe other than they had.

During the time it took to impart this information, Drouillard noticed several horsemen on the prairie. He noticed, also, that several men, women, and children had climbed the bluff and were now coming forward to join the group already there, apparently happy to see the white men. The captains and the captains' men improved upon the opportunity by striking up a trade with the Indians for fish and berries.

The explorers camped that night on an island near the middle of the river. On this island was situated a village of twenty-four houses. About a hundred of the Indians from this village visited the explorers during the evening, some bringing wood for a fire. Another smoke was held. Cruzatte and Gibson played their violins. The men danced. The Indians sat around as admiring spectators.

Along with other members of the party, Drouillard may have found the opportunity, while their guests were with them, of mingling with the Indian men and

of paying some attention to the Indian maidens. The
appearance of these women, at any rate, must have
caught his eye, not because they were young, as many
of them were, but because of the manner in which they
were dressed. Their attire consisted of a leather cloak,
open at the front, exposing the breasts, and, in the
back, scarcely reaching to the waist. "A truss or pece
of leather" was drawn "tite between ther legs and
fastened before So as bar[e]ly to hide those parts which
are so sacredly hid & s[e]cured by our women." They
wore few ornaments. They had high cheek bones and
flat heads. Neither their persons nor their attire suggested cleanliness. They were a long way from pos-
sessing those feminine qualities of grace and appearance which would have made them objects of admiration in the eyes of the male.

Running the boats through the long series of rapids
below the falls of the Columbia must have been a
thrilling experience to the men in the expedition,
Drouillard included.

At a point about a mile or so below the falls, the river
had become obstructed by a huge, black rock, below
which the channel narrowed to a width of less than
fifty paces. Through this narrow channel the river
fought its way for about a fourth of a mile. Through
this channel, to the astonishment of the Indians, who
witnessed the undertaking from their vantage point on
the rock, the explorers ran their canoes – without mishap.[2]

---

[2] It was shortly after this that the explorers sat down for a "parting
Smoke" with their two faithful helpers, the Nez Percé chiefs, who, two days
before, had sought permission to return to their people, giving as their
reasons, first, that the people below the falls were bad and would kill them;
second, that they themselves could no longer be of service to the white man;

The descent of the Columbia from the Dalles, which the explorers left on October 28, to the entrance to Gray's Bay, where they arrived on November 8, was, for the most part, uneventful. Above the Dalles, hunting had been poor. In fact, between their Canoe Camp on the Clearwater and the Dalles of the Columbia, a distance of more than three hundred miles, Drouillard had done almost no hunting at all. From now on, however, hunting became better, especially after they entered the heavily-timbered Cascade Mountains, below the Dalles. The trouble with hunting, even here, though, was that their canoes made such good time on the swiftly-flowing Columbia that to do much hunting meant a slowing up of travel; and Lewis was ever eager to reach the ocean. The result was that, instead of satisfying their keen appetites with roasted venison, they had to be content with dog, dried fish, dried berries, nuts, and wapato, obtained from the Indians.

Drouillard found much of interest on this trip down the Columbia. He saw numerous "sea otters" at and below the Dalles. Also, he found evidence to indicate that the tide came up as far as the Cascades, fifty miles below the Dalles. He had views of Mt. Hood, covered with snow, and of Mt. Adams and Mt. St. Helens

---

and, third, that they would hasten home to take care of the white men's horses. The captains had persuaded the chiefs to remain for two days, during which they were to continue to give to the explorers the valuable service they had rendered thus far – that is, by proceeding down the river ahead of the main party for the purpose, not only of preparing the minds of the natives for the coming of the white men, but of picking up such information as they could concerning the attitudes and intentions of the natives. These responsibilities the Nez Percé chiefs had now faithfully discharged. It must have been with a feeling of regret that the captains and Drouillard and, for that matter, all of the members of the expedition, saw these men leave, on horses which they had been able to purchase from the natives, at two robes per horse. – Thwaites III, p. 158.

(which the captains called *Mt. Helien*). People boiled
fish in baskets with heated stones. On one night, swans,
geese, brant, and ducks made such a "horid" noise as
to keep Clark, for one, awake.

Fleas were numerous. They were difficult to get rid
of. About the only thing the men could, and did, do
was to strip to the skin, and then attempt to exterminate
the pests, after which they would put the clothing back
on.

The weather came in for its share of attention. The
mornings were, for the most part, cool and either
cloudy or rainy. One morning, below the Cascades,
they found themselves enveloped in a fog so thick as
to make it hardly possible to see more than fifty feet.
The fog detained them until ten o'clock.

The natives were, for the most part, short in stature.
They were not good-looking, nor were they cleanly.
They possessed an abundance of wooden canoes. Fishing
appeared to be an important occupation. Crates of fish
would be prepared for winter and for the market. The
crates were the size and shape of an apple crate and
would hold from ninety to one hundred pounds of fish.
Drouillard saw hundreds of these crates, stacked up
along the river, or stored away in the houses of the
people. Put up in this way, and stored in a dry place,
this "pounded Salmon" would keep "Sound and sweet
Several years." In one village Clark counted one hundred seven stacks of these crates, twelve baskets per
stack, amounting, possibly, to ten thousand pounds.

One object of interest must have been the magnificent
canoes possessed by the Columbia Indians. Many of
these were large, artistically decorated, and raised in
the bow. At least one member of the expedition – it

may have been Drouillard – counted as many as fifty-two of these craft one day, drawn up at one place along the river. The Indians were, moreover, Drouillard learned, expert canoeists, not in the least hesitant about taking their craft out in very rough water.

On October 24, a short distance below the Dalles, Drouillard had the pleasure of casting his eyes upon the first Indian wooden house encountered since leaving Illinois. The Sioux had their commodious, artistically-decorated skin tepees; the Arikaras, Mandans, and Minnetarees their large, dome-shaped lodges constructed of earth and timber; the Shoshones their brush huts; and the Nez Percés their frame structures thatched with grass or bark. But the people of the Columbia, below the Dalles, had commodious houses constructed of split timber, which were stood on end, fastened together with thongs of cedar bark, and covered with bark. The houses above the Cascades were generally situated on the west, or on the north, side of the river, or on islands not easily accessible. Some of the houses were partly sunk into the ground. When such was the case, the inhabitants would enter by descending to the floor via a painted ladder. Upon retiring for the night, they would ascend via another painted ladder, to their beds.

Interesting, also, to Drouillard and others, must have been the evidences which bespoke of contacts which the Indians of the Columbia had with whites. One morning, for example, the explorers were visited by a group of Indians among whom was a man in possession of a "round hat Jacket," which he said he had obtained from the whites. In a village visited that same day lived an Indian in possession of a British musket, a cutlass,

and several brass tea kettles. One chief displayed, in his
lodge, a scarlet and blue piece of cloth, a jacket, a
sword, and a hat; and, incidentally, fourteen human
fingers, painted red, and taken from the hands of his
enemies to the southeast. At one point, below the Cascades, they were visited by several canoes, the men in
which were attired in sailor jackets, overalls, shirts, and
hats, which they may have put on as a special attire for
the occasion. These Indians were in possession, also,
besides scarlet and blue blankets, of a number of
muskets, pistols, and tin flasks in which to hold their
powder. At one place, near the mouth of the river, the
explorers overtook two canoes, in one of which was an
Indian who spoke some English. This man informed
them that the person with whom the Indians did most
of their trading at the mouth of the river was a man
named Haley.

The explorers were not to reach the mouth of the
Columbia without learning for themselves that the Nez
Percé chiefs had not been altogether mistaken in declaring that the people at and below the falls were bad;
so bad, in fact, as to make it seem inadvisable for themselves to accompany the white men that far on the
latters' journey.

Trouble with some of these people occurred on
November 4, the second day after the explorers had left
the Cascades. The people who caused the trouble were
none other than those who had been dressed in sailor
jackets, overalls, shirts, and hats, now on their way
down river in "Several canoes." Displaying their
muskets and pistols, their war axes, spears, and bows
"Sprung with quivers of arrows," they proved, as Clark

put it, to be "assuming and disagreeable." The captains, nevertheless, smoked with them and treated them with every consideration.

The trouble began during the "dinner" hour, when one or more of the guests stole Clark's pipe tomahawk, with which they had been smoking. A man of action, Clark ordered every Indian and every canoe to be searched. During the prosecution of the search, an Indian stole a coat. The coat was soon found, however, under the roots of a tree near which some Indians had been sitting. Having by this time discovered the determination of the white men, and perceiving the unwisdom of aggravating them further, the Indians took their departure, most of them heading downstream, the rest in the opposite direction. The stolen tomahawk, however, remained in their possession, or in the possession of other Indians, until the following spring, when it was recovered by the white men.

14

Inclement Weather

Drouillard's experiences at the mouth of the Columbia during the first month of his stay there were the kind he might wish to have written home about. Rain fell almost incessantly, night and day. Wind, waves, and tidewater, besides inundating their campsites, prevented him and his party from prosecuting their search for a place on which to establish themselves for the winter. The high bluffs rising almost sheer out of the river afforded them little room for camping.

The trying experiences began on the eighth of November. Drouillard and his companions had spent the night at a point some eight miles to the east of Gray's Bay, a body of water fifteen or more miles from the ocean. They had no difficulty in reaching the bay itself, the next day, after having got off to a delayed start caused by the necessity of changing from wet to dry clothing. At the northern end of the bay they "dined" at an old village, where they encountered their familiar friends, the fleas, whom they "treated with the greatest caution and distance." Skirting the bay after lunch, in a light rain, which fell at intervals, they arrived, after another eight miles, at a point (Gray's Point, or Portuguese Point) where they came upon waves so formidable as to compel them to land and to draw up their canoes.

Drouillard was as competent as any of them to size

up the situation: every member of the expedition, from the captains to Sacajawea's infant, soaked to the skin; the campsite, up against the steep bluffs, hardly large enough to accommodate the camp personnel clear of the tide; the water in the river too salty to drink; the waves increasing in size, making a search for a better campsite inadvisable; the men in the canoes seasick, yet compelled to remain in their craft to protect these from the waves; the baggage propped up on logs.

The situation of the gallant corps of discovery was not any better the next day. If anything, it was worse. Accompanying the rain, for example, was a hard wind from across the river, stirring up waves too formidable for their canoes. At two o'clock the flood tide inundated their camp and set adrift huge logs and other driftwood, increasing perceptibly the danger, not only to their canoes (which became filled with water) and their baggage, but to themselves. As Clark put it:

> every exertion and the Strictest attention by every individual . . . was scercely sufficient to Save our Canoes from being crushed by those monsterous trees maney of them nearly 200 feet long and from 4 to 7 feet through. our camp entirely under water dureing the hight of the *tide,* every man as wet as water could make them all the last night and today all day as the rain continued all day.

Optimistically he stated elsewhere that, in spite of this, every member of the expedition was "anxious to See further into the Ocian."

It rained during the night. It was raining in the morning (November 10) when Drouillard drew himself out of his wet blanket in obedience to the order of the captains to load the canoes and to proceed on down river to a less disagreeable camping spot.

Hugging the bluffs along the north side of the river,

they were able to make about ten miles. The ferocity
of the waves then compelled them to retreat two of the
miles they had come. Placing their baggage on driftwood, they waited, as patiently as they could, until the
waves had calmed down somewhat, when they again
loaded their canoes and started out, only to be once
more driven back by the waves.

Drouillard proceeded as cheerfully as he could,
along with his fellow travelers, to prepare his camp for
the night on the driftwood which had been deposited
at the base of the towering perpendicular bluffs. His
bedding was wet. There was nothing to eat but pounded
dried fish; nothing to drink but rain water.

The next day (November 11), at flood tide, their
camp was laid under water by the tide. The rain, which
had kept up all night, fell "in torrents." Rocks and
pebbles tumbled down the cliffs. The wind was high.
Their canoes were in one place, at the mercy of the
waves; their baggage in another. Drouillard and his
cohorts clung to floating logs or sought refuge in the
crevices of the cliffs.

At three o'clock the next morning a "Tremendious"
wind struck from the southwest, accompanied by lightning and hard claps of thunder, and followed by hail
and rain. Their situation had become so dangerous as
to make them deem it expedient, at the first low tide, to
move to a "Small wet bottom" at the mouth of a brook.
The bottom, it developed, besides being wet, was
hardly large enough to accommodate them.

Drouillard did not find the new location any great
improvement over that which they had left behind.
Their baggage had to be placed on rocks, half a mile
away. Their canoes, although sunk with "emmence

parcels of Stone," were still at the mercy of the waves. In fact, one of the canoes was, actually, washed away during the night but, luckily, became stranded, without much damage, on a rock a short distance below.

In the course of the day, Gibson, Bratten, and Willard made a heroic attempt to round the point ahead in the Indian canoe, in the hope of discovering a better campsite ahead. They were driven back by the waves. When Drouillard unpacked his bedroll before retiring he found that his blankets had rotted. Would the rain ever let up? Or the waves permit them to seek better accommodations? Drouillard had his doubts. He cast his eyes meditatively in the direction of the mountains across the river, partially covered with snow. Very likely he would have agreed with Clark, who wrote in his journal: "It would be distressing to a feeling person to see our situation at this time." Oddly enough, none of the members of the expedition were ill. None of them were discouraged.

Drouillard may have been one of those who accompanied Clark the next morning when the latter attempted to climb the hills for a view of the country. They found the hills so steep as to oblige them to grab onto the branches of trees in order to draw themselves up. The small pine was "intolerable." When they had climbed to a considerable height, they discovered to their dismay they were unable to see much of the country because of the rain and clouds.

The rain continued all day. It kept up during the night. When Drouillard crept out of his blanket in the morning he discovered that one of their canoes had been "much broken by the waves dashing it against the rocks." The wind was still strong. He felt grateful for one thing, though: Colter, Willard, and Shannon, who had been sent around the "blustering Point" ahead in the Indian canoe, to look for a better campsite, made it; an accomplishment which no doubt brought with it the sustaining hope that soon might they also be able to take the other canoes beyond that same blustering point.

They had a visit from some Indians that day. The Indians came in a canoe. Two of them were women. Hardly had they arrived than Colter also made his appearance. Colter stated the Indians had stolen his gig and basket.

Clark ordered the "Squars" to land and to give up the gig. This they refused to do, until a man "run [at them] with a gun, as if he intended to Shute them when they landed, and Colter got his gig & basket." Clark then proceeded to order "those fellows off, and they verry readily cleared out," giving Colter the opportunity he needed to bring to his news-hungry companions the welcome information that beyond the blustering point lay a sandy beach and a good harbor.

Such were the experiences of Drouillard and party during that first trying month at the mouth of the Columbia. For three long weeks, from the seventh to the twenty-fifth of November, they were confined to the base of the bluffs along the north side of the river. On the twenty-fifth, every last one of them scrambled aboard one or the other of their canoes and paddled back up the river to a spot near that on which they had camped on the night when many if not all of them believed they had arrived at the ocean. Crossing the river the next day, they again turned their canoes downstream, but were not able, because of wind and waves, to get beyond Tongue point (near present-day Astoria), which they reached on the twenty-seventh, and where they remained until December 7, when they were finally able to proceed to the spot which had been selected for their winter quarters by Lewis and Drouillard.

It became Drouillard's privilege to accompany Lewis on two trips of exploration during those weeks of waiting. The first of these was undertaken on foot on November 14, from their camp above the "blustering" point on the north side of the river. This trip took Drouillard down the beach along Baker Bay, to a point well beyond, and to the north of, Cape Disappointment on the ocean. The second trip was initiated from the camp above Tongue Point on November 29, and took him, by canoe, along Meriwether Bay (now Young's Bay), then for three miles up the Netul (now the Lewis and Clark) River, to a point on the west side of this river, which was the spot chosen on which to establish themselves for the winter.

15

Fort Clatsop

Drouillard was to lose no time in becoming acquainted with the country to the west of Fort Clatsop, the name by which their winter quarters became known. On the very day after that on which the main party arrived Clark started out, with Drouillard and four of the others, in a direct route toward the sea, to blaze a trail for the guidance of the men who would later be sent to hunt. They had as an additional purpose that of locating a place at which to make salt.

The intrepid party of explorers and workmen had not proceeded to any great distance, among lofty evergreens, and through swamps in which they waded in water to their knees, before they were delighted to discover a large herd of elk.

For three miles, they pursued those elk. The swamps over which they traveled shook for "½ an Acre" under the impact of their weight. In several places they sank to their hips in muck. But for all their exertions, their only reward was one elk.

While in the swamp they had not been able to travel very fast, with water and muck to their hips. There was also the grass in the swamp to contend with, and, possibly as bad, "a kind of Moss" which grew in abundance, not to mention submerged or protruding branches or trunks of trees, scattered "promiscuously" in all directions. To travel hip-deep in water alone, in late

December, was bad enough; to travel through all this
tangle of mud, water, grass, moss, and half-buried dead
timber was worse, to say the least. It was, therefore,
night before they realized the fact.

No better idea occurred to them than to strike camp,
then and there.

The spot selected was one of several "knobs" in the
swamp. This knob was hardly large enough to permit
them to lie clear of the water. The elkskin was used as
an improvised covering to keep out the rain. If it
covered six men, then those men must have been huddled close together, to say the least. The captain's
journal disclosed the interesting information that it
rained all night.

The herd of elk was too valuable a prize to be permitted to escape without additional effort on the part
of the explorers to prevent it. Drouillard was, therefore, commissioned by Clark the next morning to continue his pursuit of the animals. He was to be assisted
by Shannon. Clark and the other three men were, meanwhile, to continue their way to the sea.

To pursue the elk meant, to Drouillard, not merely
an attempt to overtake and kill them, but to herd them
in the direction of the explorers' camp on the Netul.
This would shorten the distance to carry the meat.

Drouillard and Shannon were gone on this assignment the better part of three days, returning to Fort
Clatsop on the thirteenth to report that they had killed
and butchered eighteen elk, and that the meat was
awaiting delivery at a distance of six miles. It may be
added that, while engaged in the task of bringing in
the meat, half of the men lost their way and were compelled to remain out all night, in the rain, and without
fire or shelter.

The task of hunting was one of no mean importance to the explorers at this time. Scarcely a day passed, during the next three months, which did not find Drouillard preoccupied in the pursuit of it. The task was by no means the easy one it had been on the Missouri. Heavy underbrush, fallen timber, mountains, hills, swamps, sink holes, rivers, sloughs, rain, fog, sleet, snow – these were some of the difficulties. Then, too, game was scarce, compared with game in the buffalo country of the Missouri. It was not an infrequent occurrence for more than one hunter to return to the fort at night to report, with discouragement, he had not had the opportunity of more than one shot, or even that. The three men who came in shortly after New Year to report they had hunted the bay area for fifteen miles but had been unable to procure more than one deer and a few fowl, were one example. Another example was furnished by Collins, who returned from the salt works one day, to report that he and five others, after hunting for five days without killing anything, had been forced to the necessity of purchasing whale blubber from Indians.

They roamed far and wide, these hunters. Drouillard knew that; he did it himself. If an animal were shot at a considerable distance from the fort, there would follow the task, the next day, of bringing in the meat and the hide.

Not infrequently the men lost their way. The heavy timber was to blame, and the seemingly endless days of cloudy or rainy weather. Under such conditions, as Lewis remarked, it was almost impossible for even the best among their woodsmen to "steer for any considerable distance the course he wishes." Drouillard may himself have got lost at times. But only temporarily. His uncanny intuition and knowledge of the signs of nature, whether in the woods or on the prairie, could not long keep him in doubt as to his whereabouts.

When he had killed one or more animal, Drouillard would ordinarily bring in the tongues and, part of the time, some of the marrow, for the special benefit of the captains, who on such occasions partook, in their opinions, of a meal comparable to a feast. The following day several of the men would be sent out to bring in the meat and skins, accompanied by Drouillard, if need be, or by one of Drouillard's hunters, to direct the way. In camp, the meat would be jerked and placed in a smoke house. The fire in this house was kept going night and day. Even so, the meat tended to spoil.

On one of his days out hunting, Drouillard came upon the Clatsop chief, Coboway (the captains called him Comowool [1]), and a number of Clatsop men in a canoe. Coboway was a frequent and, usually, welcome visitor at the fort. Drouillard bargained with him on this occasion to help bring in the meat he had killed — three elk and two deer. In return for this Drouillard promised him four elkskins. Coboway's Indians, barefoot, as per their custom, found it necessary to carry the meat, and one elkskin, six miles before the waves in the bay permitted them to load their burden into their canoe.

[1] Wheeler II, 196. At the time when Lewis and Clark were among the Clatsops, says Wheeler, "Coboway – Kob-oh-way – was the principal chief of the Clatsop tribe of Indians, within whose territory Fort Clatsop was established. Lewis and Clark erroneously gave the name of the chief as Comowool – that arose no doubt from the indistinct manner in which the Indians pronounced the name; according to their pronunciation the "b" in the name is but faintly sounded." – Wheeler II, p. 196.

"These Indians had witnessed Drewyer's shooting some of those Elk," wrote Lewis, "which has given them a very exalted opinion of us as marksmen and the superior excellence of our rifles compared with their guns." On January 16, with only three days of provisions in stock, he wrote: "Most of the party have become very expert with the rifle, if there is any game of any description in our neighborhood we can track it up and kill it." And on February 3: "About 3 oclock Drewyer LaPage returned, Drewyer had killed seven Elk."

It was not always possible to find the elk Drouillard or other hunters killed. On one occasion the men found only three out of eight killed by Shannon, Lepage, and Reuben Fields, due to a snowfall which had changed the appearance of the country. On another occasion some Indians had "purloined" five of the seven elk killed by Drouillard three days before.

With the advent of spring, the elk began to move inland, into the mountains. Hunting then became a serious problem. There were days when some of the hunters killed nothing. Not even Drouillard was able to maintain his usual record.

Then, one day, came a report, by Collins, that he had spied two large herds of elk. The expedition's prize hunter, Drouillard, accompanied by another prize hunter, Joseph Fields, was dispatched to find these herds. The two men returned the next day to report that they had not been able to catch even a glimpse of the elk. A probable explanation for this failure may be that the animals had gone so far as to make it inadvisable to follow them.

On March 11, Drouillard, Joseph Fields, and

Frazier were sent out hopefully to hunt in a territory in which hunting had not been permitted for some time. Their best efforts yielded them not more than two deer, affording a supply of meat hardly enough for three days.

Nevertheless, in spite of the meagre returns from the pursuit of game, Drouillard and his hunters brought in, between December 1, 1805, and March 20, 1806, according to Gass, one hundred and thirty-one elk, in addition to twenty deer, and a few "smaller quadrupeds," such as otter, beaver, and one raccoon.[2] Small wonder Captain Lewis was to write in his journal: "I scarcely know how we should subsist were it not for the exertions of this excellent hunter."

While Drouillard hunted, the men in camp, when not otherwise occupied, tanned skins, to be used for clothing or blankets. They prepared moccasins and other pieces of clothing for use during the winter, and for their return trip up the Columbia and down the Missouri. They stood guard, day and night, along the stockade which they had erected around the huts. They exchanged stories about their experiences in the woods. They split and carried wood for their fires and for the smoke house. They hunted fleas in their blankets.

Drouillard made moccasins for himself, and clothing, when he had time. Sacajawea helped some. But she had herself to prepare for, and Charbonneau, and Clark, and Lewis. In order to assure himself of an adequate supply, Drouillard probably had to take time to prepare it himself.

Before clothing could be made, the skins had to be

[2] Thwaites IV, p. 194.

tanned – a task which was not easy to perform without "brains," soap, or ashes. The men tried to get ashes, but the green wood they burned would hardly yield any. They were, however, able to tan enough deerskins and elkskins to provide themselves and the other members of the expedition, including Drouillard, not only with blankets, but with three hundred and fifty-eight pairs of moccasins, by actual count, and with shirts and over-alls, giving them a supply greater than at any other time during their period of service with the expedition.

Christmas was duly ushered in by the discharge of firearms. The discharge of arms was followed, accord-ing to Clark, by a salute, by cheers, and by a song in which "the whole party joined. . ." After breakfast, one-half of their remaining small supply of tobacco was divided among those who smoked (or chewed). Those who did not use tobacco were given handker-chiefs. Presents were exchanged.[3] Clark added: "we would have Spent the day the nativity of Christ in feasting, had we anything either to raise our Sperits or even gratify our appetites, our Diner concisted of pore Elk, so much Spoiled that we eate it thro' mere neces-sity, Some Spoiled pounded fish and a fiew roots." It is doubtful whether they had salt for their tainted elk.

On New Year's Day their "repast" was only slightly better. Their only beverage was *"pure water."*

Drouillard saw much of Indians – Clatsops, Chi-nooks, Cathlamahs, Killamucks, and Wahkiacums. He saw their villages, which he visited occasionally; he saw them at Fort Clatsop. Low in stature, ill-shaped, with thick, broad, flat feet and crooked legs, and with

---

[3] Among Clark's presents were two dozen weasel tails, given him by Saca-jawea.

broad, flat heads, they were much alike, in person, dress, habits, and manners. Their mouths were wide, their lips thick, their noses moderately large and fleshy, their eyes black. Coarse, well-combed, black hair, parted in the middle, hung over their shoulders. Winter or summer, men wore one and only one garment – a small skin robe reaching to the middle of the thigh. Women wore a robe similar to that worn by the men, except shorter, never reaching below the waist. In addition, women wore a short skirt made of the "tissue of white cedar bark, bruised or broken into small shreads, which are interwoven in the middle by means of several cords of the same material." Such dress, according to Lewis, was of sufficient thickness when the woman was standing, to conceal "those parts usually covered from formiliar view, but when she stoops or places herself in many other attitudes, this battery of Venus is not altogether impervious to the inquisitive and penetrating eye of the amorite." Alexander Ross, speaking of the attire of Lower Columbia women not long after the advent of Lewis and Clark, says:

> the women wear a kind of fringed petticoat suspended from the waist down to the knees, made of the inner rind of the cedar bark, and twisted into threads, which hang loose like a weaver's thrums, and keep flapping and twisting about with every motion of the body, giving them a waddle or duck gait. This garment might deserve praise for its simplicity, or rather for its oddity, but it does not screen nature from the prying eye; yet it is remarkably convenient on many occasions. In a calm the sails lie close to the mast, metaphorically speaking, but when the wind blows the bare poles are seen.[4]

Women's dresses were sometimes made of silk grass

---

[4] Alexander Ross, *Adventures of the First Settlers in Oregon, 1810-1813,* in Reuben Gold Thwaites (ed.), *Early Western Travels* VII, p. 106.

instead of bark, and sometimes of flags and rushes. Men and women occasionally threw a mat over their shoulders as a protection against rain, or wore a hat or basket of cedar bark and grass. The Indians were very fond of the attire of the whites, calling the latter "pâh-shish'-e-ooks," or "cloth men." They wore clothing whenever they could obtain it, except shoes, preferring, apparently, to go barefoot, winter and summer. They seldom tattooed themselves, but were fond of ornaments, especially blue and white beads, which they wore liberally and rather tightly around their wrists and ankles. Ornaments were also worn from the ears and, among men, from the nose, which was perforated for the purpose. Necklaces of bear claws were worn by men, and a similar ornament of elk teeth by women. Copper bracelets were not unknown. Unlike the custom prevalent among the plains Indians, the men here did much of the work, which, in addition to the building of houses, the construction of canoes, and the making of wooden utensils, included collection of fuel, building of fires, preparation of fish, and cooking for strangers. Women collected tubers and made articles from rushes, flags, cedar bark, and bear grass. Men and women alike navigated canoes.

Drouillard did not spend all of his working hours in hunting or trapping. Now and then he took a hand at interpreting, although there could not have been much time for this, since he was gone almost every day in quest of game, and since the Indians were but seldom permitted to stay at the fort overnight.

In his contacts with the Indians, it is possible he learned of the existence of a new medium of communication – Chinook jargon.

The origin of this Jargon, a conventional language similar to the Lingua Franca of the Mediterranean, the Negro-English-Dutch of Surinam, the Pigeon English of China, and several other mixed tongues, dates back to the fur droguers of the last century. Those mariners whose enterprise in the fifteen years preceding 1800, explored the intricacies of the northwest coast of America, picked up at their general rendezvous, Nootka Sound, various native words useful in barter, and thence transplanted them, with additions from the English, to the shores of Oregon. . . When, in 1792, Vancouver's officers visited Gray's Harbor, they found that the natives, though speaking a different language, understood many words of the Nootka.

On the arrival of Lewis and Clarke at the mouth of the Columbia . . . the new language, from the sentences given them, had evidently attained some form. . . The Chinooks, who are quick in catching sounds, soon acquired these words, both Nootka and English, and we find that they were in use among them as early as the visit of Lewis and Clarke in 1804.[5]

The Chinook and other Indians may, therefore, in their contacts with Drouillard and other members of the Lewis and Clark personnel, have attempted to use such forms of the jargon as they had then acquired – such as *"tilicum"* for "white man," *"cloocheman"* for "woman," *"shixe"* for "friend," *"nika"* for "I," *"mika"* for "you," *"kamook"* for "dog," *"peltkin"* for "fool." The Clatsop Cob-o-way, for example, in introducing himself, might have said: *"Nika atle* Cob-o-way, *tyee konoway* Clatsop (I am Cob-o-way, Chief of the Clatsops." If the Clatskanines, another tribe, actually did threaten to kill the explorers, as Olin D. Wheeler points out,[6] the chief, in announcing such a threat, might have

---

[5] George C. Shaw, *The Chinook Jargon,* ix-x.

[6] Wheeler, quoting, in part, Silas B. Smith, a grandson of the Clatsop chief Coboway, says: "The Indians inhabiting the upper part of Young's River Valley and the upper Nehalem Valley were known as the Klatskanin people. It was claimed by Chief Coboway that these people were disposed to attack

said: *"Nika hyas kopa nika tumtum kock mamook mika memloose* (I want very greatly in my heart to make you dead)."

Drouillard's contact with this language, if any at all, was no doubt limited to the more elemental forms of it, since the more elaborate forms had not been fully developed at the time he was there. But that he did have some contact with the language, to the extent of hearing a scattered word now and then, is not at all an improbability.

The advent of spring found at least one additional responsibility assigned to Drouillard, that of purchasing a canoe needed for the return trip. (The other responsibility was to proceed up the Columbia (on February 26) for the purpose of obtaining a supply of sturgeon and "anchovey," by catching the fish himself or by purchasing them from Indians.) Now, the purchase of a canoe from a Lower Columbia Indian could be a task of no mean difficulty. A canoe was a highly prized article, in the estimation of its owner, regarded as equal in value to that of a wife, and generally given in exchange to the father for a daughter. When Lewis and Clark decided they needed a canoe, their recourse – after having failed in an attempt themselves – was to assign to Drouillard, the dubious task of achieving their purpose. With his knowledge of the language of signs, his resourcefulness, his shrewdness, his tact, his insight into the ways of Indians, his persistency in the prosecution of a task undertaken, there was none better than he to do it.

---

the encampment at Fort Clatsop, and it was only through his influence and constant dissuasion that they were restrained, and no violence committed." – Wheeler II, p. 197.

Not in the habit of questioning a command, Drouillard started on his errand, on March 13, for the village of the Cathlamah Indians on the Columbia. He was gone the rest of the day, and all night. When he returned, accompanied by some Clatsops, he brought with him, sure enough, a canoe, but one for which the price was so high that it would require, in payment for it, more than half the stock of merchandise then possessed by the explorers; more, that is, than they could afford to pay. Moreover, in the estimation of Lewis, the canoe was an "indifferent" one. Loath, however, to let the canoe go, and knowing the fondness of Lower Columbia Indians for clothing, Lewis thought that perhaps he could do Drouillard one better by offering the Indians, as payment for the canoe, his laced uniform. To no avail. The Indians would have nothing of it. They were willing enough to sell, and did sell, some hats and roots, for a price; but when it came to their canoe – that was another matter. Net result: no sale.

Drouillard ventured forth again. Three days later he returned, not with one canoe, but with two. One of these was an excellent craft which he had been able to purchase for nothing more than a laced coat and a measly half-"carrot" of tobacco – positively a bargain; the other was a canoe which Pryor had lost nearly a week before, on a trip to buy fish from the Indians. Drouillard was continuing to serve the expedition well.

16

Horse Traders

On the return trip up the Columbia in the spring of 1806 Drouillard was to play an important role in the business of horse trading. His senior partner in the attempt was William Clark.

It may be of interest to note something about the people from whom Clark, Drouillard, and Company expected to buy their horses. They were, for the most part, the Skilloots and the Eneeshurs residing along the Dalles of the river. Along with their neighbors at the Cascades, they proved to be every bit as cocky and discourteous as they had been when the explorers made the trip down the river in the fall. They crowded the narrow trail up which the men were portaging their canoes. They crept into camp at night to pilfer. They laughed and leered at the efforts of Cruzatte, Labiche, and others struggling to draw the empty canoes up the cascades. From lofty bluffs they tossed stones upon the unprotected white men below. They stole Captain Lewis' dog – but left it and fled when they discovered that they were being pursued by three of the Lewis and Clark men. They tried to crowd Shields off the path as he was leading a dog he had purchased for his mess for supper, and might have succeeded, and taken his dog also, had he not threatened them with his knife.

Most of these incidents occurred in the vicinity of the Cascades. But the Skilloots and the Eneeshurs farther

up the river, along the Dalles, were fully as troublesome. One evening, for example, they pilfered several
small articles. That same night they got away with six
tomahawks and a knife. They stole two spoons the next
day; the morning after that, another tomahawk; on
another day, an iron socket from a canoe paddle. They
did not want to buy the explorers' canoes. They did not
want to sell their pounded fish or anything else, except
at exorbitant prices. They hung around camp. They
crowded the trail. They pretended they were interested in this, that, and everything. They laughed, leered,
pushed themselves around. These were the people from
whom Clark, Drouillard, and Company proposed to
buy horses.

The business of horse trading began in earnest on the
morning of April 16. The explorers were camped, the
night before, on Mill Creek, on the south side of the
Columbia, at or near the site of the present city of The
Dalles, Oregon. Drouillard had helped the captains in
explaining their intentions to the Indians who had
come over for a visit, and the Indians had promised to
bring their horses to the other side of the river in the
morning.

When morning came, Clark, Drouillard, Charbonneau, Sacajawea, and others crossed the river for the
purpose they had in mind. But no Indians showed up.
Drouillard, therefore, accompanied by Goodrich,
journeyed some six or seven miles up river, on foot, to
inform the Skilloot village located there that the white
man was now ready, and waiting for the horses to be
brought to him. Charbonneau and Frazier started at
the same time on a similar errand for one of the villages
a few miles below.

Drouillard succeeded in obtaining an interview with the chief of the Skilloots. This man, though apparently healthy, was unable to walk. He could ride a horse, however, and was willing to accompany Drouillard and Goodrich to the point where Clark was waiting. In his train followed not only men but women, children, and dogs.

The business of horse trading had not proceeded long before Drouillard discovered that the price asked by the Skilloot chieftain, and by the Indians brought by Charbonneau, for one horse, was almost half of all the merchandise Drouillard and the captain had. At such prohibitive prices the white men could not afford to trade.

In the afternoon, the chief said: "Come to my lodge. There will my people sell you horses." Clark took him up and, along with Drouillard, the chief, and their party, arrived in the chief's village at sunset.

After the usual ceremony of smoking, Drouillard accompanied the captain and the chief and the others into the chief's house. The chief had his women set before them a large platter of "sweated" onions, which the captain divided among his party. They found the "onion" tuber, or root, sweet. The leafy tops were tender.

After the meal, the chief asked his guests to dance. Cruzatte, who was along, got out his violin, and Drouillard, Charbonneau, Goodrich, Frazier, and the others (except Clark) danced and otherwise carried on, for the entertainment of the Indians.

Drouillard sought his bed for the night on a mat provided for the purpose. It was cold. They had no fire. Whether he slept, is not recorded. Clark, on his part, declared the next morning he had not slept at all, having been kept awake by "mice and vermin," which came to life after he had lain down.

Drouillard was up early the next morning (April 17) and assisted in arranging their stock of merchandise on a rock. The Indians, however, were in no mood for trading. They "tanterlized" Clark, Drouillard, and Company the greater part of the day, declaring they had sent for their horses and would trade as soon as the horses arrived.

Drouillard and the captain succeeded, finally, in bargaining for two horses. An hour later, the owner, as per Indian custom, cancelled the bargain. The captain, with Drouillard's help, then dickered for three additional horses. When these were brought forward, it was discovered that two of them had lame backs. Clark declined to accept these two. This so displeased the owner that he refused to part with the good one. Net result, after one day of bargaining: no horses.

Clark then sat down and penned a note to Lewis, dispatching the note with Willard and Cruzatte. In the note he stated he had not been successful in obtaining any horses. He would go on to the Eneeshur village at the falls, he said, but would return to the Skilloot village on the morrow to join Lewis there.

That evening Shannon arrived with a note from Lewis, in which Lewis suggested that Clark double his prices and try, if possible, to obtain five horses. Were Clark to succeed in this, then, he believed, they would be "enabled to proceed immediately" with their small canoes and "those horses to the village in the neighbourhood of the musselshell rapid," where horses were more abundant and cheaper; "with the remainder of our merchandise in addition to the canoes," Lewis added, "we can no doubt obtain as many horses there as will answer our purpose." He added that the "delay" they were now experiencing might prove costly, particularly at the "narrows," where they would be compelled to buy, not only food, but fuel as well, and where, besides, it would be easier for the Indians to carry out whatever evil designs these might have.

Clark did not, however, leave that day for the Eneeshur village, for no sooner had he and Drouillard started to put away the merchandise than an Indian came forward and, to their surprise, sold them two horses. A second Indian sold them a third. Several others declared they would trade also, if the white man would wait until their horses could be brought in after one sleep.

This turn of affairs induced the captain to decide to continue at this village another day. He arranged, therefore, for the purchase of three dogs for his party and, not having acquired a liking for this delectable food, reserved for himself what he called "chap-pa-lell."

Late that afternoon, or early in the evening, a chief of the Eneeshurs, along with fifteen or twenty of his people, arrived and expressed a desire to see the articles which the white men were offering for horses.

The captain, Drouillard, or one of his men, obligingly unpacked the merchandise. When the Indians had examined the goods, several of them said, if the white man would add such and such articles to such and such parcels, they would trade. This Clark agreed to do. Bundles of merchandise were, accordingly, laid aside, on the strength of the promise of these Indians to deliver the horses in the morning.

Sensing the possibility of striking a bargain, Clark proposed to them that he accompany them to their village. But this proposition the Indians turned down flat, declaring their horses were in the plain and that they would bring them the next day. Flattering though this bit of "intelligence" was, Clark had little faith in it.

Clark and Drouillard were not the only horse traders during the day. Charbonneau also tried his hand at the art and, undoubtedly to his surprise and delight, succeeded, late in the day, in purchasing a fine though somewhat unruly mare for some ermine skins, elk teeth, a belt, and sundry other articles of no great value, obtained, in part, from his self-sacrificing wife.

True to their promise, the Eneeshurs arrived at ten the next morning, with horses. But they betrayed little interest in the parcels shown them by Clark and Drouillard. When Clark laid by two additional parcels, however, they said they would bring horses after the sun had passed the middle.

By this time the captain was ready to tell the Indians they could go and take a jump in the river. He did not so express himself, however, but proceeded, instead, to dress the chief's sores. To this operation the chief submitted, not without misgivings. While performing it Clark had the satisfaction of knowing that he was being eagerly watched by the chief's children, to whom he had previously given trinkets. He had the satisfaction of knowing, also, that he was being watched by the chief's wife, a none too kindly-tempered woman with a "sulky" look on her fat, round face, who was, moreover, as the captain learned, suffering from a pain in her back. No sooner had Clark finished with the chief, therefore, than he no doubt surprised this woman not a little by stepping up to her and proceeding to rub camphor on her temple and on her back, and finishing this magnanimous act by bandaging her back with a soft flannel. The sensation produced on the skin by the medicine and the rubbing, the pungent odor of the camphor, the warm, soothing effect of the flannel, produced such an obvious change in the woman's demeanor as to cause the enthusiastic captain to decide that now was the time to strike a bargain with the old man himself. The net result was that the niggardly old chief, who owned "more horses than all the nations besides," sold the captain then and there two horses. What role Drouillard played in this drama is not recorded.

At three that afternoon Ordway and three men arrived from Lewis with several elkskins, two of Clark's coats, and four robes, to be added to Clark's stock of merchandise. Lewis also sent word that he had arrived with the canoes at the basin below (the Long Narrows) and asked Clark to get some dogs, if possible. Clark ordered Frazier to purchase and send on three dogs.

At five o'clock, Lewis himself arrived, after having walked along the Narrows from his camp. Since Clark had not slept for two nights, due to "mice and vermin," and to not having had a blanket, it was agreed that he spend the night with Lewis. Since, however, several Indians had, during the day, assured him they would be bringing in their horses, for purposes of trade, that evening, the captains decided to leave Drouillard with a stock of merchandise in the Skilloot village.

Thus did it become Drouillard's lot to spend, in the Skilloot village (with his merchandise under his head and his gun in his arms) one more of those cold nights, without benefit of fire or blanket, while "mice and vermin" carried on as on the night before. Shannon, Warner, and Goodrich were with him.

After breakfast on the following morning, he placed his parcels on display. His men stood by to lend whatever assistance they could. From his post beside his merchandise it is possible and even likely he watched his companions as these, under Lewis, transported their baggage on their backs and on the backs of their five horses, and as they drew their canoes up by means of ropes. By three o'clock they had formed a camp some distance above the Skilloot village. They were, however, still below the village of the Eneeshurs, and still below the falls of the Columbia.

Clark stated in his journal for that day (April 19) that he purchased four horses at "the village." This was in all probability the village in which he had left Drouillard, and to which he may have returned the next morning. How much help he received from Drouillard in this matter is not disclosed, nor is it indicated how long Drouillard remained in the village. When, in the evening of that day, however, Clark left for the Eneeshur village at the falls, in quest of additional horses, it is likely that Drouillard was one of the four men who accompanied him.

It had rained during the latter part of the day. A strong southwest wind was blowing. To make matters worse, when they arrived at the village at eight o'clock, they found to their surprise that the village had gone to bed. Nevertheless, they entered the largest of the houses.

The occupants obligingly enough got up. They lighted their fire with straw, since they had no wood. The captain and his companions sat down and smoked with them. The Indians said they would sell horses in the morning.

As regards the success of Clark, Drouillard, and Company the next day in trading for horses, Clark had this to say:

> My offer was a blue robe, a calico Shirt, a Silk handkerchief, 5 parcels of paint, a knife, a Wampum moon, 8 yards of ribon, several pieces of Brass, a Mockerson awl, and 6 braces of yellow beeds; and to that amount for each horse which is more than double what we gave either the Sohsohne or first flatheads we met with on Clarks river. I also offered my large blue blanket, my coat, sword & plume none of which seamed to entice those people to sell their horses. notwithstanding every exertion not a single horse could be procured of those people in the course of the day.

During the night, the captain and his men slept in the house in which they had spent the night before. The captain recorded in his journal that they lay down, "haveing our merchandise under our heads and guns &c in our arms, as we always have in similar situations."

Lewis had, meanwhile, succeeded, the day before, in obtaining a horse "at the basin." Two days later he was made the recipient of two additional horses presented or sold to him by a Nez Percé, who had joined the party at some point below and who had indicated a willingness to accompany the explorers to the Nez Percé villages.

While Drouillard and Clark were more or less unsuccessfully occupied with the business of horse trading, Lewis and his men were having difficulties with the horses already purchased. With one exception, these horses were studs and so wild as to be almost unmanageable. Now and then they would attempt to break away, only to be thrown by the ropes with which they were tethered. At night, they required the vigilant efforts of all the men on guard to keep them from getting away.

Finally, the business of horse trading was over, but not the troubles of the horse traders. These were to experience one more aggravating hour in consequence of the perfidy of the rascally Indians.

The trouble, this time, was started by Charbonneau's mare. It happened on the twenty-second of April. The explorers had succeeded in portaging their baggage past the falls of the Columbia, and, in possession of some ten or eleven horses, had gained the top of the bluffs above the river, when the mare took it upon itself to start on a wild run down the bluff toward the Eneeshur village. By the time it reached the village it had succeeded in getting rid of its saddle and a robe.

The mare was finally captured by the Nez Percé, who had decided to accompany the explorers to his people. But the robe was not recovered until after a diligent search had been made for it, when it was found by Labiche tucked away behind some baggage in the lodge of an Indian.

These incidents ended the trouble with the rogues of the Columbia. Keeping to the north side of the river, the explorers continued their journey and arrived, on April 27, among the Walla Wallas, whose village was located on the Columbia, about twelve miles below the mouth of the Snake, and across from the mouth of the Walla Walla River. Here they crossed the river, then proceeded overland, in a northeasterly direction, via a route (recommended by the Walla Wallas) that would shorten their journey by as much as eighty miles. They arrived, after another week, among the friendly Nez Percés.

17

Camp Chopunnish

The third of May, 1806, was a cold, wet, blustery day. By turn it rained, hailed, and snowed. A strong, southwest wind attacked the explorers from behind, as, partly on horseback, but mostly on foot, they made their way in a northeasterly direction, through open country, along one of the tributaries of the Snake.

Drouillard had, probably, by this time obtained a horse.[1] He had gone on ahead of the party, in search of game. But he had found nothing. Earlier that day he had eaten his share of the last of their dried meat and some dogs. They had in reserve, now, only enough food for a "scant" supper; and for the next day, no food at all.

But they experienced a piece of good fortune during the day. They met We-ah-koo-nut.

We-ah-koo-nut was one of the Nez Percés who had accompanied them on their way down the Snake the year before, as far as the mouth of this river. The captains called him Big Horn, because of the habit he had of carrying a horn of that animal suspended by a cord from his left arm. We-ah-koo-nut was a likeable fellow. Having heard that his white man friends were on their way back, he had set forth, with ten of his young men, in the face of the penetrating wind, and in the rain and

---

[1] The explorers succeeded in buying a few more horses on their route to the Nez Percés.

slush and snow, to meet them. When he discovered their plight with respect to food, he cheered them by informing them that there was a lodge at no great distance at which, he believed, when they reached it on the morrow, they might be able to obtain provisions.

They were not able, the next day, to obtain, either at this lodge or at other lodges, as much food as they needed. The truth was, We-ah-kóo-nut explained apologetically, the Nez Percés had scarcely enough food for themselves, let alone for a large band of strangers.

After four-and-a-half miles the next day (May 5) they arrived at the mouth of the Kooskooske. They began to pick their way up the northeast side of this river, and passed first one lodge of Nez Percés, then a second. They were not able to obtain food at either lodge. But at the second lodge a man surprised them by presenting Clark with a very elegant gray mare, for which he asked nothing in return except a phial of eye water.

Drouillard may have recalled an incident which had occurred the year before, at the mouth of the Kooskooske. Clark had at that time presented a man with some liniment, to be rubbed onto his knee and thigh. The man "never ceased to extol the virtues of our medicine," declared Lewis, "and the skill of my friend Capt. Clark as a phisician." It appears that the man claimed the medicine had enabled him to walk. "This occurrence," continued the captain, "added to the benefit which many of them experienced from the eyewater we gave them about the same time has given them an exalted opinion of our medicine." And this, even though the eye water was, in some instances, nothing but ordinary drinking water. The captain continued: "in our present situation I think it pardonable to continue this deseption for they will not give us any provision without compensation in merchandize and our stock is now reduced to a mere handfull. We take care to give them no article which can possibly harm them."

In the course of that afternoon, twelve miles up the river, they arrived at "much the largest" Nez Percé house Drouillard had seen. This was a house which proved, by measurement, to be one hundred and fifty-six feet long, by fifteen feet wide, with entrances on each side and a row of fires down the center. This was the house of Neesh-ne-park-ke-ook, an important Nez Percé chief whom the captains called Cutnose because of a wound received in a battle with the Shoshones.

When he arrived at this house, Drouillard was possibly as hungry as his companions. Yet no article of merchandise which the explorers then owned could induce the people in the big house, or in a house that stood close to it, to part with any food except a small quantity of "bread of cows" and some dried roots.

It seems that a number of persons suffering from some ailment or other had gathered (or resided) at these houses. They had probably heard of the reputation of the white medicine man. At any rate, upon the arrival of the explorers at this village, they came forward, seeking help.

More than likely it became Drouillard's task to tell them that the paleface medicine man would give them no help whatever unless they brought food in the form of horses or dogs.

The wife of a chief then said she would give a horse at the next sun if the paleface medicine man would help her now. She had an abscess on her back.

Obligingly, Clark lanced and dressed the abscess –
and soon found he had fifty applicants for his services.
It became Drouillard's task to explain to them that the
paleface medicine man did not wish to help them until
the next sun. Meanwhile, would they bring food?
Obligingly, they brought some dogs, which, however,
were so lean as to be unfit for consumption.

True to her promise, the wife of the chief (or rather,
the chief himself) brought a young horse the next
morning. Some of the Nez Percés offered bread. One
of them gave a horse for medicine and prescriptions for
a girl with rheumatism. We-ah-koo-nut presented a
strong, active sorrel to Lewis. He, or someone else,
donated an unbroken young horse for food (Howbeit,
the frisky young animal got away, to the "keen disappointment" of the entire party).

Two days later We-ah-koo-nut left them. They were
accompanied, however, as on the day before, by a
brother of the Twisted Hair and, part of the way, by
Neesh-ne-park-ke-ook. They had, by now, crossed to
the south side of the river, upon the recommendation
of their guide. Their camp for the night was not far
from the snow-covered Bitterroots; the mountains
which, Drouillard feared, they would not be able to
cross for another month, if the Indians spoke the truth,
as he had no reason to doubt.

As Drouillard made his way through the river bottoms of the Kooskooske the next day (May 8), in quest
of game (while the main party followed above the
bluffs of the river, in open country), he could not help
but notice the pine trees that the Indians had cut the
previous winter for the "seed" from these trees, as well
as the inner bark, for food. Some of the Indians had

informed him that the Nez Percés obtained some of
their food, during that same winter, by boiling moss
from trees. No wonder they had been so reluctant about
parting with such food as they did have, when Drouillard and his companions came among them.

When Drouillard arrived in camp that evening, a
surprise awaited him. The main party had met the
Twisted Hair on their march above the bluffs. The
Twisted Hair, instead of greeting the captains with his
usual cheerfulness and cordiality, had met them with
an air of aloofness, which, to the captains, was as "unexpected as it was unaccountable." Furthermore, hardly
had the Twisted Hair cast his eyes upon Neesh-ne-park-
ke-ook than a violent quarrel had arisen between them,
after about twenty minutes of which Lewis had sent
them word that he and his party would be going on to
the first water (about two miles distant), where they
would camp. The Indians followed, but, upon arriving
at the creek, had established separate camps, those
under the Twisted Hair on one spot, those under Neesh-
ne-park-ke-ook on another.

Lewis explained to Drouillard what had happened.
He stated that he feared the quarrel had something to
do with the horses which he and Clark had entrusted
to the Twisted Hair the year before. He was now very
desirous of knowing the whereabouts of these horses,
so that he could decide where to pitch his camp while
they were being collected. Furthermore, he desired to
talk with the Twisted Hair about serving as guide across
the Bitterroots. He had tried, he said, to persuade a
Shoshone prisoner, who was traveling with them, to act
as interpreter while he talked to the Twisted Hair, but
the prisoner had flatly refused. There was, therefore,

nothing more he could do, other than send Drouillard
to the camp of the Twisted Hair, to exert such influence as he could, in finding out about the horses and in
effecting a reconciliation between the two chiefs.

This was not the first time Drouillard had, in a time
of need, been called upon to undertake a task which he
alone, or which he better than anyone else, could perform. In situations such as this, the captains depended
upon him absolutely.

Drouillard went. He sat down beside the Twisted
Hair's fire. He offered the pipe. He got the Twisted
Hair to talk. The story the Twisted Hair told him,
either there, or at the fires of the explorers, was that
upon his return from the Dalles of the Columbia the
year before, he had collected and taken charge of the
horses. Neesh-ne-park-ke-ook and Tun-na-che-moo-
toolt (head chief of the Nez Percés) had, however,
upon their return from their war with the Shoshones,
expressed displeasure over the fact that he, a lesser
chief, should have been entrusted with the care of the
horses. They had proceeded to speak bad words to him,
he declared, to such an extent that he thought it best,
since he was an old man, to stop caring for the horses.
These had, in consequence, become scattered.

The Twisted Hair then stated that most of the horses
were not far away, and that he would send his young
men for them. As for the saddles, some of these, he
feared, might have been washed away by the rise of
the water in the river that spring. But he would bring
as many as he could; and of the horses all, except the
two to which the Shoshone guide and his son had
helped themselves the year before, when they set out
on their return journey across the Bitterroots. The cap-

tains thanked him and expressed confidence that he would do as he had promised.

Later that evening, Neesh-ne-park-ke-ook was willing to tell his version of the story. He declared, in the presence of the Twisted Hair, that the Twisted Hair was a bad old man who had permitted his young men to ride the horses instead of taking care of them. It was he himself, therefore, and the head chief of all the Nez Percés, Tun-na-che-moo-toolt, who began to take care of them. And he himself would see to it that the horses were now returned.

When Drouillard informed him of the arrangement made with the Twisted Hair, Neesh-ne-park-ke-ook apparently raised no objection. He offered to go along with the explorers and to be of such help to them as he could.

True to his promise, the Twisted Hair brought in twenty-one of the horses the next day, and half the saddles. By the end of another day he had brought in more saddles, and all but four of the horses, exclusive of the two to which old Toby and his son had helped themselves. These four horses were reported to be on the opposite side of the river, at no great distance.

Drouillard was not with the explorers when these descended the bluffs of the Commearp to the village of Tun-na-che-moo-toolt – or, as the captains called him, the Broken Arm – on the afternoon of May 10, two miles above the junction of the Commearp and the north-flowing Kooskooske. His absence was due to the fact that he had set out, with his horse, not only to hunt, but to locate, if he could, the most likely hunting grounds, since it seemed certain the explorers would remain in the vicinity for some time.

It was three o'clock in the afternoon of May 11 when he entered the village.

The village consisted of "one house only –" the house of Tun-na-che-moo-toolt. This house was one hundred and fifty feet in length, according to Lewis, and constructed, in common with other Chopunnish houses, of sticks, mats, and dried grass or bark. The house boasted twenty-four fires, which meant twice that many families – enough to muster one hundred men capable of bearing arms.

Drouillard had not been long in the village before he learned that Tun-na-che-moo-toolt had met the explorers at the time of their arrival and had turned over to them a large leather tepee for their use as long as they should choose to remain with him. Before the entrance to this tepee he had laid a bundle of wood. He had urged his people to bring food and fuel. He had refused to accept a lean horse for a fat one, to be used as food by the explorers, declaring that his young men had many horses, of which the white men could have as many as they wished, without trading any of theirs.

Lewis had already delivered himself of his address to the nation when Drouillard arrived. This had been a "tedious" process, since the captain's words had to be translated into French, and then, by Charbonneau, into the language of the Minnetarees to Sacajawea, who translated it into her own language to a Shoshone prisoner, who finally rendered it into Chopunnish to the Nez Percé chiefs – four of them. "French, Hidatsa, Shoshone, Chopunnish – four foreign tongues, four chiefs, four wonderful names, four interpreters"! This from Olin D. Wheeler. "No wonder," he continued, "that after they had 'at last,'" quoting Lewis, " 'suc-

ceeded in communicating the impression we wished,'
they 'then adjourned the council,' for nature had some
rights and demanded rest." [2] The rest consisted in showing the Nez Percés the "spye glass," compass, watch,
air gun, "and sundry other articles equally novel and
incomprehensibel" to them. The son of a chief who had
been killed not long before by the "Minnetarees of
Fort de Prarie" had, later in the day, presented the
captains with a "very fine mare colt," which he had
asked them to accept as evidence that he "had opened
his ears to their councils."

With respect to this council with the Indians, Lewis
says, in part: "the interpretation being tedious it occupied nearly half the day before we had communicated to them what we wished." Small wonder, in view
of the fact that his message had to be conveyed in five
languages – English, French, Minnetaree, Shoshone,
Chopunnish. Had Drouillard been present, the medium
of the sign language might have been used, as it was on
later occasions.

Drouillard had not been in the village long before he
met the various Nez Percé chiefs: Tun-na-che-moo-
toolt, head chief of all the Chopunnish, middle-aged,
well-built, well-dressed, with a quick step and an alert
eye; Yoom-park-kar-tim (meaning Five Big Hearts),
a short, stout man of forty summers, and of a "good
countenance"; and Ho-hast-ill-pilp, young, strongly
built, whom Drouillard came to know as active, out-
spoken, generous, and, like the other chiefs, genuinely
interested in his newly found friends. Ho-hast-ill-pilp
had distinguished his attire from that of the others by
generously adorning his tippet with human scalps and

2 Wheeler II, pp. 266-67.

with the thumbs and fingers of men whom he had slain in battle.

There was, of course, Neesh-ne-park-ke-ook, a man who, though he did not give the impression of greatness by his bearing, was, nevertheless, in point of fact, one of the four greatest – actually, second in rank. Yoom-park-kar-tim and Ho-hast-ill-pilp ranked third and fourth, respectively.

The morning after Drouillard's arrival (May 12) found the Indians in a council of their own, in which they were to decide how to answer the white men. One of the Lewis and Clark men attended this council. It is more than likely that this man was Drouillard. Upon the conclusion of the council he brought to the captains an account of what had occurred, which Lewis recorded thus:

After this council was over the principal chief or the broken Arm, took the flour of the roots of cows and thickened the soope in the kettles and baskets of all his people, this being ended he made a harangue the purport of which was making known the deliberations of their council and impressing the necessity of unanimity among them and a strict attention to the resolutions which had been agreed on in councill; he concluded by inviting all such men as had resolved to abide by the decrees of the council to come and eat and requested such as would not be so bound to show themselves by not partaking of the feast. I was told by one of our men who was present, that there was not a dissenting voice on their great national question, but all swallowed their objections if any they had, very cheerfully with their mush. during the time of this loud and animated harangue of the cheif the women cryed wrung their hands, toar their hair and appeared to be in the utmost distress. After this ceremony was over the chiefs and considerate men came in a body where we were seated at a little distance from our tent, and two young men at the instance of the nation, presented us each with a fine horse.

We caused the chiefs to be seated and gave them each a flag a pound of powder and fifty balls, we also gave powder and ball to the two young men who had presented the horses. Neeshnee-parkkeeook gave Drewyer a good horse.

The fact that Neesh-ne-park-ke-ook singled out Drouillard as the one upon whom to confer this honor no doubt indicated either that the former wished to reward Drouillard for service which Drouillard had rendered or it indicated that he recognized in Drouillard one of the important men among these white men.

The person chosen by the council to forward their answer to the white men was Ho-hast-ill-pilp's father, respected by the Nez Percés not only for the integrity of his character but for the power of his oratory. And an oration it proved to be; or, if not, then at least a speech, and a long one, judging by Lewis' summary of it. Absent from the captain's journal now are remarks about the tediousness of the occasion and the length of time involved. Not now was it necessary to employ five tongues. One was sufficient, aside from the invaluable language of signs. Drouillard was on hand to serve as interpreter.

The explorers established their camp, after two days, on the other, or east, side of the Kooskooske, on a spot designated by Tun-na-che-moo-toolt, about forty paces from the river. This spot was circular in shape, about thirty feet in diameter, and bounded by an embankment of earth three and one-half feet in height, scooped out from inside the circle, leaving the space within some four feet lower than the surface of the surrounding ground. "around this," wrote Lewis (May 14), "we formed our tents of sticks and grass facing outwards and deposited our baggage within the sunken space

under a shelter which we constructed for the purpose."
These huts ("wickiups"), he continued, were "perfectly secure as well from the heat of the sun as from
rain."

Drouillard, if he still shared his sleeping quarters
with the captains and York, and with Charbonneau,
Sacajawea, and the infant boy Pomp, as seems likely,
was not privileged at first to occupy such a comfortable
type of dwelling, for the captains thought they could
do better than their men by sleeping under part of an
old sail. The sail did not prove large enough, however,
to shelter them adequately in time of rain. The result
was that, after one week, the captains ordered to be
constructed for themselves a grass-thatched hut similar
to those occupied by their men. This they found to be
secure against rain, sun, and wind – their "most comfortable shelter" since their departure from Fort Clatsop.

At Camp Chopunnish, as the captains called it, the
explorers remained for nearly a month.

During this month, Drouillard's main occupation
was that of hunting, by no means an easy task, since
game was not nearly as abundant as on the Missouri;
besides, the region was inhabited by hundreds of Indians who, themselves, were excellent hunters.

Inside of four days after their arrival at Camp Chopunnish, he and his hunters had "scowered the country
[to the west and north] between the Kooskooske and
Collin's Creek [now Lolo Creek], and from hence to
their junction about 10 miles and had seen no deer or
bear and but little sign of either." He tried the country
to the south, to the west, and to the east, with only
limited success. Sometimes he and his men would bring

home deer, sometimes bear, sometimes "pheasants." They even penetrated to their "Quamash Flats" [3] but met with only moderate success. Their utmost exertions failed to bring in the amount of food needed. Such meat as they did succeed in bringing in had to be supplemented, now and then, by horseflesh (the Indians furnished the horses), but more frequently by kouse, camas, and possibly other tubers, obtained from the Indians.

It may have amused Drouillard to observe the ingenuity with which the captains and their men prepared the merchandise with which to tempt the cautious and conservative Nez Percés to part with their life-giving roots. The men searched among their belongings and found awls, needles, knitting pins, "scanes of th[r]ead," arm bands, fractions of ounces of vermilion, pieces of ribbon, some thread. When they learned that the Nez Percés were fond of brass buttons, they "devested themselves of all they had in possession," in order to procure a supply of roots and bread. When their supply of awls gave out, they made more from the links of a small chain taken from a steel trap. The captains severed buttons from their coats, prepared "eye water" and "Basilicon," got out some "Phials," and converted into merchandise tin boxes that had once stored their "Phosphorus." When it was discovered that antelope hair would be needed for their saddles, and when they realized, also, that they needed pack ropes, bags, and probably other articles, the men got out fish gigs, parts of an old seine, scraps of iron, old files, bullets — anything that might induce the Indians to sell them what they needed.

[3] Weippe Prairie, where the explorers first met the Nez Percés the year before. — Wheeler II, p. 282.

The sympathetic Nez Percés responded generously, giving not only of their horses, without charge, but, for a consideration, of their roots and tubers. Time and again York, Pryor, Charbonneau, and other members of the expedition returned from the village of the Broken Arm, or from the villages of other bands of Nez Percés, "laden" with supplies. When York and McNeal returned, one night, with three bushels of roots and some bread, Lewis wrote that the "successfull voyage" of these two was "not much less pleasing to us than the return of a good cargo to an East India Merchant."

Occasionally the intrepid voyageurs would have a mishap. Such happened to the Dutchman Potts and his companions, one time, when the canoe in which they were crossing the river was driven by the current broadside against some "standing trees" and sank, resulting in a loss of some blankets and a blanket coat. Out of their "pittance of merchandise," wrote Lewis, this was the greatest loss sustained by any individual since the journey began. A similar accident befell Charbonneau and Labiche the next day, when their pack horse fell into the river, resulting in a loss, not of the pack horse, but of part of their merchandise. Even the Indians, in their attempts to help, had their mishaps, as was the case on the day when a raft laden with roots and bread struck a rock and upset, spilling the entire cargo into the river. In spite of such reverses, however, and in spite of their limited supply of merchandise, the explorers found no difficulty in surviving. They did, in fact, live quite comfortably.

The stay at Camp Chopunnish afforded Drouillard an opportunity of demonstrating an art, if it may be called an art, which, if he did not already possess it, he acquired under the stress of circumstances then and there. This was the art of castration.

As it happened, several of the horses obtained by the explorers were studs, as has been mentioned, and proved to be difficult to manage. In consequence of this, the explorers attempted to trade them to the Nez Percés for mares or for geldings. This, however, the Nez Percés were reluctant to do. As a result, the captains decided that the way out was to castrate. The task of performing this operation fell to Drouillard.

The cooperative Nez Percés were ever willing to share their knowledge and experience. One of them demonstrated a method of castrating which seemed superior to that used by Drouillard. At any rate, the horses gelded by this Indian were less swollen than those operated on by Drouillard. "Others," said Lewis, "bled most but appeared much better today than the others" – that is, better than those operated on by Drouillard. Be that as it may, the need for castration served to reveal the versatile Drouillard in one additional role, howbeit, this time, a minor one.

On the first of June, Drouillard was selected by the captains to perform still another task in behalf of the expedition. This task, though nothing more than that of regaining possession of two tomahawks, proved to be a task of no small difficulty, demanding tact, judgment, patience, and resourcefulness. One of the tomahawks had inadvertently been left by Clark the year before at one of their camps. The other had been stolen, also the year before, by an Indian at their Canoe Camp at the junction of the north and the south fork of the Clearwater. The weapons were reported to be in possession, now, of some Indians residing on the other side of the river.

Drouillard knew that Clark was desirous of regaining possession of the stolen tomahawk. The weapon had belonged to Floyd, the man who died from illness on the Missouri. Floyd had been highly esteemed by both Lewis and Clark. It was now Clark's desire to regain possession of the weapon so as to enable him to present it to the sergeant's family or friends.

This mission may not, at first, have impressed Drouillard as being difficult, especially since Ho-hast-ill-pilp was to go along, and also Neesh-ne-park-ke-ook, both of them interested in the return of the tomahawk, and both of them under commitment to lend such assistance as they could. With these men along, the regaining of the tomahawk seemed all but a certainty.

In this particular case, it was not a certainty, however. For one thing, the present owner of the tomahawk had actually bought it (from the man who had stolen it), and so considered himself the rightful owner. For another thing, the man lay at the point of death when Drouillard and Neesh-ne-park-ke-ook and Ho-hast-ill-pilp arrived, and was unable to converse with them. Finally, when Drouillard and the two chiefs turned to his relatives, these refused absolutely to part with the tomahawk, for the reason that they intended to bury it with the body of its owner.

Drouillard could appreciate the position of the relatives. He recalled that, when the wife of Neesh-ne-park-ke-ook had died, recently, the chief and his relatives had felt under compulsion to sacrifice in her behalf twenty-eight horses. He recalled, also, that the Indians of the Columbia, in the hour of death, felt under compulsion to sacrifice their highly-prized canoes. It did not surprise him, therefore, to discover that the relatives of the owner of the tomahawk were not impressed by the offers he and Neesh-ne-park-ke-ook and Ho-hast-till-pilp made to them.

They did, however, finally deliver the tomahawk for a handkerchief, two strands of beads, and two horses, "to be killed agreeably to their custom at the grave of the disceased." Thus again Drouillard met with success in the performance of a difficult task, assisted in no small measure, this time, by the Nez Percé chiefs, one of whom, Neesh-ne-park-ke-ook, was mentioned by Lewis as being "principally" influential in bringing the deal to a successful conclusion.

18

The Bitterroots

When Lewis dispatched Drouillard on June 1 to retrieve the stolen tomahawk, he instructed him to make inquiries concerning the whereabouts of the Twisted Hair, in the hope that the latter, or one of his sons, might be induced to act as guide for the explorers in crossing the Bitterroots.

The matter of obtaining a guide was one about which Lewis felt no small amount of concern. It was because of this concern that he had, as far back as May 12, instructed Drouillard to invite the Twisted Hair and his family to take up their abode temporarily with the white men. It was because of this concern, again, that he had suggested to Drouillard, on June 1, that he once again try to get in touch with this particular Nez Percé chief, who, with his sons, was reputed to be familiar with the mountain trails used by the Nez Percés at that time.

It may be presumed that, acting upon the captain's instructions, Drouillard made the necessary attempts to get in touch with the Twisted Hair. If he sent a messenger for this purpose, this messenger may have been Frazier. At any rate, when, on June 6, the Twisted Hair presented himself, Frazier was with him.

Before the arrival of the Twisted Hair, however, other events had transpired. One of these was a visit to Camp Chopunnish by Tun-na-che-moo-toolt. On this

visit the Nez Percé chieftain disclosed that an "express"
had been dispatched by the Nez Percés, to ascertain
from the "Oote-lash-shoots" what had "taken place on
the East side of the mountains during that season."

If an Indian express could traverse the mountains at
this time of year, so reasoned the captains, why not
they? To which Tun-na-che-moo-toolt replied that the
mountain streams were still swollen, there was yet no
grass for their horses, the snow was deep, and the path
slippery. In twelve or fourteen sleeps, perhaps then the
path would be sufficiently open to enable the white men
to pass. As for the present, no.

This argument was not new to the captains. The same
argument had been advanced by Neesh-ne-park-ke-ook
as long ago as May 8. It had been advanced by others
since then – by Ho-hast-ill-pilp's father, for example.
The captains on their part had this to remind the Chopunnish: Would the Chopunnish furnish a guide
against the day on which the explorers would actually
start on their journey across these same, accursed mountains?

Tun-na-che-moo-toolt said the Chopunnish would.
But it was a matter on which he felt it incumbent upon
himself to speak at the forthcoming conference, to be
held on the Commearp after a few more sleeps. From
this position the captains could not budge him. He invited them, however, to pay him a visit before taking
their departure.

Clark was the one chosen to visit Tun-na-che-moo-
toolt in response to the latter's invitation. The day set
was June 6. Drouillard was chosen to accompany him,
as interpreter.

As it happened, June 6 was the day selected by the

Twisted Hair to make his visit to Camp Chopunnish, in response to Drouillard's invitation. Alas! Lewis was not able to understand what it was the Twisted Hair had come to say. He ascribed his failure in this respect to his lack of an interpreter, "Drewyer," he added, "being absent with Capt. Clark."

The Twisted Hair left in the evening. On his way he met Clark and Drouillard returning from their conference with Tun-na-che-moo-toolt. He had no difficulty in explaining to them – that is, to Drouillard – what he had intended to say to Lewis, namely, that, since his brother was ill, he would not be able to accompany the white men across the mountains.

Months had gone by during which Lewis had observed Drouillard speaking more or less freely with Indians by means of the language of signs. During these months he had been given the opportunity of seeing how Drouillard translated his own words into this medium of communication, and how the Indians used signs in speaking to Drouillard, often in direct response to a question by the captain. Yet he was not able to understand a simple, one-sentence message brought him by the Twisted Hair during Drouillard's absence. When it is recalled that Drouillard was employed in translating, not one or two sentences only, but entire speeches, (speeches given by both whites and Indians), and occasionally under trying and even dramatic situations, with the fate of the expedition at stake, then it should not be difficult to gain an appreciation of the importance to the expedition of his services in this matter of communication alone.

In their conference with Tun-na-che-moo-toolt, Clark and Drouillard once more touched on the subject

of guides. Tun-na-che-moo-toolt said he could not assure them that these guides would be supplied until his
nation had held council on the "Commearp," which
would be in another ten or twelve days. Should the
white men start on their journey, meanwhile, then two
or three young Nez Percés would overtake them in the
mountains and see them across.

Tun-na-che-moo-toolt spoke, also, of the recent arrival of a band of Shoshones, who, far from expressing
any warlike intentions, had declared that they had
opened their hearts to the talk given them by the white
men the year before on the Salmon River, and intended,
now, to follow this talk and make peace with the
Chopunnish.[1]

Tun-na-che-moo-toolt then found two pipes. Explaining that these were intended as a token of friendship
between the Chopunnish and the white men on the one
hand, and between the Chopunnish and the Shoshones
on the other, he presented one to Clark. The other, he
said, was to be reserved for the Shoshones. Clark became so impressed with this act of noble intent that he
promptly decorated with blue ribbons and white wampum the pipe which had been handed to him, and
declared, in effect: "This pipe shall serve as an emblem
of peace between your people and mine." In the declaration of pledges of friendship such as this it had become Drouillard's privilege to act, not only as witness,
but as participant. One may ask: What would the
captains have done without him?

Upon the return of Clark and Drouillard from their
conference with Tun-na-che-moo-toolt, the captains

[1] The Nez Percés called themselves the Chopunnish. In fact, Lewis and
Clark called them that too.

decided that, guides or no guides, they would start on their trek across the mountains with no more delay than necessary. The date set for the memorable event was June 10.

During the next three days, preparations for the journey were speeded up. Drouillard and other hunters went out daily in quest of game. Some of the men visited the Indian villages for pack ropes, bags, and roots. Others prepared saddles and packs. "Indifferent" horses, or horses with lame backs, were traded to the Indians for good ones.

To condition their men for the journey, especially those who had not served as hunters, the captains arranged for the staging of athletic contests: foot racing, pitching of quoits; the playing of "prison basse"; possibly wrestling, tumbling, horse racing; followed in the evening, on June 8, at least, by the playing of the violin and a dance.

Indians were invited to compete in the sports. They came with enthusiasm, these Indians, lovers of sports themselves, and robust and active and skilled in the performance of them. They proved themselves to be as fleet as Drouillard and Reuben Fields, the expedition's "swiftest runners."

Camp Chopunnish was honored by several visitors during the next few days. Tun-na-che-moo-toolt came to pay his respects, and to bid farewell to these white men who had shown themselves to be the friends of his people. Neesh-ne-park-ke-ook wished to borrow a horse to take him down the Kooskooske for some young eagles which he intended to raise for feathers. Ho-host-ill-pilp stopped for an overnight visit on his way to the plains, accompanied by some of his men, and bringing with him a horse for Frazier, in appreciation of a pair of Canadian shoes previously presented him by Frazier. There were others — one of the "two young chiefs," for instance, who came with ten of his men and stayed all night.

On June 10, the entire camp was up early. By eleven o'clock, they started, in high spirits, heading for their Quamash Flats, each man well mounted with "a light load on a second horse," besides which they had "several supenemary horses" in case of accident or want of provisions.

Their route took them north, by 22° east, three miles; then north, by 15° west, two miles to Collins Creek; then north, five miles, to the east, or remote, border of the Flats. Their camp for the night was near the spot on which they had first met the Nez Percés the year before.

During the next few days they pressed steadily, howbeit slowly, onward and upward into the mountains, hunting as they went, hampered much by fallen timber, but suffering no serious mishap, even though their horses slipped and fell, time and again.

Once they were in the mountains, Drouillard led the way. He was relieved to learn that the snow, even though from eight to ten feet deep, was hard enough to bear their horses. But for this, their horses would have bogged down completely. The hard-packed snow had this advantage, too: it made traveling easy, as compared with the year before, due to the fact that the rocks and jagged places over which they had been forced to make their way then were now completely covered, affording them a comparatively smooth, hard surface on which to advance.

But the snow offered one drawback: it hid their trail. The peeled bark and the not infrequent other telltale marks on the trees (as where the packs on Indian ponies had rubbed the bark off), so noticeable in the fall, were hidden from view now. Even much of the underbrush lay deeply buried in the thick blanket of snow. How to pick the way? That was the problem.

On the seventeenth of June, one week after their enthusiastic start, after crossing the swift and turbulent Hungry Creek twice, Drouillard led his party over the hard-packed snow, in and out among the tall trees, toward the top of the ridge separating the Chopunnish, (north fork of the Clearwater) from the Kooskooske (actually the middle fork, here called Lochsa). It was along this ridge that the trail went. That much Drouillard remembered from the year before. Mile after mile of it.

It may be presumed that he carefully scrutinized the tree trunks around him for signs that would indicate the trail. Try as he might, hardly a sign could he perceive. And no wonder. The snow lay to a depth of from twelve to fifteen feet, even on southern slopes, which had been exposed to the sun. He could judge the depth, because here and there, along these slopes, around some of the tall trees, the snow had melted sufficiently to reveal the ground.

It must have given him satisfaction to realize that the captains regarded him as their guide. In this respect they placed him above themselves. If they were to make this trip across the Bitterroots, a trip which had taken them seventeen days the year before, it would be up to him, now, to lead them.

There was a fair chance that he could. His main concern would be to hold to the main ridge between the two rivers. If he could keep from losing his way on ridges that joined up with this ridge, he would be all right. Were he to choose the wrong ridge, he would soon discover his error and be able to lead the party back to the trail before he had gone far. Such mistakes, however, with no grass for their horses, and no game for themselves, could prove fatal. Would it be wiser to return to the foothills while their horses were fresh, and then try once more, desperately, to obtain the service of a guide, or wait until the snow had melted?

This was, actually, what was decided, once the ridge had been gained. Here, in the midst of winter, with hard-packed snow to the depth of several feet all around them, their hands and feet benumbed with cold, their breath forming clouds of vapor which congealed to frost on their bearded faces – here, amid the stillness and the stateliness of the tall trees, the captains called a halt to consider what should be done.

During the conference which followed, the captains and their men weighed carefully their chances of success. They sought the opinion of Drouillard, their "principal dependance as a woodsman and guide." They questioned their other woodsmen and guides. When these expressed doubt of their ability to keep to the trail without occasionally losing it, then, but not until then, did the captains make the decision to retreat to the foothills and there await the arrival of a guide.

It was a frost-bitten, melancholy, deflated crew of men who began to erect a scaffold on which to pile their baggage of roots, "bread of cows," instruments, and records. It was an equally melancholy and disappointed crew who, when this was done, mounted their horses, at one o'clock in the afternoon, and began a "retrograde march" down the mountain – the first, as Lewis remarked, during the course of the expedition. To add to their discomfort, a cold rain set in, after they had descended a considerable distance, and kept up the rest of the day.

At their camp on Hungry Creek that evening, in a drizzle of rain, the captains held another conference, at which it was decided to send a man to the Nez Percés at once to hasten the arrival of a guide.

It should occasion no surprise to learn that the man chosen for this important mission was George Drouillard, upon whose tact and courage and resourcefulness in the discharge of important undertakings the captains had more than once come to place their dependence. Selected to accompany him was George Shannon.[2]

Drouillard's instructions were to seek an audience with the Nez Percé chiefs; to do his best to win their consent to place at the disposal of the explorers at once the guides they had previously promised. Failing in this, he was to attempt to obtain a guide anyhow. He was authorized to offer such guide a rifle. Should this prove insufficient, he was to offer two additional guns, to be paid at once; and ten horses at the falls of the Missouri.

The two delegates set off on their important mission the following morning. They may have speculated on whether the Nez Percés would be in attendance upon the council on the Commearp about which Tun-na-che-moo-toolt had spoken. It would take courage to break in upon such a council, a dignified affair, with all the Nez Percé chiefs and important men of the Nez Percé

[2] See Appendix D.

nation in attendance. Had Drouillard and Shannon
come on an errand of importance to the Nez Percés,
the task of interrupting their deliberations would have
been easier. But to have to say to these Indians, "We
started to cross the mountains. We failed. We need a
guide. Will you help us"? — that could prove a bit
humiliating. The proud Nez Percés would have ground
for saying: "So you need our help, you, who think you
know more than we. Why did you not open your ears
while yet we spoke to you? See to it. Find your guides.
We have spoken."

The main party, meanwhile, completed their "retrograde march" as far as Quamash Flats, where they
resigned themselves to the anxiety of awaiting the arrival of Drouillard and Shannon, making all sorts of
conjectures as to the probable success of the former in
his efforts to influence the strong-willed Nez Percés in
furnishing the guides whom the explorers so desperately
needed.[3]

Five days after the departure of these two, at a little
before three o'clock in the afternoon, the Lewis and
Clark men at the Flats had their attention directed to
the leisurely approach of six horsemen. Upon nearer
approach, these horsemen proved to be three Indians
and three white men. The white men were Joseph
Whitehouse, George Shannon, and George Drouillard.
The Indians were a brother of Neesh-ne-park-ke-ook
and "two young chiefs." The latter may have been the
son of Tun-na-che-moo-toolt and the son of the chief
slain by the Minnetarees of "Fort de Prairie." The
three of them were "young men of good character
. . . much respected by their nation." They had

---

[3] See Appendix E.

come, at last, upon the behest of Drouillard, to guide the white men across the mountains – another triumph for Drouillard and Drouillard's efforts at diplomacy among the Indians.

Enthusiastic young men now went out to round up and hobble the horses. Eager hands once more made ready packs and saddles. Men whistled, laughed, jostled one another, as they applied themselves to one task or another. Another attempt was to be made to conquer the formidable Bitterroots. This time, without doubt, the attempt would be crowned with success.

Two days later (June 25) found the expectant explorers on top of the "snowy mountain" on which they had stored their goods nine days before. They spent two hours re-arranging their packs, cooked a hasty meal of boiled venison and "mush of cows," then pushed on, along the ridge between the Chopunnish and the Kooskooske (Lochsa).

Four days after leaving Quamash Flats, they arrived at a cone-shaped stone mound, from four to six feet in height, erected by Indians as a place of worship. Here their guides importuned the captains to sit down to smoke.

One or the other of the captains ordered a halt. Someone got out the pipe. The ceremony of smoking that followed was one of silent, reverent meditation.

The scene before him may have brought to Drouillard's mind some of the experiences he had undergone in these same mountains: how, on their march westward, he had toiled, hunted, starved, frozen; how, from one height after another he had peeled his eyes westward; how, for days, he had the hope of catching a glimpse of the prairie country beyond; how he had exulted when finally he did. He may have recalled the doubt and misgiving with which he had gazed upon these same snow-capped mountains during the recent month at Camp Chopunnish, and the eagerness with which he and all the other members of the expedition had looked forward to the day when they should once again be getting under way. And now, as he stood beside the captains, and beside the Indians, after the ceremony of smoking, and swept his eyes once more out over the formidable mountains which surrounded them, peak after peak, for miles around, he could easily enough understand why the Nez Percés had insisted on stopping for a moment to commune with the all-seeing Spirit, whose favor they courted. He would have thought less of them had they felt otherwise. Possibly he felt that way himself.

Lewis wrote in his journal:

. . . we were entirely surrounded by those mountains from which to one unacquainted with them it would have seemed impossible ever to have escaped; in short without the assistance of our guides I doubt much whether we who had once passed them could find our way to Travellers rest in their present situation for the trees marked on which we had placed considerable reliance are much fewer and more difficult to find than we had apprehended. these fellows are most admirable pilots; we find the road wherever the snow has disappeared though it be only for a few hundred paces. after smoking the pipe and contemplating this seene sufficient to have damp[ened] the sperits of any except such hardy travellers as we have become, we continued our march. . .

At Traveler's Rest (now Lolo, Montana), which they reached on June 30, after having crossed the mountains in a week, Drouillard and most of the members of the expedition, including the Indians, sat down with the captains as these outlined their plan for the future.

Lewis expected to go by the most direct route, with a small party, to the falls of the Missouri. Here he intended to leave Thompson, Goodrich, and McNeal to assemble the carriages "and geer" with which to portage the canoes and baggage around the falls. From the falls he intended to go with some of his men up the Marias, to determine whether any tributary of that river penetrated as far north as fifty degrees latitude. He hoped to rejoin the rest of his party at the point where that river joined the Missouri; and Clark and his men at or near the junction of the Missouri with the Yellowstone.[4] Clark was to proceed to the point on the Beaverhead where they had left their canoes the year before. From there he was to send the canoes down the river with some of his men. With the other men, and with Sacajawea and her infant, he himself was to make a trip of exploration toward and down the Yellowstone.

Lewis had asked for six volunteers to accompany him on his trip up the Marias, an undertaking not devoid of danger, inasmuch as they would be penetrating a

[4] According to this plan, Clark was to proceed, with the rest of the personnel, to a point on the Beaverhead where their canoes and supplies had been cached the year before. From there, Ordway, with nine men, was to descend the Beaverhead by canoe, proceed down the Missouri to the falls of the Missouri, where they would presumably join Thompson, Goodrich, and McNeal. Clark, meanwhile, with the remaining eleven members of the party, including Sacajawea, Charbonneau, and York, was to strike out across country in the direction of the Yellowstone, find the Yellowstone, build a canoe, and descend in this canoe, with Charbonneau, Sacajawea, York, and five others, to the junction of the Yellowstone with the Missouri. If he did not find Lewis and his men at the junction, he was to wait there until they arrived. Pryor and the remaining two men under Clark were to go with the horses down the Yellowstone and down the Missouri, as far as the villages of the Mandans, and from there to the British trading posts on the Assiniboine, with a letter to a Mr. Haney soliciting his aid in prevailing upon Sioux chiefs to accompany the explorers to the seat of government at Washington.

region dominated by the disreputable Minnetarees of "Fort de Prairie" or by the Blackfeet. Drouillard was one of those who volunteered his services. In fact, among those chosen, his name heads the list: ". . . Drewyer, the two Fieldses, Werner, Frazier, and Sergt. Gass." Actually, only Lewis, Drouillard, and Joseph and Reuben Fields made the trip.

By now had time come to mean so much to the captains as to cause them to feel that they could not postpone the carrying out of their plan even as much as one day, so as to permit them to spend the Fourth of July together. They parted company on July 3; and Lewis and his party sat down, on Independence Day, at the entrance to or within Hellgate Canyon (near the present city of Missoula, Montana), for a farewell smoke with their friends, the Nez Percé guides. A week later found them at the falls of the Missouri.

19
Trailing the Horse Thieves

At the falls of the Missouri an incident occurred which was to postpone the trip to the Marias three days. The incident was the theft of several horses by Indians.

A suspicion of what had happened came to Drouillard on the morning of July 12, when two of the men rode into camp with only seven of their seventeen horses. A full realization of it came at noon, that same day, when Warner came in with three of the missing horses, and Gass with none at all. The missing horses were among their best. It fell to Drouillard and Joseph Fields to go out and track them down.

Drouillard and Fields started at once. They separated, after a short distance, to permit them to search more territory than would be the case had they kept together. Fields came in at dark, without any horses. Drouillard did not report.

Where Drouillard slept that night, or the next, or the next, is not recorded in Lewis' journal, nor did Drouillard vouchsafe the information himself. Suffice it to say that during the rest of that day, and for part of the next, he searched diligently, alone, seeking to discover the trail taken by the horses, and to follow this to wherever it might lead.

It did not seem to him likely the horses had gone up the Medicine. Gass had been along there and had found no trace of them. There was a possibility they had gone up, or crossed, the Dearborn, thirty or more miles to the southwest. It was a possibility worth investigating.

In the direction of the Dearborn he headed, and came, in due time, not only upon the spot where the horses had crossed the river, but upon an Indian encampment of fifteen lodges, abandoned, he judged, about the day the horses had disappeared. There could now be no doubt as to what had happened to their horses. They had been stolen by Indians.

The Indians must have remained here for quite some time, Drouillard judged, as he examined their camp ground. So closely had their horses cropped the grass as not to have left one blade intact; nor could he discover any clue, outside a radius of one-fourth of a mile from the camp, to indicate they had been here at all. If they had wanted a spot on which to hide, as seemed likely, they could hardly have found one better suited to their purpose than this, blocked off as it was by the steep river bluffs.

Drouillard reasoned that these Indians had not been Minnetarees of "Fort de Prairie," nor had they been Blackfeet. It was not in keeping with the natures of either of these marauding tribes, as Drouillard knew them, to keep themselves in hiding; not when there were fifteen lodges of them. They were, therefore, other Indians; some who did not wish to be discovered by any roving Blackfeet or Minnetarees.

To anyone less intent than Drouillard upon the successful prosecution of a task undertaken, the evidence revealed by the abandoned campground might have seemed sufficient to warrant the conclusion that further responsibility, in the matter of attempting to regain possession of the lost horses, could not now have been expected of him. The Indians had the advantage of a two-day start. He could not hope to overtake them. Besides, by taking too long on the present mission, he would by so much be delaying Lewis from the trip the captain was eager to take up the Marias.

But Drouillard was not satisfied. The fact that the Indians had left with the horses two days before did not prove that they had been traveling all that time. They might even be camping now at no great distance. Dangerous though the task, he determined to stay with it; at least until the trail should indicate that to continue to follow it would be impracticable.

Without hesitation, therefore, he picked up the trail left by the Indians, and followed this in the direction of the mountains to the westward.

He could not have been unaware of the danger to himself and his horse on an errand of this sort. If the Indians did not wish to meet the Blackfeet or the Minnetarees, that did not mean they would be docile or apologetic or amenable to any suggestions or demands he might choose to propose to them, once he had succeeded in overtaking them. It was more than likely that, when accused of having stolen the horses, they would either deny the fact or assume the attitude of one saying, "Yes, we did take your horses. So what?" It required but little effort to imagine the prestige that would accrue to themselves were they to return to their fellow tribesmen, not only with the stolen horses, but with the scalp of their owner.[1]

---

[1] "One thing to be noted in all the operations of the expedition was the fearlessness and absolute independence of action of these men when sent out on such errands as this [referring to Drouillard's search for the stolen horses]. Singly and in pairs they penetrated into unknown wilds, hunting, following lost horses, seeking trails, etc., apparently not knowing hesitation or fear, and risking ambushment, attack, and death." – Wheeler II, p. 296.

All this, and more, Drouillard knew very well. Yet to turn back because the culprits he sought might be lurking behind the next ridge, or be encamped on the next creek, would not be accomplishing the errand upon which he had been sent. Danger or no danger, and alone though he was, on he must go, until he had either accomplished his mission or satisfied himself that its accomplishment was unfeasible.

Lewis's journal (for July 15) states that Drouillard "struck" the mountains at a point about three miles south of their camp of July 7 – that is, near the Divide. On July 7, the explorers had traveled for about seven miles in a northerly direction, after they had crossed the Divide. Drouillard, therefore, when he struck the mountains, must have been about ten miles from the Divide, or about sixty miles from the spot on which his companions were now camping at the falls of the Missouri. Lewis' journal states that Drouillard followed the trail "over the mountains." This meant over the Divide. At any rate, Drouillard did follow the trail as long as seemed, to him, practicable. When he stopped to analyze the situation, at or near the Divide, and realized that his horse was tired, that he was a long way from the camp of his companions, that Lewis was not only anxious to start for the Marias but worried about him; and when he realized, further, that the Indians he sought might still be a long way ahead of him, and that the chances were good that they had kept on going rather than strike a camp on or near the Divide – not until then did Drouillard turn back. He arrived at the camp of his companions at one o'clock in the afternoon of July 15, almost three days after he had left them.

He learned that Lewis had, indeed, been worried about him. The captain had waited "impatiently" for his return all day on the thirteenth and on the fourteenth and, on the fifteenth until he did arrive. Wrote Lewis:

> his safe return has releived me from great anxiety. I had already settled it in my mind that a white-bear had killed him and should have set out tomorrow in surch of him, and if I could not find him to continue my rout to Maria's river. I knew that if he met with a bear in the plains even he would attack him. and that if any accedent should happen to seperate him from his horse in that situation the chances in favour of his being killed would be as 9 to 10. I felt so perfectly satisfyed that he had returned in safety that I thought but little of the horses although they were seven of the best I had.[2]

These remarks suggest, among other things, that there was in Drouillard a trait or a predisposition, be it reckless daring, or insensitivity to danger, or contempt of fear, or love of adventure, or zeal for battle, or something else, which caused him, when he met a bear, to want to attack that bear, especially were the bear a grizzly. Alone though he might be, and real though the danger, he appears to have found it as impossible to refrain from testing his prowess against that of a bear as it was for a healthy dog to refrain from barking at a suspicious-looking stranger.

The remarks suggest, also, among other things, that Lewis held in high esteem this intrepid man of the woods and plains; else he would hardly have said, "I felt so perfectly satisfyed that he had returned in safety that I thought but little of the horses although they were seven of the best I had." Or again: "his safe return has relieved me from great anxiety." Or: "I . . .

---

[2] Does Lewis mean 9 to 1? Or 10 to 1? Or 9 out of 10? The way he puts it, the chances would not be much better than 50-50.

[would] have set out tomorrow in surch of him." It must have afforded the captain no small amount of satisfaction to realize that he was to be accompanied on his dangerous sojourn into the land of the Blackfeet by a man as fearless, alert, and resourceful, and as loyal and cooperative and capable, as Drouillard. His feeling of satisfaction must have been in no small measure heightened when he realized that he was to be accompanied, also, by two men whose qualifications for the task in question were not far behind those of Drouillard. It can be said with confidence that in his choice of cohorts, Lewis was indeed fortunate, even though one of them did, on this venture, in a moment of carelessness, commit a serious error.

20

Encounter with the Blackfeet

The first half of the round-trip journey to the Marias brought to the explorers nothing more exciting than their discovery of the recent trail of a bleeding buffalo. Drouillard followed this trail in the hope of discovering whether the buffalo had been wounded by Indians. Not finding the animal, he rejoined his companions and the journey was continued.

They arrived, on July 22, after six days, and after having traveled one hundred and fifty miles by their own estimate, at a spot on the Marias toward which the river flowed from the south of west, instead of from the north of west, as it had thus far. Drouillard made out the gap through which it issued from the mountains. It was not likely that it would reach fifty degrees latitude, as Lewis had hoped, in the comparatively short distance it flowed within the confines of those mountains. To find a river reaching as far north as fifty degrees, therefore, the captain would have to pin his hopes on the Milk, to the north of them, or the White Earth.

The next morning, Drouillard and Joseph Fields explored the Marias, (here called the Cutbank), for a distance of ten miles farther west, and established conclusively, in their own minds, at least, that the river did not reach any point farther north than that, ten miles back, on which their camp was then situated. Wheeler says, of Lewis' party at their camp on the Cutbank:

> During their rest here, Drewyer – it was generally Drewyer
> who was selected when a very important mission requiring in-
> telligence and plains – or woodcraft or both was necessary – was
> sent toward the mountains to examine the further course of the
> river. On this jaunt he discovered unmistakable evidences of the
> recent proximity of Indians. This impression was confirmed by
> the fact that the hunters found no game, although they went as
> far south as the Two Medicine Fork of the Marias, a distance
> of ten miles.[1]

It might be added that, on this trip up the Cutbank,
it became Drouillard's privilege, along with Joseph
Fields, to have penetrated to a greater distance on this
river than any other member of the expedition.

It had been Lewis' intention to remain at their Camp
Disappointment, as he called it, for two days, to rest
their horses, take the latitude and longitude, and then
to start on the return trip to the Missouri. As it happened, the sun did not shine either on the day on which
they arrived (July 22) or on the twenty-third, the
twenty-fourth, or the twenty-fifth. When, by nine
o'clock on the morning of the twenty-sixth, the sun was
still out of sight, Lewis decided to bid "a lasting adieu"
to his place of encampment and to start upon his homeward journey.

They had come about eighteen miles, in a southeasterly direction, on this day, and Drouillard had just
crossed the branch of the Marias on his left (The Two
Medicine), leaving the captain and the Fields brothers
to continue along the bluffs, when, upon looking ahead,
he discovered on a hilltop, about a mile away, and on
the same side of the river as that along which the cap-

---

[1] Wheeler, II, pp. 301-02.

tain and the Fields brothers were approaching, a band of eight Indians! What was equally important, the Indians had discovered him, for they were grazing in his direction, and stood as if studying him and noting his course.

What may have been Drouillard's feelings, upon his discovery of those Indians, is a matter of conjecture. It is safe to assume he did not stop advancing, or turn his horse, or give any indication that his awareness of these Indians had given him any concern whatever.

A question, though, must have been pressing him for an answer: Were they the Minnetaries of "Fort de Prairie"?

He noted such facts about them as he could. They had thirty horses, for one thing. How many additional horses they might have, and whether there were more Indians out of sight, he had no way of knowing.

The Indians themselves were not with their horses, but stood farther up, gazing in his direction, until suddenly they began to run about, as if excited, or alarmed. Drouillard knew the reason: They had discovered the captain!

Some of the Indians dashed down and drove the horses to within a short distance of the summit. By the time these had joined their companions, the latter had stopped rushing hither and yon and appeared now to be standing at ease, as if awaiting developments.

A glance in the direction of his friends, assuming he could see them, revealed to Drouillard that Lewis was advancing alone, and that behind him were the Fields brothers, one of them (Joseph) carrying the American flag.

When the captain had come to perhaps within a fourth of a mile of the Indians, one of these suddenly mounted his horse and began to ride at full speed toward the strangers.

The captain dismounted, and began to walk toward the Indian with extended hand, followed closely by Joseph and Reuben Fields with their horses. The Indian, however, continued to ride forward at a hard clip, until he came to within a hundred paces of the captain, when he turned his horse and rode back toward his companions almost as swiftly as he had come forward.

No sooner had he rejoined his companions than these began scurrying down the hill toward their horses. After mounting these, they began to advance in the direction of the captain and his men, leaving the rest of their horses behind. They did not appear to have any thought of attacking, however, for no sooner had they come within a hundred yards of the white men than all of them but one halted. This one continued forward until he confronted the captain, who, on his part, and again mounted, extended his hand. The Indian took it! There followed a hand shaking all around.

Later, near one of three solitary trees that occupied the Two Medicine river bottom (which was here about two hundred and fifty yards in width, and hemmed in by high bluffs), the Indians pitched a large, semi-circular buffalo-skin tepee. This they wanted the captain and his men to share with themselves. The captain and Drouillard accepted. The Fields brothers chose to occupy a spot outside the tepee opening, beside the fire.[2]

---

[2] Wheeler gives the approximate location of their Camp Disappointment as longitude 113° w and latitude 48° N, on the Cutbank River, about in the center of the Blackfoot Indian Reservation, and from eight to ten miles northwest of Blackfoot, Montana. – Wheeler II, p. 303.

Thwaites places the spot on which Lewis and his party encountered the

It was not long before Drouillard learned that these Indians were exceedingly fond of the pipe; a good thing, as it developed, for, unlike most Indians they had met, these seemed strangely lacking in the warmth and cordiality and genuine courtesy which had characterized most of the Indians with whom the explorers had made contact. They seemed ill at ease among these self-assured, energetic-looking strangers. Perhaps they were afraid of them. Certainly they were mistrustful. In their hearts may have smoldered contempt, if not animosity. From what actually happened, it can be concluded they would have counted it a praiseworthy accomplishment could they have overpowered their guests and possessed themselves of their weapons and horses, and even their scalps.

Lewis and his men were not unaware of the apparent mistrust with which they themselves were being regarded. They were not the kind of men who, in a situation such as this, were likely to allow themselves to be taken off guard. They had noted the weapons possessed by the Indians, including two guns. But they figured that, should their hosts attempt violence or treachery, the four of them would be more than a match for the eight Indians.

The long evening was, with the help of Drouillard, spent in "much conversation," in the course of which Drouillard found the opportunity of becoming better acquainted with these "miscreants of the plains" (they were Piegan Blackfeet);[3] especially with the three who occupied the inner part of the tepee – that is, Wolf

Indians as being on the south side of the Two Medicine, about four miles below the mouth of Badger Creek, on the east edge of the Blackfoot Indian Reservation. – Thwaites v, p. 220.

[3] Wheeler II, pp. 311-12.

Calf, Side Hill Calf, and one to whom will be assigned
the name Standing Buffalo. These three had informed
the captain, before Drouillard arrived to act as interpreter, that they were chiefs; a bit of intelligence which
the captain had doubted. He had, nevertheless, thought
it expedient to accept them at their word and to honor
them with presents – a medal to Side Hill Calf, an
American flag to Standing Buffalo, and a handkerchief
to Wolf Calf.

At some point, in the exchange of information that
took place, the captain suggested that some of the Indians go to the rest of their nation with an invitation to
their chiefs to meet the white men at the mouth of the
Marias. To this his exemplary hosts made the un-
equivocal reply that the spot upon which they were now
camped was eminently satisfactory as a place at which
to await the arrival of the chiefs.

Anon, they lay down to sleep: Lewis and Drouillard
inside the tepee; the Fields brothers beside the fire.
They took turns at keeping watch, in this order: Lewis;
Drouillard; Reuben; Joseph. Fearing the Indians
might try to steal their horses the captain gave instructions about waking the rest of them should any of the
Indians leave the camp.

The Indians were up at daylight. They began to
crowd the fire.

Joseph Fields was on guard. He had laid down his
rifle behind him, on a spot near his brother, who was
still asleep.

Suddenly, Side Hill Calf darted forward and seized,
not only Joseph's rifle but also that of his brother. At
almost the same instant, inside the tepee, Wolf Calf
seized the gun under Drouillard's knapsack, which

Drouillard was using as a pillow. Standing Buffalo likewise seized the gun belonging to the captain.

These actions on the part of Wolf Calf and Standing Buffalo were perceived by Joseph, who promptly turned to pick up his own gun. Finding this gone, as well as that of his brother, and perceiving that Side Hill Calf was making off with both as fast as his legs could carry him, he called to his brother to wake up, and started in pursuit of the fleeing Indian, his brother at his heels.

Meanwhile, Drouillard and the captain were having a time with Wolf Calf and Standing Buffalo. Scarcely had Wolf Calf seized Drouillard's rifle than Drouillard, with a "Damn you, let go my gun," was up, on his knees at least, attempting to wrest the gun away.

Drouillard's ejaculation awakened the captain, who immediately jumped up, inquiring, "What's the matter"? Upon perceiving Drouillard in a desperate struggle with Wolf Calf for Drouillard's gun, and discovering that Standing Buffalo was darting through the tepee opening with his own gun, Lewis drew his pistol and darted out upon the heels of the fleeing Standing Buffalo, to be followed shortly afterward by Wolf Calf and then by Drouillard.

The scene outside was something like this: up ahead, sprinting like mad toward the far end of the valley (that is, toward the south), Side Hill Calf, desperately clinging to two guns; behind him but a short distance, and rapidly gaining on him, Joseph and Reuben Fields, two of the swiftest runners in the Lewis and Clark expedition; behind them, at a noticeable distance, Standing Buffalo, himself heroically clinging to two guns — that of the captain and his own; behind him, a short distance, the captain, fiery-eyed, bareheaded, with drawn pistol, barking out orders to Standing Buffalo to lay down the one gun; behind the captain, in turn, Wolf Calf, minus Drouillard's gun, but clutching Drouillard's shot pouch; finally, Drouillard himself, gun in hand, furiously pursuing the fleeing Wolf Calf. An exasperating state of affairs, not helped in the least by the fact that, up ahead, and to one side, were the five other Indians, busying themselves with the task of rounding up "all the horses."

In the matter of seconds, the Fields brothers, after having sprinted some fifty or sixty paces, overtook their fugitive. They regained possession of their guns. In the struggle which preceded this, Reuben stabbed his antagonist to the heart.

Having regained possession of their guns, the Fields brothers ran back to Lewis, who was still in pursuit of Standing Buffalo. They raised their guns as if to fire, but were forbidden from carrying their design into effect by the captain who, between gasps for air, explained that the man had offered no resistance and attempted no felony.

At that moment the astute Standing Buffalo, who had glanced back over his shoulders and possibly suspected what might happen, dropped the captain's gun promptly, and changed his headlong speed to a slow walk! The captain, followed by the Fields brothers, advanced hurriedly, and eagerly picked up the relinquished weapon.

By this time, Drouillard, puffing like a winded buck, had caught up with the captain. Having regained possession not only of his gun but of his shot pouch, and observing the strategy of the erstwhile possessor of the captain's rifle, he begged the captain, with an eagerness which indicated only too plainly his desire, "if he might not kill the fellow.   . ." This the captain forbade, on the ground that the fugitive had given no intentions of having attempted an act of violence.

Lewis wrote, "as soon as they found us all in possession of our guns, they ran and indeavored to drive off all the horses." By "they" he meant the five Indians whom he later called the "main party." They were energetically engaged in the act of running the horses "up river." Lewis promptly ordered his three men to pursue these Indians, and to shoot if they attempted to get away with any horses except their own.

After his men had gone, he gave his attention to Wolf Calf and to Standing Buffalo, who were now together, and who had started to run in the direction of the fifteen or more horses still grazing near the camp. The captain pursued them "so closely" as to make it difficult for them to carry their design into effect. They did, however, succeed in driving away his own horse, along with some of theirs.

Continuing his determined advance, Lewis pursued them until, after three hundred paces, and with the horses before them, they entered "one of those steep nitches in the bluff." Nearly out of breath, and unable to pursue them any farther, Lewis called to them several times to let his own horse go, threatening to shoot if they ignored him. He even went to the extent of raising his gun, preparatory to effecting his threat.

Wolf Calf saw him, said something to his companion, and "jumped behind a rock." Standing Buffalo, thirty paces away, turned, and raised his gun, or threatened to. Before he could carry his design into effect, whatever the design was, the captain had shot him "through the belly."

The man fell to his knees, on his right elbow, from which he partly raised himself. Without hesitation, he fired his gun, then crawled behind the rock. The bare-headed captain felt "very distinctly" the wind of the bullet whistling past his head.

Unable to reload, since he did not have his shot pouch (this had been left behind in camp), and thinking it imprudent to "rush on them" with his pistol only, which, if discharged, he would have no means of reloading, Lewis decided to walk back to camp leisurely, keeping the rock under observation, however, on the possibility Wolf Calf or Standing Buffalo might take a shot at him.

He had not gone far before he discovered Drouillard, gun in hand, making for him as fast as his well-nigh exhausted condition would permit. Drouillard had heard the shot fired by the captain. He had recognized it as having been fired from the captain's gun. When this shot was followed by a shot from another gun, he had instructed the Fields brothers to continue their pursuit of the Indians alone, while he himself hastened to the assistance of Lewis.

The captain, calmly enough, instructed him to call the Fields brothers. He and Drouillard walked back to camp to catch and saddle such horses as were still there. They were arranging the packs on these when the Fields brothers hove into sight up river, with *four* of their own horses!

While his men were preparing the horses, the captain walked back to camp, picked up his shot pouch, and threw on the fire, besides "sundry other articles," four shields, two bows, and quivers of arrows. The one gun left by the Indians he appropriated. He also reclaimed the flag which he had given to Standing Buffalo. The medal, however, he left "about the neck of the dead man," Side Hill Calf, to inform the Indians, so he said, "who we were." Picking up some of the buffalo meat, he rejoined his men, who were ready with four of the best horses of the Indians, besides all but one of their own. Mounting the bluffs, they turned their steeds in a southeasterly direction and rode for some time at a brisk pace. By two o'clock the next morning, they had arrived at a point in the vicinity of the present Fort Benton, Montana, and had covered a distance of about one hundred miles, having stopped only twice to rest, and doing the last twenty miles "leasurely." [4]

---

[4] Coues states that Lewis' estimate of sixty-three miles from the scene of action to the point reached on the Tansy at three o'clock in the afternoon is "very close." The "17 additional miles . . . should put them in the vicinity of Valleux; and 20 more by moonlight would bring them near Fort Benton." – Coues III, pp. 1105-06.

Reference to the meeting of the explorers with the Blackfeet is made by Wheeler. Wheeler points out that Bird Grinnell, in his years of affiliation with and study among the Blackfeet, made a friend of old Wolf Calf, and quotes Grinnell as saying that Wolf Calf was "for many years the most aged of the Piegan Blackfeet . . . and a mine of information on ancient lore . . . quite willing to talk freely on all historical subjects. When he died he was supposed to be considerably over one hundred years old."

In regard to the meeting with Lewis, Wheeler quotes Grinnell as follows: "He [Wolf Calf] told me [Grinnell] that he was with a war party to the south when they met the first white men that had ever come into the lower country. They met these people in a friendly fashion, but the chief directed his young men to try to steal some of their things. They did so, and the white men killed the first man with their 'big knives.' This was the man killed, I suppose, by Fields. Afterwards the Indians ran off some of the horses of the white men. The name of the first man killed was Side Hill Calf, or Calf Standing on a Side Hill." – Wheeler II, p. 312.

In regard to whether the Indians made any attempt to pursue the white men, Wheeler, again quoting Grinnell, says that Wolf Calf "distinctly gave me the idea that the Indians were badly frightened, felt that they had been punished, and I think he ended his story with, 'then we all ran away.' I have no doubt in my own mind that they flew north about as fast as Lewis flew south and east." – *Ibid.*, p. 312.

21

Drouillard and the Expedition: an Appraisal

George Drouillard was employed to serve Lewis and Clark as interpreter. Actually, he did not begin to officiate in this capacity in a large way until after he and Lewis, along with Shields and McNeal, had arrived among the Shoshones. No opportunity presented itself for so doing until then, for the reason that Lewis and Clark had, up to that time, been able to use persons who could communicate for them by word of mouth, making the more cumbersome method of communication by signs unnecessary.

It would appear that the leaders of the expedition had in mind using this oral method of communication among the Shoshones also. That is why, at the villages of the Mandans, they enlisted the services of Toussaint Charbonneau and his wife Sacajawea – Charbonneau, to speak in the language of the Minnetarees to Sacajawea; she, to render his words into the language of her people.

Which raises the question: What sort of person was Charbonneau?

According to Lewis, Charbonneau was "a man of no peculiar merit." [1] His conduct on two occasions, when a squall hit the pirogue he was sailing, has been noted,

---

[1] Thwaites VII, p. 359.

as has also his conduct of shooting into the air after Drouillard had wounded a grizzly, and after the grizzly had started to charge.[2] A few feet above one of the falls of the Missouri, when a torrent of water began to rush at them in a ravine in which he and Clark and Sacajawea with her infant had taken refuge for protection against a cloudburst, the luckless Charbonneau, even though he had taken his wife by the hand and was "endeavouring to pull her up," nevertheless became so "frightened and remained frequently [so] motionless" that had it not been for "Capt. Clark both himself and his [wo]man and child must have perished." Yet this man Lewis and Clark chose to become a member of their expedition!

Their choice of Charbonneau was consequent upon their choice of Sacajawea. It was Sacajawea, and not Charbonneau, who could speak the language of the Shoshones: Charbonneau was merely an intermediary, needed for the purpose of translating to Sacajawea the words of the captains, which would be spoken in English to Labiche or Drouillard, and rendered by one of the latter into French to Charbonneau.

But Sacajawea was a woman, and encumbered with an infant. The captains, especially Lewis, must have thought twice before deciding to take her along. They knew well enough that an Indian woman could travel as far in a day as a man. They knew that an Indian woman could pretty much be depended upon to take care of herself, and, moreover, might even be of service in and about camp. Furthermore, this woman, being a Shoshone herself, could conceivably be of service to the explorers in ways other than that of interpreter. The

[2] See Appendix B and C.

gist of the whole matter was that Sacajawea stood to be more of an asset to the expedition than a liability. This would explain the willingness of the captains to risk taking her along. This would explain their willingness to put up with Charbonneau.

The fact that Lewis and Clark were willing to employ, in the furtherance of an undertaking that meant more than life to them, a man of such "doubtful merit" as Charbonneau, and the fact that they were willing to encumber the expedition with a woman and a two-months old infant, would indicate that they regarded their arrival and subsequent dealings with the Shoshones as of primary importance. They realized beyond doubt the necessity of making themselves and their needs perfectly understood by the Shoshones, and of the almost equal necessity of being able to understand them in turn. Long before leaving the Mandans they knew, and they knew without doubt, that upon their reception among the Shoshones, (or other Indians, though the Shoshones were the most likely), and upon their ability to enlist the cooperation of the Shoshones or other Indians in supplying them with horses and a guide, depended, in no small measure if not absolutely, the success of their undertaking.

As it developed, when Lewis actually did arrive among the Shoshones, he had with him neither Charbonneau nor Sacajawea, nor anyone who could in any way assist him in the matter of communicating with them, save only the man he had originally employed to serve in just such a critical situation – George Drouillard. Had Drouillard failed the captain in this most critical situation, the Lewis and Clark expedition would, in all probability, never have reached the Pacific.

For example: Would Lewis and Clark have succeeded if the explorers had failed in obtaining horses to carry their packs across the mountains, or a guide (or directions) to show the way?

As regards the first part of the question, it seems unlikely, in view of the formidable mountains ahead of them, that they would have reached the Pacific in the absence of horses or other beasts of burden on which to transport their baggage. They would simply have been compelled to leave their baggage behind. They could not possibly themselves have carried much more than their blankets, arms, ammunition, and a supply of trinkets with which to barter with the Indians. To cross the mountains without horses would have meant that they would have had to do so at the sacrifice of most of their merchandise, as Lewis recorded in his journal on August 8.

But suppose they had, in some manner, obtained horses, but no guide, nor any directions indicating to them where to go. Would they have reached the Pacific?

They would undoubtedly have followed the Jefferson to its source, as Lewis, Drouillard, Shields and McNeal actually did. They would have crossed the Continental Divide via Lemhi Pass, descended into the narrow, mountain-enclosed valley of the Lemhi River, then into the even more hemmed-in valley of the Salmon, then down the Salmon, possibly as far as Clark and eleven of his companions went, and then, like the latter, turned back, convinced as Clark became convinced, of the utter impossibility of proceeding farther, either by canoe or on horseback or on foot.[3]

What then? Where would they go?

Back up the Salmon, to its junction with the Lemhi; or, if not that far, then to its junction with the North Fork of the Salmon. Would they, in the absence of a guide, or in the absence of even partially authentic information about the country, have ascended this fork? On the route which was actually taken, later, with horses and a guide, they did ascend this fork. But they had to chop down trees and clear others away in order to get through. The route actually took them for a second time over the Continental Divide, via an unknown pass, and in a direction which was not west but north. Their direction would continue north for another hundred miles, via the Bitterroot River; then westward, up Lolo Creek, and across another challenging mountainous divide, via Lolo Pass, in the vicinity of which, be it pointed out, even their guide lost his way. Furthermore, the formidable Bitterroots, which rank among the most rugged mountains of our country, still lay between themselves and the plateau country to the west to a distance of nearly a hundred miles. It is extremely unlikely that the explorers would have ventured upon such a route – about three hundred miles in all – unaided by the services of a guide or by information upon which they could rely. They would hardly even have found such a route in the first place, nor, in all probability, any route leading from where they were, west-

---

[3] Thwaites III, 18. On August 25, Clark gives a summary of the distances he traveled from the Indian village on the Lemhi to the ridge from which he turned back, after having become convinced that the route via the Salmon was impassable. The sum of these distances is seventy miles.

ward. Until recently, there was no route across these
mountains, in terms of a highway, other than by way of
Missoula, Coeur d'Alene, and Spokane to the north,
and by way of Pocatello, Twin Falls, and Boise to the
south.[4] Between is a vast region of rugged mountains,
three hundred miles in extent, from north to south, and
nearly one hundred miles in width. It is not likely that
the Lewis and Clark expedition, as an expedition,
would have found a way out of the Salmon River valley
by which to cross the mountains to the Pacific. All of
which points out the prime necessity of finding and
obtaining help from Indians, and lending weight to
the important role played by Lewis and Drouillard in
acting, respectively, as spokesman and interpreter
among the Shoshones. Had Drouillard done nothing
more, in his period of service to the expedition, than
function as effectively as he did among the Shoshones,
his services in this respect alone would have classified
him as an invaluable member of the expedition.

In reviewing Bernard De Voto's book, *The Journals
of Lewis and Clark,* Richard L. Neuberger, himself an
authority on this subject, states that the expedition
encountered

> three major crises: (1) when Lewis and three picked men
> wandered in the mountains, searching for Indians who could
> sell them horses to get their supplies over the Divide; (2)

---

[4] The new highway across the Bitterroots is the Lewis and Clark Highway,
shown on the maps as U.S. Highway No. 12. It follows the Lochsa River,
running parallel to the old Lolo Trail used by Lewis and Clark. The Lewis
and Clark Highway holds to the valley along this river, which is called the
Middle Fork of the Clearwater farther west. The Lolo Trail keeps to the
high ridge between the Lochsa on the south and the North Fork of the Clearwater on
the north. The highway crosses the Bitterroot Mountains via Lolo Pass (also used by
Lewis and Clark). From there, going north and west, it drops down to Lolo Hot
Springs, thence on the Missoula, Montana.

when they floundered without food in the mounting snows of
the Lolo Trail; (3) when Lewis and a small party had a
foray with the Blackfeet.

Had any of these episodes gone amiss the undertaking would
have been counted a failure. Indeed, a few more days of hunger
on the ridge between the Lochsa and the Clearwater Rivers in
Idaho and it might not have reported back with its tales of the
first grizzly bear, Bighorn sheep, and innumerable prairie
dogs. . .[5]

I would like to suggest two additional major crises
encountered by the expedition: (1) the heroic attempts of Lewis to win and to hold the confidence of
the Shoshones long enough to enable them to see for
themselves that he was telling the truth; and (2) the
determined attempts of the Teton Sioux to prevent the
expedition from continuing up river. Had Lewis failed
in the attempts which he prosecuted, or had the Teton
Sioux succeeded in theirs, it is no exaggeration to state
that the Lewis and Clark expedition might easily have
been doomed to failure. It may be important to note
that, in all of these major crises, Drouillard played a
leading role, even though he is not mentioned by name
in one of them – that involving the Teton Sioux.

It has been noted that whenever Lewis set out upon
an excursion of one kind or another he generally selected Drouillard as one of the handful of men to
accompany him. This occurred for the first time on
April 7, the day the expedition took its departure from
Fort Mandan and the captain wished to proceed up
river for a farewell smoke with his friend, Black Cat.
It occurred again on April 25, the day the captain
started out, across country, with four men, toward the
mouth of the Yellowstone. It occurred on May 31, the

[5] In "The Limits of the West," *Saturday Review of Literature,* XXXVI, p. 17.

day on which the captain explored with such enthusiasm the picturesque beauties of the badlands along
the Missouri(in the vicinity of the forks of the Yellowstone and the Missouri). It occurred on June 4
when, again with a handful of men, the captain set out
on his five-day trip of exploration up the Marias. It
occurred on June 11, when he and Drouillard and
Joseph Fields and Gibson and Goodrich started out on
an overland trip to discover the falls of the Missouri.
It occurred on June 29, when, at the falls of the Missouri, he set out to explore a giant spring discovered
by Clark. It occurred on August 1, when, along with
Gass and Charbonneau, he started out in a determined
attempt to come in contact with Indians. It occurred
when he embarked upon an even more determined attempt to come in contact with the Shoshones. It occurred again, twice, at the mouth of the Columbia, and
then, finally, for the last time, on the return trip, on
that ill-fated one hundred and fifty-mile trek toward
and up the Marias into the danger-infested country of
the Blackfeet.

Lewis made his choice of this man, not merely because he was bold, hardy, intelligent, and in every way
dependable, but because he found in him qualities of
mind and heart which must have harmonized or com-
plemented his own qualities and made him one of those
kindred spirits with whom he could enjoy fellowship
and comradship, more, possibly, than he could with any
of the other rough and ready members of the expedition save only his friend and co-equal, Clark.

It has been stated by Elliott Coues that "perhaps the
one man in the expedition with whom either of the
captains would have been most likely to meet at home

on terms of social equality," was George Shannon. But Lewis did not choose Shannon to accompany him on any of his treks into unknown country. Maybe that was because Shannon was not a sufficiently capable hunter or outdoorsman, or because he was too young. Lewis did not choose Colter, an expert hunter, like Drouillard, and all but equal to Drouillard as an outdoorsman; a man who "wore an open, ingeneous, and pleasing countenance of the Daniel Boone stamp," and whom nature "had formed . . . for hardy indurance of fatigue, privation and perils." [6] He did not, except occasionally, choose Gass, or Ordway, or Pryor, or Cruzatte, or any of the others, except two – Joseph and Reuben Fields – for whom he came, in time, to show partiality. But never did he choose the Fields brothers or any one else as frequently and as consistently as he chose Drouillard. If Drouillard served the captain, therefore, not merely as a hunter, a scout, an outdoorsman, an interpreter, an ambassador to the Indians, but as a companion and, mayhap, as a friend, that in itself alone would place greater value to the services which he gave to the expedition and, through it, to the country of his adoption.

The one regrettable blot upon the character of George Drouillard which I have been able to find is that which has risen from his neglect of, or indifference to, certain financial matters in which he was obligated, and which involved him in the entanglement of the law, as a defendant on the one hand, and as a co-plaintiff with Manuel Lisa on the other. This involvement on the part of Drouillard with the law has been dis-

<hr>

[6] Thomas James, *Three Years Among the Indians and Mexicans,* 58. (Hereafter referred to as James).

cussed elsewhere.[7] What, however, was Drouillard's conduct *outside* the pale of the law, during his period of service with Lewis and Clark? Was he inclined, as a member of the Lewis and Clark expedition, to evade a responsibility? Did he offer any protests against the performance of a duty? Did he disobey any order from a superior? Was he evasive, shiftless, unreliable? Did he speak disrespectfully of his fellows or of his commanding officers? Was he loud, arrogant, boastful, cynical? Was he a disrupting influence among his fellows? Was he dishonest, unscrupulous? Did he participate in escapades unbecoming to a member of the expedition which he served? Did he deliberately or otherwise seek to undermine the morale of the expedition? Was he ever tempted to desert? Was it ever found necessary to take disciplinary measures against him? Was he shunned or made an object of contempt by his fellows? Did he exhibit toward his fellows any air of superiority over the fact that his pay was higher than theirs, that he was associated more than they with the commanders, or that, unlike themselves, he did not have to mount guard or perform menial tasks in and about camp?

I have searched the Lewis and Clark journals almost in vain for an affirmative answer to questions such as these. The questions, directing attention as they do toward the negative rather than the positive aspects of conduct, are, possibly, misleading. It was not so much a question whether Drouillard *disobeyed* an order as a question of the willingness and ardor and persistence with which he carried an order into effect. Far from avoiding responsibilities, he sought them or shouldered

7 See Chap. XXIV and Appendix F.

them willingly. Instead of being unreliable, he proved himself time and again to be one of the most reliable of all of those who served the expedition so well. There is nothing in the records to indicate that he ever spoke disrespectfully of his fellows or of his superiors; that he was loud, arrogant, boastful, or cynical; that he was a disrupting influence; that he was dishonest or unscrupulous; that he was a partner in objectionable escapades; that he was ever tempted to desert, or that he did anything calculated to undermine the morale of the expedition. Neither is there anything to indicate he was unpopular among his fellows, or that he made any attempt to point out to them that he, George Drouillard, unlike themselves, enjoyed special privileges. The conduct of George Drouillard throughout all of the time he served under Lewis and Clark is, on the whole, an emphatic denial of anything that the questions, as first stated, imply to the contrary.

There were, however, minor exceptions. Along with John Shields and Hugh McNeal, Drouillard was upbraided once, by Lewis, for failure to exercise good judgment at a time when the captain was desperately attempting to make contact with a lone Shoshone horseman whose assistance the captain needed. On one occasion, Drouillard became involved in a "Gealousy" between himself and George Gibson, and, on another occasion, in a quarrel between himself and John Colter. These are the exceptions. A word of explanation will be offered with respect to two of them.

Under date of November 28, 1804, while the explorers were encamped among the Mandans, Ordway recorded in his journal: "Gealousy between Mr Gi[b]-son one of our intr and George Drewyer last evening.

&.c." [8] The "&.c.," added by Ordway, indicates what he might have said, but did not say, about the nature of the "Gealousy," or which of the two men, if either, was responsible for it. Since the art of interpretation was, among the Lewis and Clark men, one in which Drouillard excelled, presumably Drouillard had some justification on his side, regardless of whether he or Gibson was to blame for the difference which had arisen between them.

Under date of May 6, 1806, Lewis, on his return trip from the Pacific, made an entry in his journal with reference to a horse obtained from the Nez Percés for food for themselves and their men. "I directed the horse . . . to be led," wrote the captain, "as it was yet unbroke, in performing this duty a quarrel ensued between Drewyer and Colter."

What had precipitated the quarrel?

An angry remark, a word of criticism or blame or command, uttered by one or the other of the two men as each attempted, with varying success, to cope with the antics of an animal having intentions other than those of permitting itself to be led? The chances are fair that Drouillard was the one who, in a fit of exasperation, gave expression to that impulsive remark. The remark may have been intended as a command, or a suggestion, rather than as a rebuke, although Colter appears not to have so interpreted it, or, if he did, retorted to it with a hot remark of his own.

This may be added: Drouillard was no saint. But he was a valuable member of the Lewis and Clark expedition.

[8] Quaife, 167.

Fur Trading Ventures

22

First Fur Trading Venture

Except for a shot wound sustained by Lewis while out hunting, and except for the loss of the horses being taken by Pryor down the Yellowstone, the explorers suffered no further mishap on the remaining lap of their journey, arriving triumphantly in St. Louis at noon on the twenty-third of September.

No sooner had they arrived in the village than they discovered that the postman had just left for Cahokia. It became Drouillard's task, therefore, upon instructions from Lewis, to hasten to Cahokia to bid a Mr. May there to hold the mail until noon the following day. It became Drouillard's responsibility the next morning to go to Cahokia with the letters which the captains had written on the day before and during the night. This may have been Drouillard's last official act in behalf of the expedition.

In due time he received his pay – $833.33 1/3, for thirty-three months of service at the rate of twenty-five dollars per month. This was later doubled, by act of Congress on March 5, 1807.[1] In addition to this monetary remuneration, he received two quarter sections of land, as did the other members of the expedition.

---

[1] Thwaites VII, pp. 360-62. It appears that Drouillard bought the warrants of Whitehouse and Collins, in the land grants issued to them by Congress as a reward for their services with the Lewis and Clark expedition (Jackson, 344-45). Drouillard was also paid $197.71 for "Subsistence," which payment was "carried to the Expenses of the Expedition," as per Lewis' financial account of the expedition, and as pointed out in Jackson, 427.

One day, during that fall or winter, found Drouillard in conversation with a bold-looking, enterprising man who endeavored to interest him in joining him in a fur trading venture.

Drouillard very likely knew Manuel Lisa, the most successful of the fur traders, head and shoulders above all his competitors, characterized by Eva Emery Dye as "dark, secret, unfathomable, restless, enterprising, a very Spaniard for pride,"[2] and by Hiram Martin Chittenden as "beyond comparison the ablest of the traders so far as the actual conduct of an enterprise was concerned."[3] No man was more likely to succeed in a venture of this sort than Manuel Lisa. In the end, Drouillard joined him, in the capacity of proxy for William Morrison and Pierre Menard, of Kaskaskia.

According to Burton Harris, a man named Benito Vasquez was second in command. It was a large party – some forty-two in all – of whom thirty-seven were French Canadians. John Potts and Peter Wiser, formerly of the Lewis and Clark expedition, were members.[4]

At the mouth of the Osage, one of their *engagés,* Antoine Bissonette, took it upon himself to desert. Lisa promptly ordered a search for him. He instructed Drouillard to bring him back, dead or alive.

---

[2] Eva Emery Dye, *The Conquest,* 320.

[3] Chittenden I, p. 129.

[4] Burton Harris, *John Colter,* 117; 59, 60. (Hereafter referred to as Harris). When the Lewis and Clark expedition stopped at the Mandan villages in the month of August, 1806, on the return trip, Clark persuaded the Mandan chief Shehaka, or Big White, to accompany the explorers to St. Louis, for the purpose of making a visit to the nation's capital. Big White's squaw and young child, as well as the interpreter René Jessaume, and his wife and child, had also gone along. The captain had promised that all six would be safely returned to the Mandans (Thwaites v, p. 339). The pending departure of Lisa and Drouillard up the Missouri appeared to offer the opportunity needed for the redemption of this promise.

Upon receipt of such an order, Drouillard must have recalled the occasion, three years before, when he had been dispatched by Lewis to capture and bring back another deserter, Moses Reed. Lewis, like Lisa, had ordered Drouillard to shoot, if necessary. Fortunately, on that occasion, Drouillard had not found it necessary to resort to the extreme penalty. Now, however, in order to bring back the man at all, it appears he had to shoot, though not necessarily to kill.

The wound resulting from the shot was too serious to make it seem advisable to bring the man along. He was, accordingly, upon command of Lisa, placed in a canoe the next day and started on his journey to St. Charles.[5]

At the mouth of the Platte, the party discovered a solitary figure, that of a man, coming down the river in a canoe. This man proved to be none other than John Colter, who had been given permission by Lewis and Clark at Fort Mandan, on their return trip, to remain behind in order to join two trappers bound for the Yellowstone.

Drouillard was not slow in introducing Colter to Lisa. Lisa, on his part, seeing in Colter a man who could prove valuable to himself, lost little time in proposing to him that he join the expedition. This proposition Colter accepted. The expedition then continued northward without incident of note until the near approach to the villages of the Arikaras.

Drouillard noted with some surprise and apprehension that from two to three hundred Arikara warriors were lined up on the river bank, below the Arikara

―――――
[5] Harris, 63.

villages, as if to await the arrival of the boats. Before he knew what was up, they had fired a volley across the bow of the keelboat.

Drouillard experienced a sense of relief and a feeling of admiration at the coolness and resourcefulness of his senior partner; for hardly had the boats touched the bank than, with a loud voice and a stern look, Lisa ordered that no Indian be permitted on board. He made it plain to the chiefs on shore, by motion and looks, that he meant what he said.

The chiefs were not slow in taking the hint. Using such authority as they had, they stationed a guard to keep back the crowd. The women then came forward with bags of corn with which to trade. But no sooner had they done so, however, than an Indian sprang forward and, with deft and energetic movements, ripped open the bags with his knife. The women promptly took to their heels; the warriors started moving forward, en masse.

Lisa called his men to arms. He ordered his two swivels trained upon the mob on shore. By shouts and looks and gestures, he made it so plain that he intended to shoot that hardly had the warriors started their rush for the boats than they fell back in confusion, and, along with them, the crowd.

The chiefs were not slow in taking advantage of this change in the state of affairs. Hastening forward, with their long-stemmed pipes in front of them, they apologized for what had happened, blaming the entire regrettable incident upon some bad man among them. They spoke by signs if not by words – a language which Drouillard was eminently qualified to help Lisa understand.

Drouillard may have wondered whether Lisa would be convinced by the hastily-conceived explanation of the chiefs. He felt relieved when Lisa accepted it as true; relieved, also, when Lisa brusquely ordered the chiefs to bring forward what they had to trade so that he might complete his business with them and move on.

This reception by the Arikaras no doubt came to Drouillard as a surprise. He may have expected such treatment from the Tetons. But from the Arikaras? In view of the friendly reception accorded the Lewis and Clark expedition by these people three years before, their conduct on the present occasion was as astonishing as it was unexpected.

Had Drouillard been surprised when the expedition was challenged by the Arikaras, he must have been shocked when they were similarly challenged by the Mandans. The friendly, hard-working, peace-loving Mandans? It was unbelievable.

The skill and courage of Lisa, however, enabled the boats to proceed without serious mishap.

Several miles above the Mandans and the Minnetarees were the villages of some four or five thousand Assiniboines. These Indians also seemed bent on disputing the passage of the boats, but the resourcefulness and daring of Lisa again won the day. Lisa, on this occasion, "caused his swivels to be heavily loaded and every man to prepare his musket as if about to go into battle. Having completed his preparations he steered across the river and made directly for the place where the Indians were collected on the bank. When he had arrived within a hundred yards he ordered his swivels and musketry to be discharged, taking care, however, to aim where the projectiles could do no harm. The

Indians were appalled at the sight and sound and fell
over each other in their panic to get to the hills in
safety. A few of the chiefs and warriors remained and
asked to smoke the pipe of peace. The usual ceremonies
were gone through, presents were given, and protesta-
tions of friendship exchanged, after which the little
party, thankful for another escape, pursued its perilous
way to the river." [6]

At some point on this journey up the Missouri, and
very likely in consultation with Drouillard and Vasquez, Lisa came to the important decision of establishing his trading post on the Yellowstone instead of on
the Missouri!

The reason for the change was Colter. Colter had
been on the Yellowstone with Clark the year before,
when the latter descended this river to the Missouri.
He had trapped on the Yellowstone during the past
season as a partner of Forrest Hancock and Joseph
Dixon.[7] Though not especially successful in this venture,[8] nevertheless what he told Lisa seems to have been
sufficient to have caused the latter to come to the
decision already mentioned.

The post was established in October, at the junction

---

[6] The experiences of Lisa with the Arikaras, Mandans, and Assiniboines
are reported by Chittenden, I, pp. 117-18.

It may be added that an expedition, in charge of Ensign Pryor (the
sergeant had been promoted), headed for the Mandans with Big White and
the interpreter Jessaume and their families, was also challenged by these
same Arikaras, assisted by a number of Sioux. This time an actual battle
occurred, during which a number of men, including the Sioux chief, were
killed, and more wounded, including Jessaume and young Shannon, who were
also along. Pryor was obliged to return to St. Louis, without fulfilling his
mission. – Chittenden I, pp. 121-24; Wheeler I, pp. 121-22.

[7] Thwaites V, p. 344; Harris, 53-54.

[8] Harris, 55.

of the Big Horn with the Yellowstone, on the right
bank of each. It came variously to be known as Fort
Raymond, Fort Lisa, Fort Manuel, and Manuel's Fort.
It was the first American trading post on the upper
Missouri, and "the first building erected within the
limits of the present state of Montana."[9]

[9] Harris, 69, 70; Chittenden I, p. 119.

23
Reconnoitering for Customers

The party of fur traders had not been long at the mouth of the Big Horn before they realized there was work to be done. The work included the erection of the post itself, hunting, trapping, the location of beaver grounds, the sending of envoys to nearby Indians, and, finally, the business of trading.

It was not long before they were able to get in touch with a band of Indians, with whom they traded for horses.[1] They sent one of their members, Edward Rose, and a small party of men with trading goods and pack horses, to a nearby Crow village for the purpose of promoting trade among them. The venture proved unprofitable, due to the susceptibility of Rose to the flattery of the Crows, who succeeded in obtaining his goods without paying him for his skins.[2]

Lisa was not content to depend for pelts merely upon one establishment outside the main post, nor upon the efforts of the trappers themselves. Neither, it may be certain, was his junior partner, Drouillard. Both of them saw the need of enlisting the cooperation of Indians in the venture to which they had committed themselves. It was important, therefore, to send out envoys to acquaint the Indians with the establishment

[1] Harris, 74.
[2] Harris, 72-74; 119.

of the trading post, and to urge them to bring in their pelts.

The first of these envoys was Colter. None was better qualified for the job, except George Drouillard. On a morning in early November, or possibly in late October, in the face of an oncoming winter, with a thirty-pound pack on his back, Colter set out alone, on foot. He went in a westerly direction, either across the hills toward Pryor Mountains or else up the As-to-pah-oan-zhah, the Indian name for Elk (now Yellowstone) River, pointing his course resolutely toward a region so obstructed with mountains and valleys and canyons as frequently to "baffle those who have lived in them all their lives." [3]

Colter was not entirely unacquainted with those mountains. He had spent a winter within their recesses the year before, as a trapping partner of Hancock and Dixon, in the valley of Clark's Fork of the Yellowstone.[4] He realized full well what he was up against. Possibly he had no enthusiasm for the task ahead of him. Yet, though stupendous and dangerous it may have appeared to him, upon this task he embarked, on "one of the most difficult and hazardous journeys ever deliberately undertaken in western history," [5] covering on this trek a distance of upwards of seven hundred miles.

George Drouillard was another of the members of the party to undertake, not only one, but two, long and dangerous journeys in search of Indian customers.

The most complete and accurate information available on these journeys is that found in a map drawn by William Clark on the basis of information furnished

[3] Ibid., p. 74.   [4] Ibid., p. 85.   [5] Ibid., p. 74.

him by Drouillard upon the latter's return to St. Louis in August the following year.[6] This map proved helpful to Harris in tracing the journey of Colter. It proved helpful to Clark in correcting errors in some of his earlier maps. It also supplied Clark with information about the country of the Yellowstone. Finally, the map shows rather clearly Drouillard's two journeys.

The first day of Drouillard's first journey took him up the As-to-pah-oan-zhah (Yellowstone) River, to a place marked on the map as Pott's establishment, some ten miles above Fort Lisa. This may have been a post operated by John Potts, formerly of the Lewis and Clark expedition, but now with Lisa and Drouillard. From this establishment, Drouillard journeyed on ten or twelve miles farther, to the mouth of what he called Smalea Creek, where he spent the night.

On his second day, he passed Pompey's Pillar; then, instead of following the river, set out, across country, to the mouth of Pryor's Creek, some twenty miles farther on, in the vicinity of the present Billings, Montana. Here he came upon an Indian encampment. Referring to Colter's visit to this same encampment, Harris says :"Colter would not logically have devoted much time to this band because of their proximity to the trading post." [7] This he could have said for Drouillard, also, for Drouillard continued with his journey a short distance, then made his camp for the night just beyond a place marked "gap" on the map, which shows a range of hills or small mountains crossing the Yellowstone at this point.

---

[6] Property of the Missouri Historical Society. Used by permission of the Society. See reproduction of this map at page 339 in this volume.

[7] Harris, 83.

Drouillard talked long enough with the Indians at the mouth of Pryor's Creek, however, to gain some facts about this river, including its name, the Mere-pe-awn-zhah. He also learned that Colter had taken the well-marked trail following this river over the Pryor Mountains and down another stream to the Stinking Water, a three day's journey. Since Colter had gone this way in search of customers, Drouillard saw no need of doing the same. Instead, therefore, he continued on, up the Yellowstone, to the gap just mentioned.

The next day found him at Clark's Fork, only a few miles above present-day Billings. Turning to the left, he followed this stream, which the Indians called the As-kis-pe-pah-awn-zhah, to its junction with the A-sah-roo-ka, where he came upon a large village of Crows. In this village he spent the night.

Drouillard continued his journey the next day up the As-kis-pe-pah-awn-zhah, to its junction with what he called Dry Branch Creek. Just above the mouth of this creek, he camped. He had passed during the day an "Unfrozen" river, along which, the Crows informed him, one might obtain "gras and shelter all winter." His trail on the map does not suggest he went as far as "Blue beads mountain," plainly marked on the map farther up the As-kis-pe-pah-awn-zhah, where "the Indians obtain a clear & solid substance like glas which they manufacture into pipes." He learned, however, about this mountain and the stone quarry on it from his cooperative Crow informants.

Continuing his journey up Dry Branch Creek the next day, he arrived, toward evening, at a spot near its source, and in the vicinity of "Hart mountain," where he camped. Heart Mountain is placed correctly on this map, thanks to information furnished by Drouillard, whereas it had been incorrectly placed on previous maps drawn by Clark.[8] The following evening found Drouillard at or near the junction of "Valley river" (South Fork) with the Stinking Water, near "Sprouts' Mountain," (Cedar Mountain, or, as the Crows had it, Mah-ha-pah-mah-pah, or "Mountain of the Spirits.")

There is reason to believe that Drouillard spent at least two days in the vicinity of Cedar Mountain, gaining from the Ap-sha-roo-kees (Crows), who were camped there, not only the information that Colter had passed on up the South Fork, but information, also, about the river itself. For example, that a fourteen days' journey from the forks of the river with the Stinking Water (in the proximity of Cedar Mountain), and just above a "considerable river," was a salt cave; that from this cave, an eight-days' march farther on, and on the other side of a range of mountains (which could have been the Absaroka range), was a region wherein were located certain "Spanish settlements"; that the salt cave itself was on the "N side of a mountain"; that superior salt was found there, "pure or perfect"; that the sun never shone on this spot; that the Spaniards obtained the salt by passing over the river "Collarado"; that Indians in this region subsisted entirely on horseflesh.

The region in the vicinity, and to the south, of Cedar Mountain must have been interesting to Drouillard also because of the remarkable natural phenomena in evidence there: fumes of sulphur; steaming pools of colored, gurgling water; thunderous spouts or columns of boiling water shooting into the air from yawning

---

[8] *Ibid.,* p. 87.

caverns, – to say nothing of a pool of boiling, smelling black tar, which, together with the other phenomena, might have suggested the abode of the very devil himself.[9]

When Colter, who had witnessed these same phenomena only a few days before, returned to the post on the Big Horn and there narrated to his incredulous listeners what he had seen and heard and smelled, the latter looked at him askance, as they might at one who, because of the terrific strain to which he had been put as a result of his wanderings, was a man out of his mind. When, later, among themselves, they made reference to the place, they ungraciously dubbed it, not Drouillard's Hell, although Drouillard was the one who first described it to them, but "Colter's Hell."

It was more than likely Drouillard, in the summer of 1808, who first reported to William Clark the strange phenomena on the Stinking Water. Map maker though he was, Clark did not, on his maps, show the existence of these phenomena, other than to designate Cedar Mountain by the name Drouillard gave him, Mah-ha-pa-mah-pah (Mountain of the Spirits), and to state that out of this mountain issued "such a quantity of hot water" as to cause the river not to be "frozen in the extreem of winter for sixty miles below." It is conceivable that Clark did not believe Drouillard, any more than the men on the Big Horn had believed Colter.

The Drouillard-Clark map indicates that, on his route down the Stinking Water, Drouillard journeyed

[9] Harris gives some of the early accounts of this picturesque region. He mentions Cassius Fischer, Father De Smet, Brackenridge, Washington Irving, Joe Meek, J. K. Rollinson, and William A. Jones. In *John Colter,* 91-96.

all the way to the junction of this river with the Big
Horn, at no considerable distance below the mouth of
Gap River. The notes which he supplied to Clark state
that at the forks of these rivers resided, for the winter,
a band of Indians whom he calls "es-cup-scup-pe-ah
(who speak the same language with the Oots-lash-
shoot)." There is a suggestion in the notes that there
were additional Indians. The total amounted to "280
lodges of dressed leather or 2240 souls."

An examination of the Drouillard-Clark map would
show that Spanish settlements are mentioned as accessible by way of the Big Horn River as well as by way
of the south fork of the Stinking Water. One could get
the impression from the map, also, that Drouillard
ascended the Big Horn River to these same Spanish
settlements, a distance which could be traveled by Indians with their families in eighteen days – that is, one
hundred and eighty miles. A glance at a modern map
of this region would show approximately the same
distance.

Did Drouillard ascend the Big Horn River to these
settlements? The map clearly shows a continuation, all
the way to the settlements, of the marks used to depict
Drouillard's itinerary.

It is not likely, however, that Drouillard saw any
necessity of soliciting trade at that great distance from
the post on the Big Horn – nearly three hundred miles.
The marks, which seem to be a continuation of his
route, could simply have been placed there to indicate
that a trail ascended this river all the way to the so-
called settlements. Similar marks are placed along the
upper course of the south fork, also, presumably to
indicate a trail. It is certain these latter marks were not

placed along the south fork to indicate that Drouillard
ascended that river. Neither were they placed there to
show the route taken by Colter, for the Drouillard-
Clark map does not show Colter's route at all. The one
plausible explanation is that these marks were placed
along both rivers to show the existence of trails rather
than to indicate anyone's itinerary.

It seems likely, therefore, that after Drouillard had
visited with his Es-cup-scup-pe-âh friends at the forks
of the Stinking Water and the Big Horn, he retraced
his steps up the former river to its junction with Gap
River. Then, ascending this river, he crossed the Pryor
Mountains and descended Pryor Creek and the Yellowstone to the post at the mouth of the Big Horn – a
journey which appears to have taken him at least five
days, making his total journey one of fifteen days. It
could easily have taken longer, depending on the dura-
tion of his stopovers at the various Indian encampments which he visited. Harris is also of the opinion
that Drouillard turned back at the mouth of Gap River.

It should be pointed out that the Greybull River
follows a course between the south fork of the Shoshone
and the Big Horn which is about two-fifths of the distance from the former, and about three-fifths of the
distance from the latter. The Drouillard-Clark map
shows no such river at all. This could again suggest
that Drouillard did not ascend the Big Horn, for if he
had he would, after some thirty miles, have arrived at
the junction of the Greybull with this river. The Greybull is a river sufficiently large to have attracted his
attention and to have caused him to mention it to Clark.
The fact that the Greybull is not shown on the Drouillard-Clark map suggests, not that Drouillard did not

see this river, but that he saw it from the top of some ridge or peak, and thought it to be the Big Horn. The Greybull is, in fact, one of the forks of the Big Horn – the west fork. The Big Horn proper, or east fork, was so much farther away that it may have caused Drouillard to conclude, if he saw it at all, that it was a stream of no great size.

Drouillard's second journey in search of Indian customers was made in the spring of 1808, close upon his first journey, and before Colter's return to the post. Starting at the post on the Big Horn he made his way, on foot, up the Yellowstone as before, as far as the mouth of the Smalea Creek, a day's journey away. At this point, however, instead of continuing on up the Yellowstone as on his first trip, he turned to the left, or south, arriving, at the end of his second day, at the forks of the Big Horn and the Little Big Horn at a point which he called Antelope Bend. Continuing his route the next morning along the west side of the meandering Little Big Horn, he arrived, after another two days, at an Indian encampment at the mouths of two streams emptying into the Little Big Horn, one from the south, the other from the north. Harris thinks the Indians he encountered here could have been Crows, or Cheyennes, or Sioux, or Arapahos.[10]

Drouillard continued his journey the next morning, for another day, along the west bank of the Little Big Horn. Here he found excellent beaver grounds, as indicated by the notations on the Drouillard-Clark map.

Turning eastward the next day, he journeyed on to

---

[10] *Ibid.,* p. 89.

the headwaters of a creek flowing into what he supposed was one of the tributaries of the Tongue. This creek he followed to its confluence with the tributary itself, up which he continued his route for several miles. Then, three days after leaving the Little Big Horn, and the eighth after leaving Lisa's Fort, he struck camp.

The river on which he was now camped would appear to have been the Rosebud, emptying into the Yellowstone some sixty or more miles to the north, and not, as he supposed, into the Tongue. He called it the Minna-e-sa, or "big water river." He did not follow the Minna-e-sa to its mouth, but continued on eastward instead, to the Tongue. He followed it for two days, when he turned west and crossed the Minna-e-sa; then struck out across country for the mouth of the Big Horn. Since he did not descend the Minna-e-sa to its mouth, nor the Tongue either, he had no way of knowing that the former flowed directly into the Yellowstone instead of into the Tongue. It did not occur to him to make inquiry among the Indians on this point.

In proximity to his camp on the upper Minna-e-sa, Drouillard came upon a "remarkable lake under the foot of a high ridge of mountains. . ." Clark wrote:

> on the side next these mountains, the rocks rise from the waters edge, to the hight of [word illegible] feet – this rock occupies about half the circumpherence of this lake – which is nearly circular the other side is surrounded by a beautiful plain – the lake is about 440 yards in diameter – the water is clear and affords a handsome little river which discharges itself into a northern branch of tongue river which bears its name or Minna-e-sa or *big water*.

There may have been an Indian encampment at Drouillard's camp on the upper Minna-e-sa. These, or other Indians whom he met later, told him that "at the

head of this river [the Minna-e-sa] could be heard frequently a loud noise . . . like thunder – which
makes the earth tremble – they state that they seldom go
there because their children cannot sleep at night for
this nois and conseive it posesed of spirits who are
averse that men should be near them."

A day's journey to the eastward took Drouillard to
another Indian encampment, this one at the fork of a
creek with Tongue River. A short distance below this
he came, the next day, to still another encampment.
The Indians at this latter encampment may have told
him of excellent beaver grounds on a creek, the Neah-
pah-to-awn-zhah, or Otter Creek, to the northeast, and
Drouillard struck off, across country, in that direction,
on that same day. He made extensive explorations
along this creek and its tributaries, then returned to
the Tongue River, but below the Indian encampment,
and there put up for the night. Crossing the river the
next morning, he made his way, a day's journey, westward, across country, until he struck the Minna-e-sa, as
before indicated. On the west side of this river he
camped for the night. Three days later, after traversing
by a zigzag route across country, and over a range of
mountains which he called the "Chatish or Woolf
teeth mountains," found him back at the post on the
Big Horn, having been gone at least fifteen days, and
longer if he made more than one-night stops at Indian
encampments. He had traveled upwards of two hundred miles, as against over three hundred on his first
trip. He had visited several Indian encampments, and
had discovered the location of excellent beaver grounds.

Drouillard, on his second journey, passed in proximity to the spot on which General George Custer was

later to make his historic last stand, and through the valley in which Sitting Bull and his legions were encamped prior to the battle. Like Colter, he spread the news of the establishment of the post on the Yellowstone and invited the various bands to bring in their pelts. If the fur trading venture of Lisa and Drouillard were to fail, such failure would not be due to any lack of effort on the part of men like Drouillard and Colter. These intrepid men served the present enterprise as they had served the Lewis and Clark expedition: with courage; with intelligence; and with willing subjugation of self to whatever the task might demand.

24

The Grip of the Law

Scarcely had Drouillard set foot in St. Louis early in August, 1808, than he was confronted with the necessity of defending himself in court on a charge of murder. The following piece of sworn testimony, taken on August 5, of that year, may be of interest.[1]

On the day when we had to leave the River of Osages to continue our trip Mr Manuel Lisa ordered the crew to go on the open [river]; as soon as the boat started going the crew exclaimed that one man was missing. Manuel ordered to land and to go and search for "Bazine." And he told Mr. George Drouillard, "George, go and find this Bazine." Mr. Drouillard took his rifle and went away in the company of Benito. Some time after they left I heard a rifle shot and about half an hour later Mr. George Drouillard came back and said that he shot "Bazine" but he did not die. And he came to bring some more men with him to take the wounded man to the camp. He took some men and went away to find him and he brought him in. Manuel Lisa was also gone saying that he was going to the river *"marie"* where he could find him. He took a boat and two men and when he left he said "If I meet him I will shoot him on first sight"; he came back two or three hours afterwards and as soon as he landed George Drouillard announced to him that he had wounded the man. He said, "It is well done. He's a rascal who got what he deserved." He went up to "bazine" and spoke to him in an angry tone, blaming him for the condition in which

[1] Translated from the French by Thomas Molnar, while Professor of Modern Languages, Pacific University, from a document owned by the Missouri Historical Society.

he had put himself and which was purely his fault. The man remained until the following day when he sent him with some one from St. Charles whose name I do not remember.

ANTE. DUBREUIL

The order for Drouillard's arrest in connection with this affair was issued on August 6 by Thomas F. Riddick, a justice of the peace, District of St. Louis. The trial was held on Friday, the twenty-third of September. An illuminating account of it is given below:

On Friday the 23d ultime the trial of Geo. Druillard for the alledged murder of Antoine Bissonnette, came on before the Court of Oyer and Terminer, held for the district of St. Louis: The hon. J. B. C. Lucas presiding Judge, and the hon. August Chouteau associate justice – John Scott, Esq. Attorney General, prosecuted, and Edward Hempstead, Wm C. Carr and Rufus Easton, Esquires, were counsel for the prisoner.

The facts were briefly these: Mr. Manuel Lisa & the prisoner had embarked, in the spring of 1807, goods and merchandise, which, with their outfits and equipments, amounted to $16,000, as an adventure on a trading and hunting voyage up to the sources of the Missouri river. They had enlisted the deceased as a hand for the term of three years; he had engaged to do duty, not only as a hunter, but also expressly convenanted, by articles of agreement, "to obey the command of his patroons, to mount guard, to give them timely notice of everything that might prove injurious to their interest, and not to leave their service on any pretext whatever."

The party arrived at the mouth of the Osage river, about 120 miles up the Missouri on the 14th of May 1807, and when again putting off it was discovered that the deceased was missing – Mr. Lisa, the commander of the party, directed them to call him, but he made no answer: Lisa then said to Druillard, "go and bring him, DEAD OR ALIVE." Druillard returned in about half an hour, and said he had wounded the deceased, and was sorry for it. Four men were sent to bring him to the boat: He was then asked "why he had deserted?" – he replied he "could give no reason – it was a misfortune for him." He was also asked "if any one treated him ill?" He answered "no, it was an unlucky fate that awaited him." The bullet penetrated his back near one of his shoulders.

Mr. Lisa procured him a canoe, gave every possible accommodation, and hastened him to St. Charles, to receive surgical aid – but he died in the canoe the next day about 10 o'clock, A.M. before his arrival at St. Charles.

It was proved that the deceased, previous to deserting, had bundled up blankets and other articles, forming the equipment furnished to him as a hand, and secreted them at the aforesaid river Au Marie; and also another bundle containing a shirt lent him by one of the party, and hid it in the trunk of an old tree near where he deserted. . .[2]

At this trial Drouillard was ably defended by his attorneys. Hempstead spoke, "in a forcible and impressive manner," for about forty-five minutes. Easton, quoting law and "HOLY WRIT," spoke an hour and a half. Carr, "with his usual elegance of style and beauty of thought and expression," used about an hour. "The Jury retired from the bar, and in about fifteen minutes returned a verdict of NOT GUILTY." [3]

---

[2] *Missouri Gazette,* October 12, 1808, in Missouri Historical Society Papers. Courtesy of the Society.

[3] "The counsel for the prisoner contended that the crime would only amount to man-slaughter, in case it had not been proved that the deceased committed a felony – The desertion from a voyage so peculiarly important to the prisoner and hazzardous in its nature, and a refusal on the part of the deceased to be taken, was a sufficient provocation to do away the least possible presumption of malice prepense, on the part of the prisoner. Mr. Hempstead read a variety of law-cases in point, to support this position. . .

"Mr. Easton . . . maintained that the deceased had committed larceny in taking away and secreting the articles of equipment which had been furnished him by the prisoners and his partners, for the use and benefit of the voyage; and that over the said articles the deceased had no right to exercise acts of ownership, except whilst he continued in the service of his employers. – That the clandestine manner of deserting with the blankets, &c. was a complete evidence of a felonious intent . . . that therefore, the killing was

It may have been his trial for the murder of Bissonnette which prompted Drouillard to write, on May 23
the following spring, the letter to his half-sister to
which reference has been made. He says:

You have without doubt learned of the misfortune which happened to me last spring on my way to the Upper Missouri. I
admit that this misfortune was very fatal to us but at the same
time, I would have you observe without trying to excuse myself,
that this has not been done through malice, hatred or any evil
intent. Thoughtlessness on my part and lack of reflection in this
unhappy moment is the only cause of it, and moreover encouraged
and urged by my partner, Manuel Lisa, who we ought to consider in this affair as guilty as myself for without him the thing
would never have taken place. The recollection of this unhappy
affair throws me very often in the most profound reflections, and
certainly I think it has caused a great deal of grief to my family
for which I am very sorry and very much mortified. That I have
not lost the affection of my old friends proves that they did not

---

perfectly justifiable, both by the laws of God and man – it being for the
advancement of public justice. . .

"He took an extensive view of the Law and the testimony – of the importance of such expeditions up the Missouri – that the success of those enter-
prises depended entirely on the fidelity of the hands, and that if treachery be
suffered with impunity, all commerce with that rich country would be frus-
trated forever. He pourtrayed with the liveliest animation, the persevering
and unshaken fidelity of the prisoner in ascending the Missouri with the intrepid and brave captains Lewis and Clark. . . The force of his argu-
ments carried conviction to the minds of the Jury and audience that the
defence of his client was founded on a just and legal basis.

"Mr. Carr endeavoured to justify the defendant because his habits being
military, and he being used to implicit obedience – that therefore, he could
not be charged with having a bad heart for fulfilling the commands of his
superior in this instance; and that if any one was to blame it was Mr. Lisa
who ordered him to bring the deceased, 'dead or alive!' He reminded the
Jury of the punishment of manslaughter, and besought them not to fix such
infamous stigma upon so deserving a character. . .

"The Attorney General contended that the desertion of the deceased, and
carrying off the articles of equipment, was only a breach of trust in him. –
That the killing was perpetrated thro' express malice, and that it was murder
in the fullest and most strict sense of the term. . ." – *Missouri Gazette,*
October 12, 1808. Courtesy of the Missouri Historical Society.

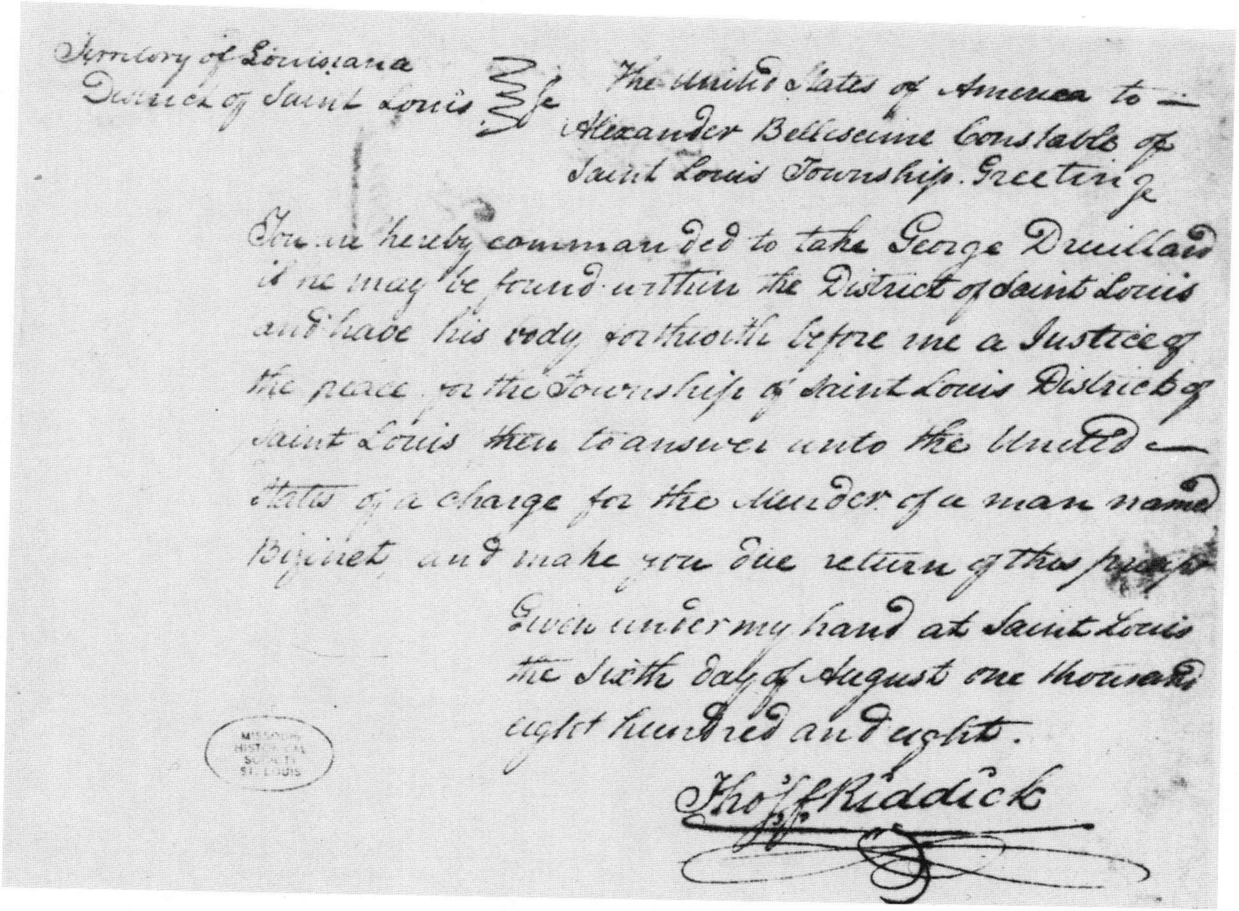

LIST OF JURORS AT DROUILLARD'S TRIAL, SEPTEMBER 23, 1808
Showing the name of George Shannon, probably the same man who had accompanied
the Lewis and Clark Expedition, and who accompanied Drouillard on the
mission to the Nez Percé chiefs.
Courtesy of the Missouri Historical Society, St. Louis.

believe me capable of an action so terrible through malice and bad intent. . .[4]

There is no reason to doubt Drouillard's expressions of regret over the shooting of Bissonnette, nor his statement that he felt "mortified" over any sorrow this incident may have brought to his family. Drouillard was ever faithful in the discharge of a duty. It was unfortunate that this time his zeal in this respect should have carried him too far.

It may be of interest to note that, in the list of jurors, appears the name of one, George Shannon. This was in all probability the same Shannon who accompanied Lewis and Clark, and therefore Drouillard, to the Pacific — the same Shannon who was with Drouillard on that important mission to the Nez Percé chiefs when Drouillard successfully bargained with the latter for the guides whom the explorers needed to lead them over the Bitterroot Mountains.

Scarcely had Drouillard been acquitted of the murder of Bissonnette than he was confronted with the necessity of attending to the matter of the non-payment of his debt to Frederick Graeter, assumed by him on February 11, 1804 — a debt now of four and one-half years standing. There is reason to believe, not only that the debt was paid, but that other litigations, involving the indebtedness of one, Paul Primeau, to Drouillard and Lisa, were also satisfactorily consummated.[5]

---

[4] Wheeler I, p. 110. Also in Missouri Historical Society Papers, the Voorhis Memorial Collection.

[5] Jackson points out that Drouillard conveyed the land warrant granted him by Congress, along with the two warrants he had purchased from Whitehouse and Collins, to Thomas F. Riddick and Alexander McNair for $1,300. Thomas F. Riddick was Clerk of the Court of Common Pleas, District of St. Louis. Jackson, p. 345; also see Appendix F.

25

Second Fur Trading Venture

In the spring of 1809, Drouillard was again ready for a fur trading venture up the Missouri. The man in charge was again Manuel Lisa, who had busied himself during the winter in promoting the organization of the St. Louis Missouri Fur Company. The company, composed of the ablest fur traders of the west, was backed by a capital of $40,000.[1] The plan provided for the establishment of posts along the Missouri, from the Sioux to the Minnetarees. The main force was to proceed to Lisa's Fort on the Yellowstone, from whence, the following spring, a strong party would be dispatched to establish a post at the Three Forks of the Missouri, the main objective. For a consideration of $7,000, the company was to conduct the Mandan chief She-ha-ka and his family and friends as far as the Mandan villages.[2]

---

[1] Chittenden I, p. 140.

[2] Chittenden (I, p. 139) states that the contract price for the return of the Mandan chief was $7,000. Harris (p. 137) puts the figure at $10,000. In the Appendix to James, Douglas (pp. 269-70) gives the contract itself, from which is here quoted: ". . . To pay . . . the sum of Seven thousand dollars lawful money of the United States. . . "; and "For the true and faithful performance of each and every of the Conditions, Covenants, and Stipulations, herein before sustained the said parties respectively, do hereby jointly and severally bind themselves, their Heirs, Executors, Administrators and Assigns each to the other in the penal sum of Ten thousand dollars lawful money of the United States."

Drouillard's connection with the expedition is not stated. He had many qualifications, among which his ability to act as interpreter was not the least. Moreover, he knew the country in which the operations would be carried on. He could be depended upon to do a commendable job as an emissary to the Indians, should his services as such be needed. He was cooperative. He had on numerous occasions demonstrated strict fidelity to duty. He was a man of courage, an able outdoorsman, an expert hunter, a man amply capable of leading parties to the best beaver grounds. Other than all of this, he was an excellent trapper himself. In brief, George Drouillard possessed in no small measure qualifications which should have made him all but invaluable to almost any fur trading venture.

It may be assumed that Drouillard was with the expedition when it left St. Louis in May or June.[3] He was one of those who saw the flotilla make its way through the territory of the Sioux, who, though they made threats against the advancing party, nevertheless permitted the party to proceed unharmed, no doubt impressed by the numerical strength arraigned against them. Drouillard witnessed, also, the delivery of the Mandan chief to his people. He was present when the expedition arrived among the Minnetarees of Knife River, and there picked up an invaluable recruit in the person of John Colter,[4] who, on his part, had journeyed to the villages of these people from Lisa's Fort, after having undergone some harrowing experiences at the hands of the Blackfeet. Drouillard was also on hand, and available for service at various points along the river, where supplies and personnel were diverted

---

[3] Chittenden I, pp. 140-41.   [4] Harris, 136.

from the main party and left behind to establish the posts to which reference has been made. He was with the expedition as this made its way up the Yellowstone. It arrived, finally, late in the fall, at Lisa's Fort, and proceeded at once to the business of trapping and bartering in furs with the Indians.

Drouillard must have noticed several differences between this expedition and that of which he had been a member under Lewis and Clark four years before. The Lewis and Clark men had been carefully selected and trained. The men in the present expedition appear not to have been either highly selected or adequately trained. Both expeditions had proceeded on the assumption that discipline was a necessity; but whereas, in the Lewis and Clark expedition, the men submitted to this discipline willingly and even gladly, in the case of the Lisa expedition, there was much complaining, frequent dissension, several desertions, and even open rebellion. The men under Lewis and Clark had shown respect and even admiration for their leaders; a goodly number of those under Lisa appeared to regard their leader with contempt, disrespectfully referring to him as Esau.[5] From the standpoint of morale, the two expeditions were as different as black and white.

What Drouillard thought of these men, is not known. He is mentioned only infrequently in the absorbing narrative which one of them, Thomas James, subsequently wrote concerning this venture.[6] In one of these references, James calls Drouillard "a brave man." In

---

[5] James, 16, 17.

[6] James, *Three Years among the Indians and Mexicans,* published by the Missouri Historical Society. The author is indebted to James and to the Society for quotations from the book, and for information contained therein, that is pertinent to the present study and used by the author as indicated in the footnotes to this and the two chapters that follow.

another, he refers to him as "the principal hunter of
Lewis & Clark's party."[7] In a third, he states that
Drouillard was influential in thwarting a cowardly
attempt on the part of one, Bouché, to seek revenge
against Lisa.[8] The fourth reference was in connection
with an incident which occurred in May the following
year. Why James does not mention Drouillard more
often is not known. He may have looked askance at
Drouillard as not being one of the "Americans" of
whom the expedition was composed, due to Drouillard's French or Indian extraction. In his book, he
states that the "French hands were much better treated
on all occasions than the Americans."[9] He seems to
have felt resentful of this apparent show of partiality,
and he may have assigned Drouillard to the category
of those thus apparently favored by Lisa, and therefore
excluded Drouillard from the class of those with whom
he did identify himself.

Whatever the reason for James' failure to mention
Drouillard more frequently, the fact remains that
Drouillard did not accomplish – nor perhaps saw any
need for attempting to accomplish – anything outstanding, good or bad, on the journey up the Missouri. Since
he was obviously not one of the French "hands," nor
yet one of the "Americans," he did not especially seek
to ingratiate himself with either, preferring, rather,
more or less to mind his own business. He was content
to allow events to take their course until such time as
he should arrive at the post on the Yellowstone, and,
even more, at the Three Forks, where he hoped to find
the fruition of his plans in pursuit of the much sought-

---

[7] James, 80.   [8] Harris, 65.   [9] James, 19.

after beaver. It should be added that James did not accompany the main party while this made its way up the Yellowstone.[10] This may to some extent account for the few times Drouillard was mentioned in the latter's narrative.

Late in March the next year (1810), Drouillard was one of a party of thirty-two French and Americans under Pierre Menard, including James, who set out from Lisa's Fort to establish the long planned-for post at the Three Forks of the Missouri. Since those who composed the party anticipated opposition from the Blackfeet, they went equipped for doing their own trapping, on the chance that no Indians would come in to trade. Among the thirty-two, and serving as guide, was Colter, "who thoroughly knew the road, having twice escaped over it from capture and death at the hands of the Indians."

The travelers made their way on horseback up the Yellowstone, over Bozeman Pass – the same pass over which Clark had come four years before. Continuing their journey down the Gallatin, they arrived, on April 3, at the Three Forks.

Not many miles out of Lisa's Fort they came upon a scene which must have left an indelible impression, if not upon Drouillard and Colter, then, at least, upon many of those in the party, who, as compared with the former, were tenderfeet in so far as their experience with Indians was concerned. The scene, moreover, and the incident which had contributed to it, awakened in the latter a vivid realization of the dangers which could

---

[10] *Ibid.,* pp. 35-45.

be expected in the country through which they were then traveling.

The incident referred to is given in some detail by James.

> On first arriving at the Fort, I had learned that two of the men with an Indian chief of the Snake tribe and his two wives and a son had gone forward, with the intention of killing game for our company and awaiting our approach on the route. Our second day's journey brought us to an Indian lodge; stripped, and near by, we saw a woman and boy lying on the ground, with their heads split open, evidently by a tomahawk. These were the Snakes's elder wife and son, he having saved himself and his younger wife by flight on horseback. Our two men who had started out in company with him, were not molested. They told us that a party of Gros Ventres had come upon them, committed these murders, and passed on as if engaged in a lawful and praiseworthy business.

What may have been Drouillard's thoughts and feelings as he sat on his horse and contemplated the mutilated bodies of the unfortunate Shoshones, can perhaps better be imagined than described. It is not likely that he experienced any apprehension lest the Gros Ventres inflict a like outrage upon himself or upon any of his companions, even were he or they to find themselves unexpectedly alone, or in much reduced numbers, in the presence of these people. Against the Shoshones the Gros Ventres could be presumed to take liberties. But against white men, people of a sturdier cast – against himself – no. Any thought to the contrary did not enter his mind, or if it did, he banished it as not worthy of consideration.

The journey up the Yellowstone had not proceeded far before one of their men, Brown, became blind from the reflection of the sun upon the snow. According to

James, this man "implored" his companions to put an end to his torment by shooting him.

Had Drouillard or any of the other members of the party felt inclined to poke fun at the unfortunate Brown, they may have changed their minds when, several days later, they themselves became stricken with the same malady. Before that happened, however, they found it necessary to make their way through a heavy snow which began to fall "most violently" while they were attempting to negotiate Bozeman Pass. According to James (who may have been inclined to exaggerate), the snow continued to fall all night. James continued:

> The morning showed us the heads and backs of our horses just visible above the snow which had crushed down all our tents. We proceeded on with the greatest difficulty. As we entered the ravine or opening of the mountain the snow greatly increased in depth being in places from fifty to sixty feet on the ground, a third of which had fallen and drifted in that night. The wind had heaped it up in many places to a prodigious height. The strongest horses took the front to make a road for us, but soon gave out and the ablest bodied men took their places as pioneers. A horse occasionally stepped out of the beaten track and sunk entirely out of sight in the snow. By night we had made about four miles for that day's travel. By that night we passed the ravine and reached the Gallatin river. . ."

Then, after they had plowed through the worst of the snow, and after the bright sun had begun to produce a glare upon the unrelieved whiteness all around them, then was it that the affliction of blindness smote them.

They had suffered from "indestinct vision" during the last two days. But now

> the hot tears trickled from the swollen eyes nearly blistering the cheeks, and the eye-balls seemed bursting from our heads. At

first, the sight was obscured as by a silk veil or handkerchief, and we were unable to hunt. Now we could not even see our way before us, and in this dreadful situation we remained two days and nights. Hunger was again inflicting its sharp pangs upon us, and we were upon the point of killing one of the pack-horses, when on the fourth day after crossing the Gallatin, one of the men killed a goose, of which, being now somewhat recovered from our blindness, we made a soup and stayed the gnawings of hunger.

Upon joining their companions down the river, they found that these had suffered "more severely than we from the same causes. They had killed three dogs, one a present to me from an Indian, and two horses to appease the demands of hunger. . ."

Again referring to the party which had gone ahead, James continued:

While in this distressed situation enveloped by thick darkness at midday, thirty Snake Indians came among them, and left without committing any depredation. Brown and another, who suffered less than the others, saw and counted these Indians, who might have killed them all and escaped with their effects with perfect umpunity. Their preservation was wonderful.[11]

The conduct of the admirable Shoshones, who could easily have killed the white men and helped themselves not only to their horses but, and especially, to their guns and ammunition, might have given Drouillard cause for meditation. Had these Shoshones been members of that band under Cameahwait, on the Lemhi, and at the Two Forks, who had met Lewis and Clark four years before? If not, had they heard of Lewis and Clark? Was there any connection between what Lewis and Clark had done or said four years before, and the conduct of these Shoshones on this occasion – an occasion

---

[11] *Ibid.,* pp. 47-51; 66.

which, had they willed it, could have supplied them with additional means of defending themselves against their enemies?

Another question suggests itself: Was it Drouillard "who suffered less than the others," and who, with Brown, "saw and counted these Indians"? At any rate, Drouillard, who was more of an outdoorsman than any other member of the party save Colter, would have known more than they how to protect himself against an affliction such as that which overtook them.

The discovery of the mutilated bodies of the Shoshones who had gone ahead of the main party from Fort Lisa was impressive enough. It could hardly have been as impressive as the sight which was to meet the eyes of the travelers when these arrived at a spot about a day's journey from the Three Forks. Here, scattered over the ground, lay a "vast" number of human skulls and bones, in mute evidence of a tragic battle that had transpired some time in the past.

The battle had occurred in the late summer, or in the fall, of 1808 (two years before). It was none other than Colter who now told the story to James, and to as many as were there to listen, which may have been the entire party, including Drouillard.

After his return, in the spring of 1808,[12] from his epic tour in quest of Indian customers, Colter had remained at Fort Lisa for some time. Before his departure for St. Louis, in July of that year, Lisa had commissioned him to start on a second journey, this time in search of the Blackfeet. The purpose of this journey was to invite the Blackfeet to come to the fort to trade.

Colter was making his way up the Yellowstone, in

---

[12] Harris, 117.

obedience to the order which had sent him out, when
he came upon a band of five hundred Flatheads. He
had not been with these long before they were attacked
by fifteen hundred Blackfeet.

The Blackfeet, says James, who later retold Colter's
story, fell upon the Flatheads "in such numbers as
seemingly to make their destruction certain." The
"desparate courage" of the Flatheads, however, "saved
them from a general massacre," until a band of Crows,
three hundred of them (who also happened to be in the
vicinity) attracted by the "noise, shouts, and firing,"
came to their rescue. The Flatheads, meanwhile, had
been "fighting with great spirit and defending the
ground manfully." This fighting, coupled with the rein-
forcement by the Crows, finally caused the Blackfeet,
in spite of their superior numbers, to withdraw, but
not until they had discovered that on the side of the
Flatheads was a white man, who though wounded,
"crawled to a small thicket and there loaded and fired
while sitting on the ground." The white man was John
Colter.[13]

There may have been a question in the mind of
Drouillard and other members of the party as they
strolled over the battlefield, and as they reflected on the
part that Colter had played in the battle proper: What
would be the ultimate effect upon the Blackfeet of this
encounter? Would their realization of the fact that a
white man had fought valiantly against them cause
them to stay away from the post which Drouillard and
those with him were hoping to establish at the Three
Forks? Would they try to keep other Indians away?

Another event, namely, Colter's second contact with

---

[13] James, 52-53.

the Blackfeet, was to give Drouillard and his companions even greater cause for speculation.

After the battle just described, Colter spent some time at the fort on the Yellowstone, nurturing his leg. In due time, mindful of Lisa's commission to him to visit the Blackfeet, he started once more, on foot, for the Three Forks, accompanied by Potts.

The story of his second encounter with the Blackfeet, first narrated by the English botanist Bradbury, who got it direct from Colter, has become an epic among stories of American adventure. An excellent version is given also by Washington Irving (who got his from Bradbury).[14] Another excellent version is given by Thomas James, who "passed over the scene" with Colter as Colter told the story to him direct, and as Colter "described his emotions during the whole adventure with great minuteness." [15]

This time Colter and his companion succeeded in reaching the Three Forks. Not finding the Blackfeet there, the two men spent their time trapping on the Jefferson, having prepared or procured a canoe for the purpose.

Their encounter with the Blackfeet occurred early one morning while they were ascending a creek in their canoe. In the incidents which followed, Potts was riddled with arrows, after he had shot an Indian. Colter was stripped of his clothing and given the opportunity of running for his life. Run he did as he had never run before, outdistancing the entire pack of five or six hundred Indians, except one, who kept gaining on him.

In his heroic attempt at escape, Colter "exerted him-

---

[14] Irving, *Astoria,* I, pp. 155-59.   [15] James, 58-63.

self to such a degree, that the blood gushed from his nostrils, and soon almost covered the fore part of his body." Turning his head, he

> saw the savage not twenty yards from him. Determined if possible to avoid the expected blow, he suddenly stopped, turned round, and spread out his arms. The Indian, surprised by the suddenness of the action, and perhaps at the bloody appearance of Colter, also attempted to stop; but exhausted with running, he fell whilst endeavoring to throw his spear, which struck in the ground, and broke in his hand. Colter instantly snatched up the pointed part, with which he pinned him to the earth, and then continued his flight.

Arriving at the Jefferson, he dove under a "raft of drift timber" which had become lodged against an island.[16] Here he remained concealed until night, when, naked, shivering, minus a weapon, his feet pierced by a hundred spines from the prickly pear, he started out on his way over the seven-day stretch that separated him from Lisa's Fort.[17] Fearing to cross the mountains by way of Bozeman Pass, he "ascended," according to James,

> the almost perpendicular mountain before him, the tops and sides of which a great way down, were covered with perpetual snow. He clambered up this fearful ascent about four miles below the gap, holding on by the rocks, shrubs and branches of trees, and by morning had reached the top. He lay there concealed all that day, and at night proceeded on in the descent of the mountain, which he accomplished by dawn. . .

This feat James holds to have been not "the least of his exploits," inasmuch as the mountain seemed to him

---

[16] John Bradbury, *Travels in the Interior of North America,* 27-28. Bradbury says it was toward the Jefferson he ran. James (p. 60) says it was toward the Madison. In Washington Irving's version (I, p. 157) he is described as running toward the Jefferson. In Irving (I, p. 155) also, the statement is made that Colter and Potts "set their traps at night, about six miles up a small river that empties into the fork."

[17] Bradbury, *op. cit.,* 28-29.

impassible even by the mountain goat. As I looked at its rugged and perpendicular sides, I wondered how he ever reached the top – a feat probably never performed before by mortal man. . .

As we passed over the ground where Colter ran his race, and listened to his story an undefinable fear crept over all. We felt awe-struck by the nameless and numerous dangers that evidently beset us on every side.

Even the courage of Cheek, a tall, well-built man from Tennessee; a leader among the malcontents; rash, headstrong, obstinate; "his courage . . . equal to any enterprise" – even Cheek's courage

sunk and his hitherto buoyant and cheerful spirit was depressed at hearing of the perils of the place. He spoke despondingly and his mind was uneasy, restless and fearful. "I am afraid," said he, "and I acknowledge it. I never felt fear before but now I feel it." A melancholy that seemed like a presentiment of his own fate, possessed him, and to us he was serious almost to sadness, until he met his death a few days afterwards from the same Blackfeet from whom Colter escaped.

Colter had not even yet finished with stories.

Just before his encounter with the Blackfeet on that early morning in December, he had dropped his traps into the water. During the ensuing winter, after he had recovered, says James,

from the fatigues of his long race and journey, he wished to recover the traps which he had dropped into the Jefferson Fork on the first appearance of the Indians who captured him. He supposed the Indians were all quiet in winter quarters, and retraced his steps to the Gallatin Fork. He had just passed the mountain gap, and encamped on the bank of the river for the night and kindled a fire to cook his supper of buffalo meat when he heard the crackling of leaves and branches behind him in the direction of the river. He could see nothing, it being quite dark, but quickly heard the cocking of guns and instantly leaped over the fire. Several shots followed and bullets whistled around him, knocking the coals off his fire over the ground. Again he fled for

life, and the second time, ascended the perpendicular mountain
which he had gone up in his former flight fearing now as then,
that the pass might be guarded by Indians. He reached the top
before morning and resting for the day descended the next night,
and then made his way with all possible speed, to the Fort.   . .[18]

Colter's experiences with the Blackfeet must have
brought into sharp relief in Drouillard's mind one important point: the intense hostility of the Blackfeet
toward the traders as a result of what had happened.
How was he or Menard or any and all of his comrades
singly or together to cope with this hostility?

There were three tribes of these Indians, besides a
fourth which, though not Blackfoot, was affiliated with
them and generally considered as a member of the
Blackfoot confederation. The Blackfoot tribes were the
Siksikau, or Blackfoot proper; the *Pikuni,* or Piegans;
and the *Kainah,* or Bloods. The affiliated tribe consisted of the *Atsina,* or Gros Ventres of the Prairies.

Of these tribes, the Gros Ventres of the Prairies were
the most bitter in their hatred of the traders. The "most
relentlessly hostile tribe ever encountered by the whites
in any part of the West, if not in any part of America,"
was the way Chittenden characterized the tribe. They
were followed, in point of hostility, by the Bloods, who
"were the most troublesome to the traders," and "bit-
terly hostile"; and these, in turn, by the Siksikau, who
"were also very hostile." The least hostile were the
Piegans, who were not, by any stretch of the imagination, friendly.

Not only were these four tribes hostile to the whites,
they "were hostile to nearly all the surrounding
tribes.   . ."[19] Wheeler calls them the "devils of the

[18] James, 62. See also, Chittenden II, pp. 851-54.
[19] Wheeler I, p. 298.

prairies and mountains," and, also, "copper-colored Ishmaelites." [20]

Why were the Blackfeet so implacable? This question Drouillard may well have pondered. Was it because of the affair which he and Lewis and Joseph and Reuben Fields had had with the Piegans four years before, when Reuben had stabbed one of the Indians to the death and the captain had shot another "through the belly"? That affair must have been felt by them as a humiliating defeat, to be avenged at the first opportunity. Yet when Lisa's men first came into contact with the Blackfeet, the latter evinced no disposition to be hostile. If they recalled the unhappy affair on the Marias four years before, their conduct, upon meeting Lisa's men, did not indicate they were resentful. On the contrary, they treated the white men "civilly," apparently entertaining toward them at that time no hostile intentions whatever. [21] They may at this time have held that what had happened four years before on the Marias afforded them now no equitable cause for resentment: the white men had been justified in committing the acts which occurred at that time.

There was, however, the battle in which they had discovered a white man fighting valiantly on the side of their enemies. That discovery was not of a kind likely to inspire them with any strong love for the white men. Yet when they encountered Colter and Potts at the Three Forks a few months later, their first act could not be said to have been one of hostility. They had simply ordered the men to step ashore. It was not until after they had suffered the humiliation of having one of their number killed by Potts, to be followed in less

---

[20] *Ibid.*

[21] Harris, 123, Quoting Biddle in Sen. doc. 1, 16 Cong., 1 sess., p. 47.

than an hour by the death of another at the hands of
Colter, and to have this followed, in turn, by the unfor-
givable disgrace of having Colter escape – it was not
until then that they had begun to evince toward the
traders the intense hostility which they demonstrated
time and again in the months to come.

Even so, the humiliation which they suffered at the
Three Forks could hardly have been the main cause of
their hostility toward the whites. The main cause lay
in the fact that the whites had established their trading
post, not among themselves, but among their enemies,
the Crows and Flatheads. In committing this unpardon-
able offense, the traders placed themselves in the position of supplying these enemies with weapons and
equipment which would make the latter more formidable, more unconquerable, and more taunting than ever.
The fact that a band of Piegans, in the summer of 1809,
"lost sixteen warriors in a humiliating defeat before the
newly acquired guns of the Flat Heads," did not miti-
gate this feeling of resentment toward the traders.[22]

Commenting upon Lisa's decision to establish his
post on the Yellowstone instead of on the Missouri,
Chittenden says:

> Whatever might be his real intentions, this act of going to the
> Crows to build his post could not but make the jealous Black-
> feet suspect that he was in league with their enemies. Lisa prob-
> ably did not realize the far-reaching consequences of this act at
> the time and very likely ascended the Yellowstone on the advice
> of Colter, who had found it a good fur country and who had
> little occasion to observe the political situation of the various
> tribes.[23]

---

[22] Harris, 143.   [23] Chittenden I, pp. 118-19.

26

The Three Forks

The trading post of which Drouillard had dreamed for months was finally established, in April of that year (1810), on the "neck of land between the Jefferson and the Madison rivers, about two miles above their confluence." [1]

Work in the construction of the fort was started without delay.

It is not likely that Drouillard was one of the workmen. It is more likely he went up one or the other of the forks of the Missouri, from day to day, to set his traps for beaver, and to reconnoiter for beaver grounds.

The work on the fort progressed rapidly. In a few days, Menard was able to release some of the workmen for the all-important task of trapping. Chittenden relates:

> Fortune at first smiled upon them most encouragingly. It was evident that they were in the midst of virgin territory unsurpassed in its wealth of beaver. The daily catch was heavy and the prospect was excellent that the company would take out from the Three Forks fully three hundred packs of beavers the first year.
>
> In the midst of this sunshine of prosperity a black storm of disaster broke upon the unsuspecting company. It was the morning of the 12th of April and the trappers as usual had gone to examine their traps when a band of Blackfeet [Gros Ventres of the Prairie. – Chittenden] came down upon them with the sud-

---

[1] Chittenden I, p. 141.

denness of a lightning flash. Before the least warning could be
given five of the men were killed, and all their horses, guns,
ammunition, traps, and furs were stolen. Only two of the Indians
are known to have been killed. This most unfortunate affair
spread gloom and discouragement throughout the camp, and it
was with difficulty that the men could be induced to resume
their work. . .[2]

The narrative by James, though less dramatic, is
given in greater detail.

According to James, it was decided to send a group
of eighteen men up the Jefferson, and a group of four
down the Missouri, leaving the remaining nine under
Menard to complete the construction of the fort and
trading post.

The group headed upstream left the fort on April 9,
only six days after their arrival at the Three Forks in
the first place. Drouillard was one of those who accompanied this group. So was Colter. So was Cheeks, the
man who had said a week before, after he had listened
to Colter's recital of the latter's escape from the Blackfeet by plunging into a beaver dam: "I am afraid and
I acknowledge it. I never felt fear before but now I
feel it."

According to James, the party reached, in three days,
a point on the Jefferson forty miles above their base of
supplies and source of reinforcements – a fact not without portent in a country in which at any moment they
might be set upon by hostile Indians. Scarcely had they
arrived at this point on their third day than the majority
of them "dispersed in various directions to kill game,"
leaving Cheeks, Hull, Ayers, Vallé, and two others to

[2] *Ibid.*, pp. 141-42. Chittenden states that the Indians who made the attack
were Gros Ventres of the Prairie.

prepare the camp. These latter pitched their tents for
the night near the river, but were still

employed in preparing the camp . . . when some thirty or
forty Indians appeared on the prairie south of them, running
afoot and on horses, toward the camp. Vallé and two men whose
names I forget, came running up to Cheek and others and told
them to catch their horses and escape. This Cheek refused to do,
but seizing his rifle and pistols, said he would stay and abide his
fate. "My time has come, but I will kill at least two of them, and
then I don't care." . . Ayres ran frantically about, paralysed
by fear and crying, "O God, O God, what can I do." Though a
horse was within reach he was disabled by terror from mounting
and saving his life. Courage and cowardice met the same fate,
though in very different manners. Hull stood cooly examining
his rifle as if for battle. The enemy were coming swiftly toward
them, and Vallé and his two companions started off pursued by
mounted Indians. The sharp reports of Cheek's rifle and pistols
were soon heard, doing the work of death upon the savages, and
then a volley of musketry sent the poor fellow to his long
home. . .

Early the next morning the whole garrison [at the fort] was
aroused by an alarm made by Vallé and several Frenchmen who
came in, as if pursued by enemies, and informed them that the
whole party who had gone up the Jefferson . . . had been
killed by the Indians, and that they expected an immediate attack
on the Fort. The whole garrison prepared for resistance.

Upon receipt of news of the tragedy, Menard, at the
fort, dispatched Dougherty and Brown to James and
Ware, who were still trapping down the river, with
instructions to them, according to James:

to hasten to the Fort to assist in its defence. Being well
mounted, they came up to our camp as we were preparing dinner.
Their faces were pale with fright, and in great trepidation they
told us they had seen Indian "signs" on the route from the
Fort. . . Everything indicated that Indians were near, and
we hastened to depart for the Fort. . .

[At] two o'clock the next morning, we reached the Jefferson
Fork, opposite the Fort. . . when we entered the Fort, the
whole garrison was drawn up with fingers upon triggers. . .
They were all in the greatest consternation. Lieutenant Immel
. . . had come in and they supposed that all the rest had been
killed. They had had a very narrow escape themselves. . .

As a matter of fact, only Cheeks and Ayres are known
to have lost their lives as a result of the attack by the
Indians. Three others, however, (Hull, Rucker, and
Fleehart), were missing. One Indian was, later, found
dead, "with two bullets in his body, supposed to be from
Cheeks' pistol."

On the morning after the day of the tragedy, "Colter
came in unhurt, with a few others, and said there were
no Indians near the Fort." Those who came in ahead of
him appear to have had a "very narrow escape   . . .
as all but Colter probably considered it; he with his
large experience, naturally looked upon the whole as
an ordinary occurrence." Colter, a man of courage
though he was, and though he may have regarded his
present experience as an ordinary occurrence, nevertheless on this morning, after he had entered the fort,
undoubtedly caused a sensation by declaring that "he
had promised his Maker to leave the country, and 'now'
said he, throwing down his hat on the ground, 'if God
will only forgive me this time and let me off I *will*
leave the country day after tomorrow – and be d--d if
I ever come into it again.' "

It may be added that this was not the first time Colter
had made such a declaration. He had made it a year-
and-a-half before, in connection with his miraculous
escape from the Blackfeet by fleeing for his life and
plunging into a beaver dam. That promise, however,

he broke. This one he did not break. Within ten days he had left the fort.[3]

A party under the command of Menard was soon organized to visit the scene of the conflict and to pursue the Indians.[4] The men in this party buried the bodies of Cheeks and Ayres. They searched for, but did not find, the body of Hull; neither did they find the bodies of Rucker and Fleehart, whose camp had been located two miles up the river.[5] They scalped the Indian presumably killed by Cheeks. Starting out in pursuit of the culprits, they recovered forty-four beaver traps and three horses, but failed to overtake the Indians. After a march of two days, upon orders of Menard, they returned to the fort.[6]

It had long been evident that the Blackfeet would not come in to trade. It also became evident that they saw to it that no other Indians came in either. Furthermore, they seemed bent on starving the traders out, by driving the game away. At least, so thought James. Whether the scarcity of game in the vicinity of the fort was due to the Blackfeet or not, this fact remained: the hunters were compelled to go twenty to thirty miles from the fort in order to find game at all, making hunting as dangerous an enterprise as trapping.

Drouillard was well aware of the fact that Indians continued to show themselves in the vicinity of the fort from time to time. He saw them himself, as James saw

[3] The quotations are from James, 64-65; 70-75.
[4] Douglas states that Pierre Menard had been commissioned captain prior to starting up the Missouri in 1809. James (262-63) however, continued to refer to him as colonel.
[5] Harris, 145.
[6] James, 74-75.

them, as every member of the fort saw them. He was
one of those who, whenever Indians hove into sight,
went out from the fort in an attempt to get in touch with
them. But whenever the parties from the fort came out,
the Indians would flee. Nor did it do any good to pursue them. The Indians would not permit themselves to
be overtaken.

What was to be done about the present sad state of
affairs? It seemed obvious that, could they but capture
a Blackfoot, treat him well, and send him to his people
with a message of goodwill, their hope of establishing
some system of communication, and eventually a more
amenable relationship between themselves and their
enemies, might meet with some degree of success, especially if they should promise, as they would, to erect a
post for the Blackfeet at the mouth of the Marias. For
the purpose of putting some such plan as this into effect,
Menard even went so far as to propose that a messenger
be sent to the Shoshones and the Flatheads to urge upon
these the practicability of waging war upon the Blackfeet until such time as one or more prisoners be obtained.[7]

Who was to be chosen as messenger in the carrying
out of this plan? Who but Drouillard? Drouillard was
the best man for such an undertaking. He had no fear
of long excursions into Indian country. He knew Indians as he knew his father and mother. He could speak
with Indians. He had undertaken successful missions
to Indians in the past. He was a man not only of courage but of determination and resourcefulness. He could
be depended upon to prosecute to the fullest extent, and

7 Chittenden I, p. 142; II, p. 898.

better than any other member of the party, the plan proposed. Drouillard, therefore, was their man.

But would Drouillard accede to such a plan?

Actually, the plan was not as bad as may appear on the surface. Warlike skirmishes among the plains Indians were common. It would not seem unusual or even unethical, either to the Shoshones or the Flatheads, for a band of one or another of them to venture forth to do battle against the dreaded Blackfeet, especially since the object this time was nothing more than that of obtaining a prisoner; who, moreover, was to be treated kindly, showered with presents, and returned, unharmed, to his people, all for the sake of promoting amicable relations, not only between the traders and the Blackfeet, but between the Blackfeet and all other Indians. Fouler plans than this had verily been concocted by the minds of men.

Drouillard may have had a plan of his own, however, for establishing some measure of goodwill between the traders and the Blackfeet. His plan may have involved setting out, alone, in search of a band of these people. Could he but gain admittance to one of their villages or encampments, he would, in a measure, have placed himself in a position which would all but compel them, in conformity with their concept of hospitality, to treat him as a guest. He would then sit down and smoke with them. He would show them samples of goods they could expect to receive in trade if they came to the fort to trade. He would explain to them how it happened that the trading post was placed on the Yellowstone instead of on their own river. He would say to them, "Let the Crows and Flatheads trade with the white man on the

Yellowstone. Come and trade with me at the Three Forks. For your beaver skins, I will give you all the guns and knives and blankets that you need." He would help them see that, even if they did not love the white man or wish to be his friends, it would be to their advantage, from a business standpoint, to come in anyhow, to obtain the weapons and supplies that would enable them to compete on equal terms with their enemies.

Drouillard may have reasoned, however, that the trouble with his plan, aside from the length of time it might take to get in touch with the Blackfeet, was that once the Blackfeet saw him approaching, whatever his intentions, and whether he approached unarmed or not, their present animosity was such as to make it more than likely they would pounce upon him and cut him to pieces, and scatter his flesh to the four winds, without allowing him the slightest opportunity of stating his errand.

Before Drouillard could put his plan into effect, if he had a plan, and before Menard could do likewise with the plan he had proposed, the Blackfeet struck again, as suddenly and as unexpectedly, apparently, as on April 12, and with results which left Menard, for one, with little inclination for putting his plan into operation. Instead he left the country.[8]

---

[8] *Ibid.* I, p. 143.

27

The Prairie Wind

The men at the post continued to make sporadic, half-hearted attempts at trapping, emerging from the fort in parties of varying size. They had "narrow escapes from Indians and still narrower from the Grizzly and White Bears." [1] The American flag was hauled down, to be replaced by the scalplock of the Indian killed by Cheeks, as a taunt to the Indians to come and get it. "The Blackfeet," wrote James, "manifested so determined a hatred and jealousy of our presence, that we could entertain no hope of successfully prosecuting our business, even if we could save our lives. . ." And again: "We all became tired of this kind of life, cooped up in a small enclosure and in perpetual danger of assassination when outside the pickets."

Before giving up altogether, they were willing, once more, to go up the Jefferson, in a party sufficiently large to afford them reasonable protection against the Blackfeet.

Twenty-one men formed this party. They got under way early in May, at a time while Menard was still with them.

They had not worked long in their new location, however, before they realized that trapping in large

---

[1] Quotes unless otherwise indicated, are from James, 78, 79, 80, 82, 83.

numbers was "not very profitable." Accordingly, they changed their plan, and began to go out in smaller parties.

All went well for awhile. As no Blackfeet, in so far as they could tell, came near to bother them, their fear gradually "began to wear off," causing them to "become more ventureous."

One day, impatient at the ineffective efforts of trapping being employed, Drouillard announced to the men in camp that he intended to go up the river, alone, if need be, to set his traps.

The men in camp stared at him. Had he gone mad?

James, for one, warned him of his danger. Drouillard said: "I am too much of an Indian to be caught by Indians."

Drouillard was sincere when he made this boast. But he was also yielding, once again, to that disposition in his nature which made it well nigh impossible for him to refrain, for example, from matching his prowess against the prowess of a grizzly, once he had encountered this animal. Except that, this time, his antagonist was not a grizzly but Indians – a whole pack of them.

Drouillard had become disgusted with the cringing attitude of the men in camp. He had perceived, plainly enough, that neither he nor they were making progress in catching beaver. The chances were good that in the matter of days the majority of the men now with him, as well as those at the fort, including Menard, would be returning to the post on the Yellowstone, or to St. Louis; at least, they seemed determined to get away from the Three Forks. Danger or no danger, it behooved him, as it behooved them, to take as many pelts as possible. They would then at least have *something* to show for their trouble. As for danger – he was not a woman, nor yet even as one of these danger-fearing men in camp. Besides, did he not know how to take care of himself? Would it not give him pleasure to prove, in as convincing a manner as possible, that he, for one, had no fear of the vengeance-seeking Blackfeet? As far as that went, it gave him pleasure to taunt the Blackfeet themselves, as an Indian brave might, after having plucked the hair from his scalp, save for a lock at the top reserved as a challenge to his enemy to come and get it – if he could.

These were the circumstances, therefore, which led Drouillard to pick up his traps and his gun, mount his horse and start out, alone, for a trip up the Jefferson.

He kept close to the river. The willows there would serve as a screen to obstruct the view of any who might be lurking on the other side. As for any who might discover him from the near side of the river, that did not matter. He would perceive them as soon as they perceived him, and could make his escape.

He went some little distance – a mile; perhaps two. He set his traps. He returned to the camp. In the morning, he went out again and returned, after some time – with six beaver pelts!

He repeated the performance the next morning, keeping a lookout for Indians who might be lurking off to his left, while being screened, as on the day before, by the willows along the river. When his work was completed, he returned to camp – with beaver! He flung the pelts at the feet of the goggle-eyed men in camp. He taunted them with the remark: "This is the way to catch beaver."

On yet one other morning he ventured forth, accompanied, this time, by two Delawares, who, like himself, irked by the timidity and the indolence of the men in camp, had decided to go out for a hunt.

He made his way, ahead of the Delawares, up the Jefferson, keeping a lookout for Indians.

A strong wind was blowing – the rollicking, robust, romping wind of the prairie, against which he had braced himself on many an occasion. He may even on this day have entertained memories of moments when he had filled his lungs to capacity with the pure, invigorating air brought to him by this same playful prairie wind, and of the times when, in reckless glee, this same wind had swooped down upon the boats of Lewis and Clark and sent these scurrying for shore. He loved this wind of the prairie. It is not inconceivable he may even have talked to it at times, as Indians sometimes talk to birds and beasts with whom they associate, or from whom they seek assistance.

As he leaned his face against the play of the wind, coming, say, from the left, he may have given himself again to a contemplation of the probable outcome of the well-planned but ill-fated venture of himself and his partners into the land of the Black Moccasins. They could still be placated, these Black Moccasins, and brought to some terms of agreement, *could he but gain an audience with them;* could he but sit down with them, and smoke with them, and make them see. . .

Was that a noise? A yip? A yell? Had he been dreaming? Of all times!

He jerked his head in the direction from which the sound had come. A band of feathered Indians was swooping down upon him as fast as their horses could carry them; and from a direction which precluded the possibility of escape! Well, if he could not flee, he could dismount, throw down his gun, approach the Indians in the guise of friendship. He discarded the idea at once as useless. He might as well have decided to plead for mercy. They would cut him down with no more compunction than they would a cornered coyote. There remained but the one alternative, that of fighting; and fighting "to the last drop," as his friend, Captain Lewis, might have said.[2]

Where were the Delawares? Had they been here now, he, an excellent marksman, could have fired their guns as well as his, as fast as they could reload. They might then have a chance. As for now – well, the men at the camp might hear the report of his gun – or was the wind too strong? – and come to his rescue. They had planned to come this way anyhow, this very morning. They had told him so; had begged him to wait until they could go with him. That was what he should have done. As for his chances now, alone, two miles from the camp, with the Delawares off somewhere by themselves – those chances were none too good. But he would fight. *Par tous les saints,* yes! He would show the Black Moccasins that he could die as bravely as any of them. Black Moccasins or not, he, George Drouillard, was ready for them.

He got down from his horse. He used his rifle until there was no longer time to reload. He used his pistol. He placed his horse between himself and his enemies. When the horse fell, he used it as a breastwork. When

---

[2] The actual words used by Lewis on July 28, 1806, on the occasion of his flight from the Blackfeet, were ". . . sell our lives as dear as we could." – Thwaites v, p. 227.

the savages pounced upon him, he had recourse to his tomahawk, the butt of his gun, his hunting knife. Could he but pull down a rider from off his horse, and mount the horse himself, possibly then, amid the shouts and yells and dust and confusion; amid the sounds of hoof-beats and the clash and clatter of weapons, and the howling, srhieking prairie wind – possibly then would he find an opportunity of making good his escape.

But there were too many of them. In the matter of minutes at the most, the entire affair was over. And when the plunderers had gone, there remained but the pitiful wailing of what had once been the robust, rollicking, prairie wind; that, and a few scattered pieces of flesh and bones on the scene of battle.

James, an eyewitness to the scene of conflict, says:

> We started forward in company, and soon found the dead bodies of the last mentioned hunters [the two Delawares, whom he calls Shawnees], pierced with lances, arrows and bullets and lying near each other. Further on, about one hundred and fifty yards, Druyer and his horse lay dead, the former mangled in a horrible manner; his head was cut off, his entrails torn out and his body hacked to pieces. We saw from the marks on the ground that he must have fought in a circle on horseback, and probably killed some of his enemies, being a brave man, and well armed with a rifle, pistol, knife and tomahawk. We pursued the trail of the Indians till night, without overtaking them, and then returned, having buried our dead, with saddened hearts to Fort.

From information obtained in an interview with Menard, the *Louisiana Gazette* for Thursday, July 26, 1810, published an account of the venture of the Missouri Fur Company into the land of the Blackfeet, a part of which follows:

> A few days ago Mr. Menard with some of the gentlemen attached to the Missouri Fur Company arrived here from their

Fort at the head waters of the Missouri, by whom we learn that
they had experienced considerable opposition from the Blackfoot
Indians; this adverse feeling arose from the jealousy prevalent
among all savage (and some civilized) nations of those who trade
with their enemies. The Crows and Blackfeet are almost con-
tinually at war. The Company detached a party to trade with
the latter. This gave offense to the Blackfeet who had not the
same opportunity of procuring Arms, &c. The Hudson Bay
Factory being several days journey from their hunting grounds,
and with whom they cannot trade with equal advantage. . .

Early in May George Druilard accompanied by some Delawares, who were in the employ of the Company, went out to
hunt, contrary to the wishes of the rest of the party who were
confident the Indians were in motion around them, and that
from a hostile disposition they had already shown it would be
attended with danger, their presages were too true, he had not
proceeded more than two miles from the camp before he was
attacked by a party in ambush by which himself and two of his
men were literally cut to pieces. It appears from circumstances
that Druilard made a most obstinate resistance as he made a
kind of breastwork of his horse, whom he made to turn in order
to receive the enemy's fire, his bulwark, of course, soon failed and
he became the next victim of their fury. It is lamentable that
although this happened within a short distance of relief, the fire
was not heard so as to afford it, in consequence of a high wind
which prevailed at the time.[3]

Chittenden has a statement which may have a bearing
on this case. The statement is a quotation from Alexander Henry. It reads:

. . . The Bloods were at war on the Missouri about the
same time as the Falls Indians [who had attacked the Drouillard-
Lisa trappers on April 12]. They also fell upon a party of
Americans, murdered them all, and brought away considerable
booty in goods of various kinds, such as fine cotton shirts, beaver
traps, hats, knives, dirks, handkerchiefs, Russia sheeting tents,
and a number of bank notes, some signed New Jersey and

[3] Quoted by Douglas, in James, 283-84.

Trenton Banking Company. From the description the Bloods
gave of the dress and behavior of one whom they murdered, he
must have been an officer or trader; they said he killed two
Bloods before he fell. This exasperated them, and I have reason
to suppose they butchered him in a horrible manner and then ate
him partly raw, and partly boiled. They said his skin was exceedingly white and tatooed from the hips to the feet.

Chittenden adds:

"It is possible that the officer or trader referred to
was Drouillard. . .[4]

This assumption by Chittenden is probably correct.
There are errors, however, in the statement itself. For
example, Drouillard did not have in his possession, on
the morning on which he was attacked, a considerable
supply of goods of various kinds, including fine cotton
shirts, Russia sheeting tents, and a number of bank
notes. It is possible that Henry, in furnishing these
details, was confusing this attack by the Bloods on
Drouillard and the Delawares with the attack by the
Gros Ventres of the Prairies on the larger body of
trappers on April 12. One thing is certain: the life of
George Drouillard, the Lewis and Clark hunter and
interpreter, came to an untimely and tragic end. But
for the robust, rollicking prairie wind, Drouillard
might have lived to make a dream come true – the
establishment of a fur trading post *somewhere* on the
Missouri.

On January 15, 1807, Meriwether Lewis sat down to
write to General H. Dearborn, Secretary of War, in
behalf of the men who had served him. What he said
of these men was particularly true of Drouillard:

---

[4] Chittenden I, p. 146.

With respect to all those persons whose names are entered on this roll, I feel a peculiar pleasure in declaring, that the ample support which they gave me under every difficulty; the manly firmness which they evinced on every necessary occasion; and the patience and fortitude with which they submitted to, and bore, the fatigues and painful sufferings incident to my late tour to the Pacific Ocean, entitles them to my warmest approbation and thanks. . .

Of Drouillard himself he had this to say:

A man of much merit; he has been peculiarly useful from his knowledge of the common language of gesticulation, and his uncommon skill as a hunter and woodsman; those several duties he performed in good faith, and with an ardor which deserves the highest commendation. It was his fate also to have encountered, on various occasions, with either Captain Clarke or myself, all the most dangerous and trying scenes of the voyage, in which he uniformly acquitted himself with honor. . .[5]

Wheeler, a student of Lewis and Clark, who, a century later, traveled over much of the route taken by the intrepid explorers, declared, in the book which he published on his tour, that George Drouillard was beyond question one of the two or three most valuable men of the expedition. "Where so many were deserving," he added, "it is rather difficult to discriminate, but in this case it is a safe proposition." [6] Elliott Coues, another student of Lewis and Clark, gave it as his opinion that, as a member of the Lewis and Clark expedition, Drouillard was "simply invaluable." [7]

Dare one hope that some day a marker will be erected in commemoration of the services of this man in behalf of the Lewis and Clark expedition and the country he had come to regard as his own?

---

[5] Thwaites VII, p. 359. [6] Wheeler I, p. 105.
[7] Coues I, p. 257.

Appendices

A

Indian Sign Language

One of George Drouillard's accomplishments was the proficiency with which he used the Indian language of signs. Time after time, in intercourse with one tribe or another, he used this language with satisfactory results, if one may judge from the accounts given of these discourses in the journals of Lewis and Clark.

In his journal for August 14, 1806, for example, the day on which Lewis had such a nerve-racking time bargaining with Cameahwait and his Shoshones for horses to transport the explorers' baggage over the Divide to the Shoshone village, the captain stated that he spoke to the Indians through Drouillard, "who understood perfectly the common language of jesticulation or signs which seems to be universally understood by all the Nations we have yet seen." The language, the captain added, is imperfect and "liable to error," but "much less so than would be expected. the strong part of the ideas are seldom mistaken."

Reuben Gold Thwaites has this to say with respect to the Indian language of signs:

> Communication by signs and gestures is doubtless the most primitive form of human language; but it has also largely taken the place of vocal utterance among persons or peoples of differing tongues. Certain signs and gestures are at once so universal and obvious that they can be understood by all; accordingly, our North American aborigines have therein a limited means of communication between all their polyglot races and tribes. A regular code of signs has arisen, however, among the Plains tribes of Indians, among whom so many varying languages exist, while their mutual need of intercourse has been much greater than among the mountain tribes.[1]

An authority on this language is William Philo Clark, whose

---

[1] Thwaites II, pp. 346-47.

knowledge of this medium of communication came to him on contacts which he had with tribes west of the Mississippi River.

During the Sioux and Cheyenne war of 1876-7, in November of 1876, I found myself in command of three hundred friendly enlisted Indian scouts of the Pawnee, Shoshone, Arapahoe, Cheyenne, Crow, and Sioux tribes; six tribes having six different vocal languages. . . I observed that these Indians, having different vocal languages, had no difficulty in communicating with each other, and held constant intercourse by means of gestures.[2]

It was at this time Clark learned the language. His ability to use the language was later improved through further contacts with Indians in an official capacity. For example, he was thrown into intimate relations with Cheyennes, Sioux, Crows, Bannocks, Assiniboines, Hidatsa, Mandans, Arikaras, and other tribes and had almost constant use of his knowledge of this form of communication. In 1881 he was directed by Lieutenant-General Sheridan to submit to him a work on this medium of communication. In furtherance of this directive, Mr. Clark visited tribes in Indian Territory, and in Minnesota, Manitoba, Northwest Territory, the Dakotas, Montana, Nebraska, Utah, Wyoming, and Idaho, using the language frequently and making such notations with respect to it as he deemed necessary. Samples from his book are given below:

YES. Conception: Bowing the head and body. Hold right hand, back to right, in front of right breast, height of shoulder, index finger extended and pointing upwards, other fingers nearly closed, thumb resting on side of second finger; move the hand slightly to left and a little upwards, at the same time closing index over thumb.
The index finger represents a person standing, and the bending of the body and head in assent.

No. Hold extended right hand, back up, in front of body, fingers pointing to left and front; move the hand to right and front, at same time turning hand, thumb up, so that back of hand will be to right and downwards; the hand is swept into its position on a curve.

COME. Carry right hand, back out, index finger extended and pointing upwards, others and thumb closed, well out in front of body (or towards person you wish to cause to ap-

---

[2] Clark, *Indian Sign Language.*

proach . . .); draw the hand rather sharply in towards the body, lowering it slightly. The index finger is usually kept elevated, though it is sometimes curved as the hand is brought in towards the body.

GO. Hold right hand in front of body, back to right, fingers extended, touching, pointing to front and downwards; move the hand to front, at same time, by wrist action, raise the fingers, so as to point to front and upwards. The hand can, of course, be held to right or left of body, making the motion to indicate the direction, and is usually so made.

I AM GOING. Make sign for "I" and above sign.

FRIEND. Conception: Brother, and growing up united, together. The most common sign in the North is to hold the right hand in front of and towards neck, index and second fingers extended, touching, pointing upwards and slightly to front, others and thumb closed; raise the hand, moving it slightly to front at same time until tips of fingers are about as high as the top of head. (Some tribes the index finger of each hand is used, and the hands raised similarly. The hand is fixed as in BROTHER, and raised as in GROW).

ENEMY. Make sign for FRIEND and NO.

For Drouillard to have mastered this art to the extent that he could communicate with the various tribes with whom the explorers came in contact on their route from St. Louis to the mouth of the Columbia was no small accomplishment.

Maximilian, Prince of Wied, who in 1833 accompanied the fur trading party under Wilson P. Hunt up the Missouri, and who published vocabularies of several Indian tribes, apparently doubted the universality of the Indian language of gesticulation. "The Arikkaras, Mandans, Minnitarris, Crows, Chayennes, Snakes, and Blackfeet," he says, "all understand a system of signs, which, as we are told, are unintelligible to the Dacotas, Assiniboins, Ojibuas, Krihs, and other nations." [3]

Garrick Mallery, an authority on the Indian language of signs, has this to say about Maximilian's pronouncement:

It is worthy of note that the distinguished explorer . . . is the only printed authority agreeing with the present writer in

[3] Maximilian, *Travels in the Interior of North America, 1832-4,* in R. G. Thwaites (ed.) *Early Western Travels,* XXIV, pp. 300-01.

denying the existence of a universal sign language among the several tribes, in the sense of a common code, the report of which has generally been accepted without question.

He states that the signs described, gathered by him from the tribes above mentioned, are unintelligible to the Dakotas (probably Sioux), Assiniboine, Ojibwas, Krees, and other nations. Mallery then goes on to say that Maximilian probably meant

> that different signs prevailed among the two bodies of Indians, so divided by himself, and that the individuals who had only learned by rote one set of those signs, would not understand the other set which they had never seen, unless they were accomplished in the gesture speech as an art, and not as a mere memorized list of arbitrary motions. It has been clearly ascertained that two Indians of different tribes who have neither oral language nor previously adopted signs in common, can, after a short trial, communicate through familiarity with the principles of gesture speech, signs being mutually invented and accepted.[4]

There is, then, the possibility that the Teton Sioux did not employ the system of signs used by Drouillard. This does not mean, however, that Drouillard could not have improvised signs that they would have understood. He probably did, in the various conversations and conferences which the captains had with the Tetons later. That is, he supplemented the Frenchman's oral speech, either by his own signs, or by signs improvised by him on the spot – more likely, by a combination of these.

---

[4] *Ibid.,* p. 302.

B

The Squall on May 14

On the afternoon of May 14, 1805, while the explorers were westward bound on the Missouri, Drouillard had steered the white pirogue until relieved by Charbonneau. Toward evening of that day a squall came up and struck the pirogue with such force as to bring the pirogue nearly broadside against the force of the wind. The unfortunate Charbonneau, instead of steering the vessel into the wind, turned it the other way. The result was that the wind knocked the squaresail out of the hands of the man who held it. Before anyone on board realized what had happened the pirogue had keeled over and would have turned completely on its side but for the resistance offered by the sail as it lay flapping on the rough water.

Lewis, who witnessed the incident from shore, wrote that, "such was their confusion and consternation at this moment that they suffered the perogue to lye on her side for half a minute before they took the sail in. . ." When, finally, this was done, the pirogue, relieved of its top-heaviness, righted itself immediately, but not until it had filled with water to within an inch of the gunwales.

During this emergency the helpless Charbonneau had, apparently, done nothing but lift his voice in supplication "to his god for mercy," while at the same time attempting to keep himself from being washed overboard. The rudder, which he was supposed now more than ever to manage, he seemed entirely to have forgotten, "nor could the repeated orders of the Bowsman, Cruzat, bring him to his recollection until he threatened to shoot him instantly if he did not take hold of the rudder and do his duty." [5]

When Drouillard and his companions entered camp in the early part of the evening, they found the pirogue drawn up, safely enough, on the gravel. They beheld the various papers, instruments, books,

---

[5] Thwaites, II, p. 35.

medicines, merchandise, and, in short, "almost every article indispens-
ably necessary" to the success of the expedition, opened up and carefully spread out to dry. The men, for the most part, went about their
tasks silently, efficiently. Lewis was none too cheerful. Clark, who
had also been on shore when the accident occurred (very seldom were
both of them away from the boats at the same time), was observing
the men who may still have been bailing water from the luckless
pirogue.

Drouillard learned that it was Sacajawea who, at some risk to
herself and her infant, had leaned over the gunwales to rescue most
of the bundles which had been washed overboard. He learned that
but for the "fortitude, resolution, and good conduct" of Cruzatte,
the pirogue might have been completely wrecked. It was because of
Cruzatte's commands and threats that Charbonneau had finally been
made to take hold of the rudder. It was due to Cruzatte's commands,
also, that the only two other men on board, neither of them swim-
mers, had been compelled to bail out water as fast as they could with
kettles. It was Cruzatte, with the help of these two men, who eventually brought the vessel to safety.

In narrating this incident, Lewis compliments Cruzatte, Sacajawea,
and Drouillard. He does not compliment Drouillard in so many
words. He simply said: "It happened unfortunately for us . . .
that Charbono was at the helm at this Perogue, in stead of Drewyer,
who had previously steered her." The implication is that, had Drouillard steered the pirogue instead of Charbonneau, the accident might
have been averted, or at least mitigated. Drouillard is shown in one
more role in which he had acquitted himself well.

C

The Grizzly

Among the most thrilling adventures which came to the explorers on their epoch-making trip to the Pacific were those resulting from their encounters with the grizzly. Two hunters, for example, were compelled to jump over a twenty-foot precipice into the river one day, only to discover that Brother Bruin, unable to stop himself, had jumped in after them.[6] Joseph Fields, a swift runner, was chased by a bear which had compelled him to leap "down a steep bank of the river." Drouillard, Colter, and others were forced to seek refuge in trees, or behind flimsy clumps of willows. Lewis was, on one occasion, driven into a river, after which he turned to confront an infuriated grizzly with his only weapon, an espontoon. Joseph Fields was once pursued by a bear so closely as to have his "foot" struck, presumably by the bear's claws. Charbonneau, in a fit of panic, discharged his gun into the air on one occasion, instead of at an oncoming grizzly which Drouillard had just wounded – and so on, one nerve-shattering adventure after another.[7]

On June 27, at the Great Falls of the Missouri, Drouillard and Joseph Fields killed a bear which was "by far," according to Lewis:

> [the largest] we have yet seen; the skin appear[ed] to me to be as large as a common ox. while hunting they saw a thick brushey bottom on the bank of the river where from the tracks along shore they therefore landed without making any nois and climbed a leaning tree and placed themselves on it's branches about 20 feet above the ground, when thus securely fixed they gave a [w]hoop and this large bear instantly rushed forward to the place from whence he had heard the human voice issue, when he arrived at the tree he made a short paus and Drewyer shot him in the head.[8]

[6] Thwaites, II, p. 34.   [7] *Ibid.*, II, pp. 109, 191; 158; 122; 109.
[8] *Ibid.*, II, p. 191.

The westward-bound Lewis wrote on May 11:

About 5. P.M. my attention was struck by one of the Party runing at a distance towards us and making signs and hollowing as if in distress, I ordered the perogues to put too, and waited untill he arrived; I now found that it was Bratton the man with the soar hand whom I had permitted to walk on shore, he arrived so much out of breath that it was several minutes before he could tell what had happened; at length he informed me that in the woody bottom on the Lard. side about 1½ [miles] below us he had shot a brown bear which immediately turned on him and pursued him a considerable distance but he had wounded it so badly that it could not overtake him; I immediately turned out with seven of the party in quest of this monster, we at length found his trale and persued him about a mile by the blood through very thick brush of rosbushes and the large leafed willow; we finally found him concealed in some very thick brush and shot him through the skull with two balls; we proceeded [to] dress him as soon as possible, we found him in good order; it was a monstrous beast, not quite so large as that we killed a few days past but in all other rispects much the same. . . we now found that Bratton had shot him through the center of the lungs, notwithstanding which he had persued him near half a mile and had returned more than double that distance and with his tallons had prepared himself a bed in the earth of about 2 feet deep and five long and was perfectly alive when we found him which could not have been less than 2 hours after he received the wound. . . these bear being so hard to die reather intimedates us all; I must confess that I do not like the gentlemen and had reather fight two Indians than one bear; there is no other chance to conquer them by a single shot but by shooting them through the brains, and this becomes difficult in consequence of two large muscles which cover the sides of the forehead and the sharp projection of the center of the frontal bone, which is also of a pretty good thickness. the fleece and skin were as much as two men could possible carry.[9]

Three days later (the day on which their white pirogue had almost been swamped, after Drouillard had turned over the helm to Charbonneau), the men in the two "rear" canoes discovered a large grizzly reposing in the "open grounds" at a distance of about 300 paces from the river. Six of these men, all good hunters, stole forth to the attack. Taking advantage of a slight elevation in the ground, they were able to come within forty paces of the unsuspecting animal. Two of them

[9] *Ibid.*, II, p. 25.

reserved their fire, as agreed upon; the other four fired at nearly the same time, each of them putting a bullet through their intended victim, two of these balls penetrating the bulk of both lobes of the bear's lungs. Lewis' account continues:

> in an instant this monster ran at them with open mouth, the two who had reserved their fir[e]s discharged their pieces at him as he came towards them, boath of them struck him, one only slightly and the other fortunately broke his shoulder, this however only retarded his motion for a moment only, the men unable to reload their guns took to flight, the bear pursued and had very nearly overtaken them before they reached the river; two of the party betook themselves to a canoe and the others seperated an[d] concealed themselves among the willows, reloaded their pieces, each discharged his piece at him as they had an opportunity   they struck him several times again but the guns served only to direct the bear to them, in this manner he pursued two of them separately so close that they were obliged to throw aside their guns and pouches and throw themselves into the river altho' the bank was nearly twenty feet perpendicular; so enraged was this anamal that he plunged into the river only a few feet behind the second man he had compelled [to] take refuge in the water, when one of those who still remained on shore shot him through the head and finally killed him; they then took him on shore and butch[er]ed him when they found eight balls had passed through him in different directions.   . .[10]

Indians, the explorers learned, had great respect for the grizzly. They did not attack this animal except in parties of from six to ten men, and even then were frequently defeated with the loss of one or more of their number. If a hunter missed his aim, or if he did not shoot the animal through the brain or heart, the chances were good that he would himself become the victim instead of the bear. The grizzly, it seemed, had the reputation of attacking a man more often than it would flee. The Indians made preparations for a bear hunt comparable to the preparations they made when bound for the warpath.

[10] *Ibid.*, II, p. 34.

D

The Crossed-out Sentence

In commenting (on June 17) on their chances of finding their way, eastward bound, over the Bitterroot Mountains without the benefit of Indian guides, Lewis stated that Drouillard, their "principal dependance as a woodsman and guide was entirely doubtfull." Reuben Gold Thwaites, who edited this journal, says, in a footnote: "This sentence is crossed out with ink (of another color) in the MS." [11] If Lewis was the one who crossed out the sentence, then he used ink of a different color – a possibility, though not a probability, unless the sentence was crossed out later, say, after his arrival in St. Louis. If some one other than Lewis crossed it out, this some one may have been Nicholas Biddle, who was engaged by Clark to prepare the Lewis and Clark journals for publication. George Shannon was appointed by Clark to give to Biddle the benefit of such firsthand information as Shannon might be able to furnish. Biddle was, moreover, in correspondence with Clark during the period of time which he devoted to the task assigned him.[12] Was it upon information furnished by Shannon that Biddle crossed out the sentence, assuming that Biddle was the one who crossed it out? That is, did Shannon doubt the veracity of the statement in Lewis' journal as of June 17 – the statement which said ". . . our principal dependance as a woodsman and guide was entirely doubtfull" and so ordered Biddle to draw a line through it? In other words, did Drouillard tell Shannon on their journey to the Nez Percé villages that he, George Drouillard, felt that he *could* have guided the explorers all the way to the fish weirs of Colt Creek?

On his own part, Clark also made a statement in his own journal

---

[11] Thwaites, v, p. 141.

[12] Thwaites, "Story of the Lewis and Clark Journals," in American Historical Association *Annual Report 1903*, I, pp. 112ff.

for that memorable day. Referring, as had Lewis, to their chances of keeping to the trail all the way, Clark said that of this "all of our most expert woodsmen and principal guides were extreemly doubtfull." [13] Therefore it could hardly have been Clark who was instrumental in having Lewis' statement crossed out — at least, not any more so than Lewis himself. Whoever crossed it out, and for whatever reason, at least this much can be said about the decision made on June 17: it was a decision on the side of caution and, in view of the uncertainties involved had they pushed on instead of turning back, a wise one.

[13] Thwaites, V, p. 143.

E

Crossing the Bitterroots

While Drouillard and Shannon were gone on an errand to attempt to persuade the Nez Percé Indians to furnish guides for crossing the Bitterroot Mountains, Lewis and Clark evolved a plan which they intended to put into effect in the event Drouillard and Shannon were to fail. According to this plan, either Lewis or Clark would start with four of their best woodsmen (which would include Drouillard) and three or four of their best horses, and, amply fortified with "provisions," go a two days' journey ahead of the main party, in an attempt to follow the trail over the Bitterroots as evidenced by telltale marks on the trees along their trail. In the performance of this task they would blaze a trail for the main party. After having gone two days beyond Hungry Creek, two of the men would be sent back to report to the main party on the probable chances of success. It was expected that these two men would meet the main party on Hungry Creek. Should the report of the two men be favorable, then the main party would continue their march without delay. Should, however, the advance party of five, after a two-day attempt, fail to find or keep to the trail, then all five of the men, instead of merely two, would return to the main party, when all of them – the five men and the entire party – would venture forth in a desperate effort to cross the mountains via a pass to the south, of which not only the Nez Percés had told them but the Shoshones as well. A journey via this pass would, however, be considerably longer than one via the trail over which they had come in the fall, and not only longer but dangerous, through a region in which it would be difficult for them to support themselves. At least so they had been given to understand by the Shoshones. They were convinced, moreover, that, had the trail to the south been better than the one over which they had come the year before, then the Shoshones would have directed them over this trail instead of the other. The trail over which they had come in the fall – the trail used by the Nez Percés – was the trail they wished to take, and would take – if Drouillard and Shannon obtained a guide!

F

Litigations[14]

On February 11, 1804, George Drouillard executed a promissory note for $301.63 1/3, payable in two months to one Frederick Graeter, as has been mentioned in this volume on pages 23-25 and 279.

Some time after the contraction of the debt, Graeter furnished a statement in which he declared that he had been "obliged" to accept in part payment of this debt from one, Louis Provot, a [word illegible] for the amount of twenty-three dollars.

On February 11, 1807, that is, three years after the negotiation of the debt, Graeter executed a statement showing interest due of $50.15 1/3, and an additional reduction of the debt by goods received from Indians in the amount of $10.69½, and a balance due of $318.09. See illustration on page 335.

Some time in 1807, William C. Carr, attorney for Graeter, prepared for the June Term of the Court of Common Pleas, District of St. Louis, a statement in which, for failure on the part of George Drouillard to pay the principal of the debt "or any part thereof," the said George Drouillard was, for costs or damages or both, assessed the sum of 100 dollars.

Drouillard had a friend who was willing to assume some responsibility in connection with the debt, as witness the following writ:

District of Saint Louis, Lsa
FREDERICK GRAETER   In the Court of Common
          vs   Pleas, for said Frederick
GEORGE DROUILLR   Damages $100 ....
                                     Debt $400 ....

Whereas George Druiller has been asserted in the above case,
    Now therefore you Benjamin Wilkinson do acknowledge
yourself indebted to Frederick Graeter in the sum of five

---

[14] Summarized from legal documents, photostat copies of which were supplied by, and used by permission of, the Missouri Historical Society.

Hundred Dollars to be levied of your Goods, and Chattels,
Lands and Tenements if default be made in the Condition
underwritten — that if the said George Drouiller be cast in the
said action he shall pay the cost and condemn his money, or
surrender his body in prison in discharge thereof, or that you
the said Benjamin Wilkinson will do it for him —
Taken and acknowledged
before me one of the Judges
of the Court of Common Pleas
for Saint Louis District
the 10th of August 1807 —
     BERN PRATTE

On February 8, 1808, William C. Carr, attorney for the plaintiff
Graeter, made motion in the Court of Common Pleas, District of
St. Louis, to the effect that a "Deposition" be taken of "Antoine
Laselle," in the case of Frederick Graeter vs. George Drouillard. In
accord with this motion, which appears to have been duly passed,
Thomas F. Riddick, Clerk of the said Court of Common Pleas, in
behalf of the Honorable Silas Bent, Presiding Judge of said Court,
on the "8th of February one thousand eight hundred & eight and of
the Independence of the United States the Thirty Second," issued an
order to "any Justice of the peace for the District of S Louis" to
obtain sworn testimony from the said Antoine Laselle concerning his
knowledge of the controversy then pending in court between Frederick
Graeter, plaintiff, and George Drouillard, defendant.

The content of this deposition I do not know. Be it noted, however, that on Drouillard's promissory note as of February 11, 1804,
appears the name (which is probably the signature) of "Ant. Laselle."
The same signature appears also on the statement by Graeter, in
which the latter testifies that he was "obliged" to accept payment
equivalent to twenty-three dollars in part payment of the debt owed
him by Drouillard.

William C. Carr, on his part, duly served notice (on February
13) upon Edward Hempstead, attorney for Drouillard, informing
the latter that "in the aforesaid suit the deposition of Antoine Laselle
will be taken at the home of Major William Christy, in the town of
St. Louis before Thomas F. Riddick esquire . . . to be read as
evidence in the aforesaid suit." The serving of this notice Edward
Hempstead acknowledged, on the same February 13.

On March 24, 1808, Thomas F. Riddick executed another order

commanding the Sheriff of the Territory of Louisiana and the District of St. Louis to confiscate the "goods and chattels, lands and tenements of the said George Douiler" for the payment of a debt of "Three hundred & Seventeen Dollars & eight cents" and also in damages, "the sum of Nineteen Dollars & 17½ cts," or a total of $330.17½, the debt of George Drouillard to Frederick Graeter. The amount of the debt was certified to by William C. Carr as amounting to the sum given above. "Jer. Conner, Shf.," certified that "Neither property nor body to be found."

On April 10, 1808, under the signature of Charles Gratiot, Esquire, First Justice of the Court of Common Pleas, at the town of St. Louis, and "in and for the District of St. Louis," was issued an order to the Sheriff of said District, "to take George Drouillard if he may be found in your District and him Safely keep so that you may have him before the Judges of our Court of Common pleas, same Court to be holden at the Town of Saint Louis in and for the District of Saint Louis on the Third Thursday of June next, then there to answer onto Frederick Graeter in a plea of debt Three hundred & one dollars sixty three & third cents, and to the damage of the Said Frederick Graeter the Sum of one hundred Dollars as it is Said, and have you then there this writ."

Once again, Drouillard's friend, Benjamin Wilkinson, comes into the picture, this time in no less a matter than that of appearing in the St. Louis Court of Common Pleas on the first Monday of November next, to show cause why execution of judgment should not be made against him "as special Bail for the said George Druillier," in an action instituted by Frederick Graeter to recover the "sums of Three hundred & seventeen Dollars and eight Cents costs of Suit together with the further costs and the costs of this. . ." The order, signed by Silas Bent, "Principal Judge of our said Court in the town of St. Louis," was issued to the Sheriff of the said District of St. Louis by "Thos. F. Riddick, Clk.," and dated July 13, 1808.

All this while, from May 3, 1807, to August 5, 1808, a period of fifteen months, Drouillard, the defendant in the case, was not even near the said District of St. Louis, since he was engaged with Manuel Lisa in the Lisa-Drouillard fur trading venture on the Yellowstone. Small wonder the Sheriff of the District of St. Louis found it necessary to certify that the "body" of the man he had been ordered to apprehend was not "to be found," nor, for that matter, his property.

After August 5, however, and after the conclusion of his trial for
the murder of Bissonnette, Drouillard had ample time to devote to
the matter of his debt to Graeter. It seems probable that Drouillard
found the means with which to defray this sadly-neglected debt.

Evidence tending to support this conclusion is furnished by a document bearing on the case and showing the payment of fees, not only
to Jeremiah Conner, Sheriff, but to certain "Att.y & Clks." On this
particular document, the sheriff's signature appears twice, once evidently in acknowledgement of fees paid to himself, and again, "in
presence of . . . H. Price & Baptiste Norin," for [the word is
indistinct]. There appears on the document, also, the initials, "[illeg-
ible], Attorney," placed there in acknowledgment of some service or
other. The presence of these notations and signatures indicates that
something was done about the payment of the debt. So does the statement in Jackson (page 345), to the effect that Drouillard paid to
Thomas F. Riddick and Alexander McNair the equivalent of
$1,300.[15]

On April 11, 1807, shortly before Drouillard and Lisa departed
from St. Louis on their first fur trading venture, one, Paul Primeau,
executed a promissory note payable to Manuel Lisa and George
Drouillard, or to their order, in an amount equal to $292.05. This
note was given for "value received . . . in so much money by
them paid to divers persons for the said Paul. . ." When, later,
upon refusal of Primeau to repay this amount, either in whole or in
part, even "though often thereto requested," Lisa and Drouillard,
through their attorney, Edward Hempstead, instituted suit against
him, for the recovery of principal, plus interest and costs. An order
for Primeau's arrest was, accordingly, on December 16, 1807, issued
by Thomas F. Riddick, Clerk of the Court of Common Pleas, District
of St. Louis, and by the Honorable Silas Bent, Judge of said Court.
The order was administered by "Jer. Connor, Shf., who "committed"
Primeau to jail but was obliged to liberate him soon afterward in consequence of the "Insolvent Act."

The case dragged on until April 1, 1808 (when Drouillard and
Lisa were on the Yellowstone). On this date, Thomas F. Riddick,
Clerk, and the Honorable Silas Bent, Judge, again issued an order to
the Sheriff of the District and Town of St. Louis, to confiscate, for

[15] Jackson, p. 345; also see herein chap. XXIV, note 7.

the redemption of the debt, such "goods and chattels, lands and tenements" of the said Paul Primeau as he could find, failing in which he was once more to commit the said Paul Primeau to jail, where he was to be kept until the date of his forthcoming trial on July 4. See illustration on page 336.

Again Jeremiah Connor, Sheriff, found it necessary to certify that "Neither property can be found, nor body to be touched, Deft. having been liberated under the insolvent law." Frederick Graeter was not the only man who found it difficult to collect money on a debt. Drouillard and Lisa were experiencing the same difficulty. It may be added, in this case, however, that Paul Primeau's debt, amounting now to $305.55, appears to have been taken care of, if the word "Recd.," in the notation, "Recd. 6th. April, 1808," appearing on one of the court papers pertaining to this case, means "received," as it presumably does, instead of merely "recorded."

On April 26, 1809, Drouillard found himself participating as a witness in a legal action involving one, Etienne Brant, on the one hand, and Manuel Lisa on the other. See illustration on page 337.

Etienne Brant had been one of the engagés employed by Lisa in the first Lisa-Drouillard fur trading venture. It appears that goods used by the fur traders as money with which to purchase furs from the Indians were being stored in the "loft" above the room occupied by Lisa, Drouillard, Brant, and one, Baptiste Mayelk. According to Drouillard's testimony, only four persons – those just mentioned – were permitted access to the loft, for the purpose of drawing upon the goods there contained.

In the "deposition" taken in connection with this case, one of the witnesses, Baptiste Mayelk, testified that "about december 1807 . . . he Saw Etienne Brant . . . at repeated times Steal Whiskey, Scarlet Cloth, beads, & other articles"; that there had been altercations between Brant and Lisa; that Brant had called Lisa a "thief and threatened him with his knife"; and that Lisa had forthwith ordered Brant to go and live in the house where the men were." Drouillard's testimony pertained pretty much to the same subject, including information to the effect that Lisa ordered Brant to "go and live in the other room provided for the men," and that Brant "deserted & went to [live] among the Indians," to whom he appears to have made sales amounting to "$50."

Brant was involved in additional legal complications with Lisa, or with Drouillard and Lisa. For example, he was, "on the fifth day of this present month [April, 1809] . . . taken into custody by the Sheriff of the district aforesaid [District of St. Louis] on civil process at the Suit of Manuel Lisa and George Drouillard for seven hundred dollars damage and confined in the common jail of said district for want of bail." After a confinement in this jail of "twenty days," he took advantage of the "Act concerning insolvent debtors' & the Act supplementary thereto."

The outcomes of the legal disputes between Brant and Lisa, also involving Drouillard as they did, could not be determined. It may be added, however, that it was not at all uncommon for Lisa to find his acts and motives criticized and condemned, not only by his subordinates, but by his contemporaries, many of whom made no bones about the resentment and hostility they bore toward him. As a result, Lisa succeeded in drawing upon himself the ire and vituperation of many of those with whom he had dealings. This was the man with whom Drouillard had, up to this time, served as a partner for more than a year; a man who may be characterized as bold, vigorous, strong-willed, relentless, enterprising, alert, shrewd, resourceful, domineering; a man who cared neither whether his acts elicited praise or condemnation.

FREDERICK GRAETER'S STATEMENT OF FEBRUARY 11, 1807, REGARDING
THE BALANCE DUE ON DROUILLARD'S NOTE TO HIM
Courtesy of the Missouri Historical Society, St. Louis.

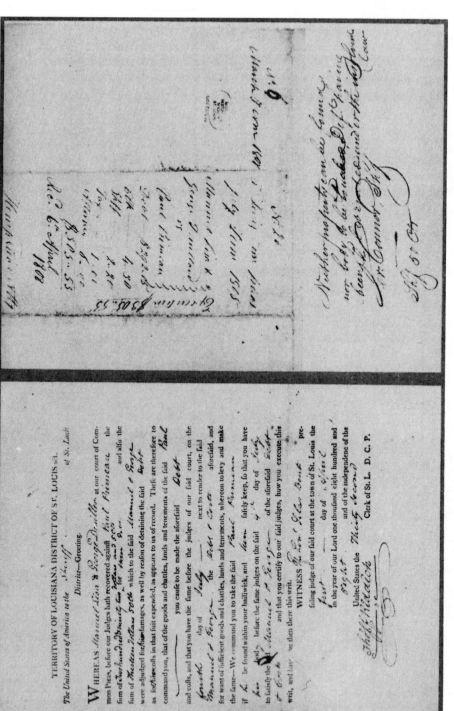

THE COURT ORDER CALLING FOR CONFISCATION OF PROPERTY OF PAUL PRIMEAU
FOR NON-PAYMENT OF HIS DEBT TO MANUEL LISA AND GEORGE DROUILLARD
Courtesy of the Missouri Historical Society, St. Louis.

TERRITORY OF LOUISIANA DISTRICT OF ST. LOUIS sc̄.

The United States of America to the *Sheriff* ——— of St. Louis

District—Greeting.

YOU are hereby commanded to summons *Pierre Deserve, John B Mayette. George Druillard & John McPherson*

that setting aside all manner of excuse and delays *they and each* ——— be and

and appear in proper person before the judges of our Court of common pleas on the

ninth ——— day of *March* next *at the Court now in S Louis* then there to testify and the truth to say in a cer-

tain matter of controversy now pending in our said court, wherein *Etienne Brant.* is plaintiff and *Manuel Lisa* ———

defendant on the part of the *Defendant* ——— and have you then there this writ.

WITNESS *the Hon. Silas Bent* pre-

siding judge of our said court at the town of St. Louis the

first ——— day of *february*

in the year of our Lord one thousand eight hundred and

nine . and of the independenc of the

United States the *thirty third*

Thos. F. Riddick ——— Clerk of St. L. D. C. P.

Bibliography

Adair, James, *History of the American Indian.* Edited by Samuel Cole Williams. Johnson City, Tennessee: The Watauga Press, 1930.

Allen, Paul, *History of the Expedition under the Command of Captains Lewis and Clark.* 2 vols. New York: Harper and Brothers, 1842.
A reprint of the Biddle edition of 1814, with an introduction by Archibald M'Vickar.

Bakeless, John, *Lewis and Clark: Partners in Discovery.* New York: William Morrow and Co., 1947.

Bradbury, John, *Travels in the Interior of North America.* London: Sherwood, Neely, and Jones, 1819.

Chittenden, Hiram Martin, *The American Fur Trade of the Far West.* 2 vols. New York: Francis P. Harper, 1902.

Clark, William Philo, *The Indian Sign Language.* Philadelphia: L. R. Hammersley and Co., 1885.

Coman, Katherine, *Economic Beginnings of the Far West.* 2 vols. New York: The Macmillan Co., 1912.

Coues, Elliott (ed.), *History of the Expedition under the Command of Lewis and Clark.* 3 vols. New York: Francis P. Harper, 1893.

De Voto, Bernard, *Across the Wide Missouri.* Boston: Houghton Mifflin Co., 1947.

———, *The Journals of Lewis and Clark.* Boston: Houghton Mifflin Co., 1953.

Dorsey, Florence L., *Master of the Mississippi.* Boston: Houghton Mifflin Co., 1941.

Douglas, Walter B., editorial material and biographical sketches in "Appendix" to Thomas James, *Three Years Among the Indians and Mexicans.* St. Louis: The Missouri Historical Society, 1916.

Dryden, Cecil, *Up the Columbia for Furs.* Caldwell, Idaho: The Caxton Printers, Ltd., 1949.

Dye, Eva Emery, *The Conquest.* Chicago: A. C. McClurg and Co., 1903.

Fuller, George W., *A History of the Pacific Northwest.* New York: A. A. Knopf, 1931.

Ghent, William James, *The Early Far West.* New York: Longmans, Green, and Co., 1931.

Harris, Burton, *John Colter.* New York: Charles Scribner's Sons, 1952.

Hosmer, James Kendall, *Gass's Journal of the Lewis and Clark Expedition.* Chicago: A. C. McClurg and Co., 1904.

Irving, Washington, *Astoria.* 2 vols. Philadelphia: Corey, Lea, and Blanchard, 1836.

Jackson, Donald, *Letters of the Lewis and Clark Expedition, with Related Documents, 1783-1844.* Urbana: University of Illinois Press, 1962.

James, Thomas, *Three Years Among the Indians and Mexicans.* Edited by Walter B. Douglas. St. Louis: The Missouri Historical Society, 1916.

Laut, Agnes C., *Pathfinders of the West.* New York: The Macmillan Co., 1904.

Louisiana Gazette, July 26, 1810. Quoted by Walter B. Douglas in Appendix to Thomas James, *Three Years Among the Indians and Mexicans.* St. Louis: The Missouri Historical Society, 1916.

Lyman, Horace S., *History of Oregon.* 4 vols. New York: The North Pacific Publishing Society, 1903.

Maximilian, Prince of Weid, *Travels in the Interior of North America, 1832-34.* In Reuben Gold Thwaites (ed.), *Early Western Travels,* XXII-XXV. Cleveland: The Arthur H. Clark Co., 1904.

Missouri Gazette, October 12, 1808. Contains account of Drouillard's trial for the murder of Antoine Bissonette.

Missouri Historical Society, St. Louis. Collection of maps and papers, including early litigation papers, Lisa papers, and one map and one paper of the Voorhis Memorial Collection.

Neuberger, Richard L., *The Lewis and Clark Expedition.* New York: Random House, 1951.

———, "The Limits of the West," *Saturday Review of Literature,* XXVI no. 9, 1954.

———, "They're Taming the Lolo Trail." *Saturday Evening Post,* CCVI no. 41, 1954.

Oudard, Georges, *Four Cents an Acre*. New York: Brewer and Warren, Inc., 1931.

Quaife, Milo M. (ed.), *The Journals of Captain Meriwether Lewis and Sergeant John Ordway*. Madison: State Historical Society of Wisconsin, 1916.

Robinson, Doan, "The Lewis and Clark Expedition." *South Dakota Historical Collections*, IX. Pierre, South Dakota: 1918.

Ross, Alexander, *Adventures of the First Settlers of Oregon, 1810-1813*. In Reuben Gold Thwaites (ed.), *Early Western Travels*, VII. Cleveland: The Arthur H. Clark Co., 1904.

Schafer, Joseph, *History of the Pacific Northwest*. New York: The Macmillan Company, 1938.

Shaw, George C., *Chinook Jargon*. Seattle:Rainier Printing Co., 1909.

Teggert, Frederick J., "Notes Supplementary to Any Edition of Lewis and Clark," American Historical Association *Annual Report, 1908*, vol. I.

Thwaites, Reuben Gold (ed.), *Original Journals of the Lewis and Clark Expedition*. 8 vols. New York: Dodd, Mead and Company, 1904.

————, *"The Story of Lewis and Clark's Journals,"* American Historical Association *Annual Report, 1903*, vol. I.

Turner, Frederick Jackson, *The Frontier in American History*. New York: Henry Holt and Co., 1921.

Wheeler, Olin D., *The Trail of Lewis and Clark*. 2 vols. London and New York: G. P. Putnam's Sons, 1904.

Winther, Oscar Osborn, *The Great Northwest*. New York: Alfred A. Knopf, 1950.

Index